European Diplomacy 1870-1939

Simon Peaple

Series Editors
Martin Collier
Erica Lewis

Heinemann

HEINEMANN ADVANCED HISTORY

Heinemann Educational Publishers
Halley Court, Jordan Hill, Oxford, OX2 8EJ
a division of Reed Educational & Professional Publishing Ltd
Heinemann is a registered trademark of Reed Educational & Professional Publishing Ltd

OXFORD MELBOURNE AUCKLAND
JOHANNESBURG BLANTYRE GABORONE
IBADAN PORTSMOUTH NH (USA) CHICAGO

First published 2002

ISBN 0 435 32734 8
04 03 02
10 9 8 7 6 5 4 3 2 1

Designed, illustrated and typeset by Wyvern 21 Ltd, Bristol
Printed and bound in Great Britain by The Bath Press Ltd, Bath
Index compiled by Ian D. Crane

Photographic acknowledgements
The authors and publisher would like to thank the following for permission to reproduce
photographs: Art Archive/Eileen Tweedy: 50; Associated Press: 116; Bridgeman Art Library:
2; Centre for the Study of Cartoons and Caricature/Daily Mirror: 158; Corbis: 41 (both),
49, 71 (both), 94, 132 (right), 148, 150, 168; David Low/Solo Syndication: 115; Hulton
Archive: 39; Popperfoto: 44, 132 (left); Punch: 16, 53, 186 (right); Topham Picturepoint:
204

Cover photograph: © Mary Evans Picture Library
Picture research by Sally Smith

Written source acknowledgements
The author and publisher gratefully acknowledge the following publications from which
written sources in the book are drawn. In some sentences the wording or sentence structure
has been simplified: J. Charmley, *Chamberlain and the Lost Peace* (Papermac, 1989): 209,
211; J. Charmley, *Duff Cooper* (Papermac, 1986): 209; T. Howarth, *Twentieth Century
History: the world since 1900* (Longman, 1979) © Longman Group Limited 1979, reprinted
by permission of Pearson Education Limited: 209; J.V. Polisensky, *History of Czechoslovakia
in Outline* (Bohemia International, 1947): 209; Lord Birkenhead, *Halifax – The Life of Lord
Halifax* (Hamish Hamilton, 1965): 211; D. Stevenson, *Armaments and the Coming of War*
(Clarendon Press, 1996): 121
The publishers have made every effort to trace copyright holders of material in this book.
Any omissions will be rectified in subsequent printings if notice is given to the publishers.

Dedication
To Sheree, Thomas and Edward.

For their help in producing this book I would like to thank Caroline Souter and Victoria
Cuthill of Heinemann, as well as Martin Collier and Barbara Massam for their invaluable
help in bringing a new author into print. Andrew Forrest, Malcolm Lambert and John
Vincent taught me so well I would like to take this opportunity to thank them.

The author is Head of History and Politics at Princethorpe College.

CONTENTS

HOW TO USE THIS BOOK

This book is divided into two distinct parts. The first part, Chapters 1–10, is designed to meet the needs of AS Level History students who are studying the relationship between the European powers between 1870 and 1939. The titles of the different chapters reflect the various modules offered by the three awarding bodies – Edexcel, AQA and OCR, including those offered as coursework. These chapters provide an analytical narrative of international relations both from 1870 to 1914 and from 1918 to 1939. There are summary questions at the end of each chapter to challenge students to use the information to develop their skills in analysis and explanation, and to reinforce their understanding of the key issues. The AS chapters also provide a solid basis for the more analytical work required at A2 Level.

The A2 part of the book is more analytical in style and is designed to challenge students not only to assess the evidence but also the claims of rival historiographical schools of thought. These interpretations should be read in conjunction with the relevant AS chapters. Since the subject matter covered at AS is so broad the A2 sections may draw upon more than one AS chapter. Each A2 section is directed at specific modules offered by Edexcel, AQA and OCR.

At the end of both the AS and A2 parts there are assessment sections which have been designed to give guidance on how students can meet the requirements of the new AS and A2 specifications of the three awarding bodies – Edexcel, AQA and OCR – when answering questions both in traditional examinations and for coursework.

It is hoped that the book will interest the general reader who is seeking to explore this dynamic and ultimately destructive period in relations between the European powers.

HEINEMANN ADVANCED HISTORY

European Diplomacy 1870–1939

AS SECTION: EUROPEAN DIPLOMACY 1870–1939

INTRODUCTION

The AS part of the book will enable you to acquire the knowledge and understanding you need at AS Level. Whichever AS Level modules you are studying you will find that there are chapters designed for you, and other chapters that will provide the context of what you are studying. In particular, the first chapter provides you with an overview of the entire period of international relations in Europe between 1870 and 1939.

The first seven chapters focus on the various factors which are seen as contributing to the origins of the First World War. In producing homework on its origins, you will often be asked to focus on a particular 'cause', such as the military alliances, in which case you can use the appropriate chapter. When asked to provide an overview of the causes, you should use material from different chapters to balance your answer. There is also a historiography of the origins of the First World War, which appears in Chapter 7.

Some of the AS chapters are deliberately focused on a particular factor in European relations. For example, the chapter on military plans is heavily weighted towards the Schlieffen Plan because this was the crucial factor in 1914. Recent specialist German scholarship points firmly towards the key role of the German General Staff in seeking war in 1914, and so a clear case is put forward. Equally, it is impossible to understand events in Europe after 1919 without comprehending how insecure France felt, so significant space is devoted to French plans and aspirations after 1919.

CHAPTER 1

What was the diplomatic situation in Europe in 1870 and how did it develop?

WHAT WAS THE IMPORTANCE OF THE FRANCO-PRUSSIAN WAR, 1870–1?

In 1870, Prussia, with the support of the other German states, successfully invaded France. Through a combination of military errors and political weakness, France was unable to meet the challenge and the French Emperor Napoleon III was captured following the Battle of Sedan (1870).

Whilst the Prussian generals, led by **Moltke the Elder** (Count Helmuth von Moltke)**,** destroyed the French army, the Prussian Chancellor **Otto von Bismarck** negotiated with the other German states to forge a new Germany dominated by Prussia. The result, after lengthy negotiations, was the proclamation on 21 January 1871 of the German Empire, with the Prussian King Wilhelm becoming German Emperor (Kaiser) Wilhelm I. The decision to make this ceremonial proclamation in the Hall

KEY PEOPLE

Moltke the Elder (Count Helmuth von Moltke) (1800–91) Moltke was appointed Chief of the Prussian General Staff in 1857. His distinguished service against the Danes in 1864 was followed by his brilliant use of railways to defeat Austria in 1866. Moltke's reputation reached its climax in 1870–1 when he masterminded the defeat of France.

Otto von Bismarck (1815–98) Prussian diplomat and statesman, chief minister of Prussia in 1862 during the constitutional crisis over the powers of the Diet (Prussian parliament). This he solved by declaring that there was a 'gap' in the Prussian constitution of 1848, which then allowed him to collect taxes without the Reichstag's consent, and thus to finance the expansion of the Prussian army. After a victorious war against Denmark to gain control (with Austria) over Schleswig-Holstein the parliamentary opposition faded. The army's subsequent victories over Austria (1866) and France (1870–1) made Bismarck unassailable. In 1871 he became Chancellor of the new united Germany.

The Proclamation of the German Reich in the Hall of Mirrors at Versailles, 1871.

of Mirrors at Versailles was calculated to humiliate the French. The royal hunting lodge at Versailles had been transformed into a magnificent palace on the orders of the French King Louis XIV, to symbolise his power, and Louis XIV had dominated continental European affairs from Versailles in the seventeenth and early eighteenth centuries. The ceremony thus symbolised the eclipse of France by Germany. To add to this insult, the victorious Prussian army insisted upon a victory parade through Paris despite Bismarck's wishes.

A harsh peace

By the Treaty of Frankfurt of May 1871 the new German government imposed a harsh peace settlement on France:

- France was forced to pay a huge indemnity of 5 billion gold francs;
- France lost the ore-rich provinces of Alsace-Lorraine.

The German Reich (Empire), 1871.

The defeat and the harshness of the peace treaty caused much bitterness in France. Successive governments of the

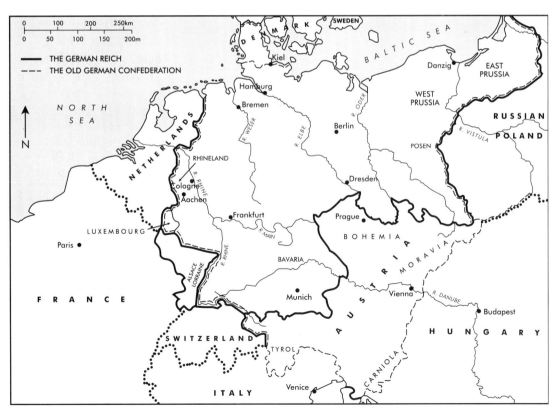

The German Reich (Empire), 1871.

French Third Republic made the return of these lost provinces a priority – in political terms this desire for their return was called **revanchism**.

After 1871, all German leaders had to take into account France's desire for revenge and therefore of the potential division of Europe into two camps – one based on France and the other based on Germany. The ultimate failure of these alliances to deter aggression would lead to war in 1914.

WHAT WERE THE CONSEQUENCES OF THE GERMAN VICTORY IN 1871?

The consequences of the German victory of 1871 were considerable and went way beyond just Germany and France.

- **Italy.** France had to use all its available troops in the war against Germany including those previously guarding Rome. When these troops left, there was nothing to stop the Italian army occupying Rome and completing the unification of Italy, despite the Pope's opposition and his decision to lock himself in the Vatican. In 1871 statesmen therefore had to deal with two new countries, Germany and Italy.
- **Britain** and the **balance of power**. Great Britain had taken no part in the conflict between France and Prussia. The German decision to invade France from the east and follow the most direct route to Paris had kept the fighting away from Belgium. Great Britain, France and Prussia had all agreed to guarantee Belgian neutrality under the Treaty of London in 1839. As France had declared war on Prussia, it was easier for Britain to remain neutral, especially given the belief in British royal circles that Crown Prince Frederick would soon succeed his father and therefore Queen Victoria's favourite daughter, as Frederick's wife, would become Empress. However, the creation of a united Germany changed the balance of power in Europe. From now on Britain recognised that it couldn't amend the balance of power in its favour by siding with either France or Prussia. The aims of British foreign policy after 1890 will be examined in depth in Section 1.

KEY TERMS

French Third Republic
After the defeat of Napoleon III at Sedan, a new republic was established in France. As there had been two previous periods when France had been a republic (1789–1804 and 1848–51) it was logical to call this the Third Republic. The Third Republic, which gave most power to the Chamber of Deputies, was to last until 1944.

Revanchism The name for both the French desire for revenge on Prussia for the loss of the provinces of Alsace-Lorraine and for the determination to recover them. Louis XIV had secured these provinces in the 1680s so the contrast with earlier French military glory was emphasised by their loss.

Balance of power This refers to the comparative importance of the main powers. Before 1870, the 'French question' was a dominating issue in Europe. It was obvious that after 1870 the balance of power had swung to Germany. This is what the historian A.J.P. Taylor meant by saying that in 1870 the French question had become the German question: since 1670, Britain had been concerned about the French dominating the whole coast of Europe along the English Channel, but after 1870 it was clear that the only power which might be strong enough to do this was Germany.

- **Russia and Austria-Hungary.** Also watching the events in western Europe were Russia and Austria-Hungary. These two empires had played a major role in European affairs before the Franco-Prussian conflict but, for different reasons, were sidelined in 1870–1. Austria-Hungary was still recovering from its defeat by Prussia in 1866. Bismarck had helped Russia to suppress the Polish Revolt in 1863 and this helped to ensure that Russia remained neutral.

WHAT WERE THE REASONS FOR THE DECLINE OF AUSTRIA-HUNGARY?

The period from 1866 to 1918 marked the decline of the once-dominant Austrian Empire. It began when Austria and Prussia went to war over Schleswig-Holstein in 1866. The Austrian army was defeated at the Battle of Sadowa, and the consequences for the Austro-Hungarian Empire were considerable.

- Up until the 1860s Austria-Hungary was considered the leading German power. After Sadowa, Austria lost the leadership of Germany to Prussia.
- Austria was also forced to grant concessions to the Hungarians in the empire. The result was the creation of Austria-Hungary (the Dual Monarchy) in 1867.
- The Austrians in the empire felt humiliated and this made them even more concerned to maintain their prestige in the Balkans. This was to have important consequences in 1914.
- The weak Austrian economy meant that they did not have the resources to recover from their relegation to fifth place amongst the 'European great powers'.
- Austrian weaknesses had been exposed in the war against Prussia. The Prussians had made excellent use of railways for moving their troops and at Sadowa a fierce fight had eventually turned partly on the ability of Prussian guns, made of steel, to keep firing accurately. In contrast, Austrian bronze cannon overheated and their fire became inaccurate.

WHAT WAS RUSSIA'S POSITION?

In 1861 Tsar Alexander II introduced the **emancipation of the serfs**, together with various legal and local government reforms, and it seemed that Russia was finally moving to catch up economically with the western European powers. However, Russia was held back by the increasing tension between the attempts to create a modern industrial economy and the refusal of the tsars to introduce significant political reforms. For example, after Alexander II was assassinated in 1881, his successors refused to give the Russian people a parliament (Duma) until the **Revolution of 1905**, and even then the Tsar cut back on the Duma's powers as soon as he felt strong enough. In the period prior to 1914 it was therefore Russia's potential to mobilise a numerically larger army rather than its proven power that European statesmen had to balance in their calculations. In 1914 the German leadership decided they could not risk waiting any longer to go to war because Russia might be too strong by 1917.

KEY TERM

Emancipation of the serfs 1861 Emancipation meant that the serfs would no longer belong to their landlords and their status as peasants would thus be similar to that of peasants elsewhere in Europe. However, the Russian peasants were obliged to make redemption payments to the government, to cover the compensation payments made by the government to their former owners. And in order for the government to collect these taxes, the peasants had to remain within their commune (mir). As a result, peasant farming continued along the antiquated strip system, so little actually improved.

The Revolution of 1905 A combination of factors led to the revolutionary situation in Russia in 1905. General discontent among peasants and industrial workers was fuelled by a repressive government and a lack of political reforms, and defeat in the unpopular war against Japan had led to food shortages and an economic slump. When demonstrators marching to the Winter Palace in 1905 were fired on by the Tsar's troops, this proved the final straw: a wave of strikes and unrest followed. Although the Tsar was eventually able to restore control by 1907, he had been forced to end redemption payments and to create a parliament (Duma).

Russia, Austria-Hungary and the Ottoman Empire, 1871.

Russian foreign policy. Despite domestic problems, all Russian rulers shared the same foreign policy objectives.

KEY EVENT

Alvensleben Convention
By signing this agreement in February 1863, Bismarck strengthened Russia's hand in Poland and ensured Russia's benevolent neutrality in the 1866 war against Austria.

- Russia's main interest in western Europe was to maintain its position in its Polish lands where it had had to crush a serious revolt in 1861. Russia knew it was important to maintain forces there. In this aim it was assisted by Prussia, and under the **Alvensleben Convention** Prussia was to return any escaping Polish nationalists to the Russian authorities. The agreement shocked Prussian liberals but Bismarck cynically used it to make sure Russia stayed out of his war with Austria in 1866.
- In the past Russia had been an ally of Austria-Hungary, both of which were conservative powers determined to prevent revolutions. So, for example, in 1848 Russia had lent Austria 100,000 troops to help suppress the revolution in its Hungarian lands. However, when in 1854 Turkey, Britain and France went to war against Russia (the Crimean War), Austria stayed neutral and did not assist Russia. This proved to be a major error by Austria since it was left without allies when Prussia attacked it in the 1860s over the ownership of Schleswig-Holstein.
- While not a question of expansionism, one of Russia's goals was to maintain secure passage of Russian vessels through to the Black Sea. The significance of **Constantinople** was that it dominated the mouth of the Black Sea and therefore the channels (known as the Bosphorus and the Dardanelles) from the Black Sea to the Mediterranean. The Black Sea offered Russia warm-water ports that it could use all year round, unlike those on the Baltic and Arctic coasts. Increasingly, Russia needed these ports so that it could export grain; money from these exports enabled Russia to import the industrial goods it needed to develop its economy.

KEY PLACE

Constantinople This city was the capital of the Ottoman Empire and guarded the mouth of the Bosphorous. As the Ottoman Empire declined, so it became an important consideration to the Russians that Constantinople did not fall into the hands of other powers, e.g. Austria, who might prevent access of Russian vessels to the Black Sea.

THE OTTOMAN EMPIRE

Geographically the Ottoman Empire was centred on modern Turkey, but it also included part of south-eastern Europe and stretched down through what is today called the Middle East. Politically the Ottoman Empire had declined since failing to capture Vienna in 1683, and during the eighteenth and nineteenth centuries the Russians had pushed it back by advancing towards the Black Sea. Turkey's hold on south-east Europe had therefore gradually weakened.

- **The Ottoman Empire and Austria.** During the nineteenth century the Austrians had gained control over the areas of **Bosnia and Herzegovina** but they were not formally part of the Austrian Empire until they were annexed in 1908.
- **Ottoman Empire and Russia.** The tension between Turkey and Austria was made worse as Russia's influence expanded into the Balkans. To limit Russian power, the other great powers therefore insisted that some of Russia's conquests become independent states. In practice this made the situation more complicated, for example the **Slavs** living under Turkish rule could see that they might become independent and not just swap one ruler for another. (Chapters 2 and 3 provide a history of the Balkans in this critical period, when Turkish-owned areas were the focus of intense rivalry between Russia and Austria-Hungary.)
- **Ottoman Empire and Britain.** In support of Turkey lay Great Britain, who was very reluctant to see Russia gain access to the Mediterranean. At the end of the Crimean War, Russia had agreed the Treaty of Paris, which contained the 'Black Sea Clauses'. These denied all warships, including Russian warships, access from the Black Sea into the Mediterranean through the Dardanelles. The important thing about the Treaty of Paris was thus that it neutralised the Black Sea.

After Britain purchased control of the Suez Canal in 1875 its concern to prevent Russia from reaching the eastern Mediterranean became even more acute. Britain's main concern here was the security of the Suez Canal as it provided a shorter and safer route to India, and the increasingly important **Middle East**, than the route round the Cape. At the same time Russia seemed to pose a threat to India through its interests in Persia (modern Iran) where Britain too was developing trade links.

KEY TERMS

Entente This French word meaning 'understanding' is the term given to Britain's informal agreements with France (1904) and Russia (1907). Although there were no formal treaties binding Britain to go to war, by 1912 the cabinet had been told that this would be the probable result of a German attack on France.

Schlieffen Plan This is the name given to the German operational plan for conducting war, used in 1914 and named after the man who originally conceived it in 1895, Field Marshal Count Alfred von Schlieffen. Neither the original plan, nor the revised version agreed by Schlieffen before he retired, was implemented in 1914, but this is the name by which it is known as the strategic concept remained unaltered.

KEY PERSON

Count Alfred von Schlieffen (1833–1913)
Born into one of the wealthiest Prussian families, Schlieffen attended the Prussian War Academy in 1858 and developed expertise in map-making, but this only led to slow promotion before 1865. Moltke's early impressions of Schlieffen were not good, but by 1888 he was on the General Staff and well known to the Kaiser and his favourite, Philipp von Eulenberg. Schlieffen then served as Chief of the General Staff from 1891 until his retirement in 1906.

WHAT EFFECT DID COLONIAL RIVALRY HAVE ON EUROPEAN DIPLOMACY?

One of the ironies of the period 1870–1914 is the **Entente** of Britain, France and Russia: so often colonial rivals between 1870 and 1900, these countries ended up on the same side in the First World War. Prior to 1900 the sharpest colonial disputes were between Britain and France in Africa, and Britain and Russia in the Middle East. (The importance of colonial rivalries will be explored in Chapter 3. In Section 3 the relationship between these three powers will be looked at further.)

WHAT WERE GERMAN PRIORITIES BEFORE 1914?

Given all these conflicting tensions and rivalries it is perhaps surprising that no major conflict broke out before 1914. The role played by Bismarck in the period 1870–90 is frequently used to explain why conflict did not occur sooner. He is often quoted as having said that the Balkans were not worth the 'bones of a single Pomeranian Grenadier'. The view is that if Bismarck had been alive and still in charge he would never have allowed Germany to become involved in a war over the Balkans as it did in 1914.

Bismarck managed to make his dismissal as Chancellor in 1890 by Wilhelm II appear connected with the Reinsurance Treaty with Russia (see Chapter 5). Linking his departure to this treaty made it look as if a headstrong monarch, Wilhelm II, had upset Bismarck's careful diplomacy. However, Chapter 5 will explore how far Bismarck's mistakes had already committed Germany to an alliance with Austria-Hungary that would lead to war. Prior to 1914, and as a result of German victories over the Austrians and French, the German General Staff was admired by military leaders around the world. Its role and importance are often discussed solely in relation to the **Schlieffen Plan**, but its influence on the decisions made in 1914 will also be analysed.

Arms race and Sarajevo

The overall impact of military planning and the 'arms race' will be assessed in Chapter 5. All the great powers developed military plans and this had a crucial impact in the lead-up to the declaration of war in 1914. Assessing the interaction between the military and their civilian counterparts will lead us, in Chapter 6, to consider why the assassination in Sarajevo, the capital of Bosnia-Herzegovina, led to the outbreak of war amongst the five 'great powers'. War should have been avoidable, but many leaders encouraged it. They did not have any idea of the developments in warfare that were to prolong the conflict into a worldwide one lasting four years. Since war may have been avoidable, we will explore why key decision-makers chose war. The reasons why Britain decided to enter the conflict will be examined in more detail in Section 4, whilst the broader issue of Anglo-German rivalry is the focus of Section 2.

WHAT WAS THE IMPACT OF THE FIRST WORLD WAR?

War guilt

At Versailles in 1919, the victorious powers could certainly agree that Germany had caused and started the war and this became enshrined in the famous Article 231 of the Treaty of Versailles, otherwise known as the 'war guilt' clause. Chapter 8 will explore the question of Germany's guilt. It has been argued that Germany was making a 'bid for world power' and this view almost seems to justify the Allied view, but it is very important to explore the critical role played by Austria-Hungary during the crisis of 1914.

Diplomatic consequences

The enormous impact of the First World War on the map of Europe meant that diplomats had to reassess their aims and objectives, as well as the methods by which they would achieve them in the post-war order. The diplomatic consequences of the war will be explored in Chapter 8 and British foreign policy objectives will be analysed in Section 5. Relationships between the European powers during the 1920s will then be considered in Chapter 9, and the role of the League of Nations will provide the focus of Chapter 10. The importance of the League will be balanced against the exhaustion of Europe as a whole and the weakness of Germany in particular. An important thread running through these chapters will be the French search for security following the decision of the United States not to ratify the Treaty of Versailles. Ultimately, the French sought security in a policy of **appeasement** in which they found an ally in Britain. Sections 6 and 7 will explore the motives for appeasement and whether recent scholarship justifies a reappraisal of the role of Neville Chamberlain as Chancellor between 1931 and 1937 and as Prime Minister of Great Britain from 1937 to 1940.

KEY TERM

Appeasement The policy of seeking to avoid war by agreeing to Hitler's reasonable demands. This was the object of British and French foreign policy. Britain and France wanted to keep peace in Europe by renegotiating the Treaty of Versailles. Germany was expected to play a conciliatory role in this, i.e. to make concessions for peace.

SUMMARY QUESTIONS

1 What were the main priorities for France between 1871 and 1939?

2 What were Russia's objectives between 1871 and 1914 and what were its fears?

CHAPTER 2

What were the long-term tensions in the Balkans and why did these tensions lead to war?

The Balkans are in the south-eastern corner of Europe, between the Adriatic and Black Seas. Their proximity to Turkey affected their history in a way not experienced by the rest of Europe, for they were invaded and for centuries occupied by Turks and ruled by the Ottoman Empire. This led to tensions normal between ruled and rulers, but there were also tensions between the various different races within the Balkans which became increasingly apparent as the Turkish grip on the area weakened.

THE OTTOMAN EMPIRE

From their original heartland in Asia in the fourteenth century, the Turks (who were Muslims) had advanced into and conquered most of south-east Europe. By 1685 the Ottoman Empire (so-called after Osman, its first leader) had reached its peak. It had been checked to the north by Russia, who had taken back land north of the Black Sea by 1800, and to the west by Austria when it failed to capture Vienna in 1683, but the Ottoman Empire's European possessions still comprised all the area of what became present-day Hungary, Romania, Bulgaria, Yugoslavia, Albania and Greece.

THE BALKANS

The Balkans is the part of south-east Europe closest to Asia Minor (modern-day Turkey) that includes Greece, Bulgaria, the former Yugoslavia and Romania. In 1870, the Turks still ruled much of the Balkans. However, as Turkish authority began to crumble, independent states were set up, the first being Greece in the 1820s.

Throughout their occupation of the Balkans, the Turks failed to subdue the non-Turkish peoples who lived there. In addition, the Balkans contained lots of different tensions. These were based upon:

- Religious differences, e.g. Orthodox Serbs and Catholic Croatians. There were three different religious groups – Turkish Muslims, Christians of the Western Church (usually Roman Catholics) and Christians of the Eastern **Orthodox Church.**
- Ethnic differences. There were ethnic differences between Slavs and Turks, and between the Slavs themselves; the different groups were often intermingled.

These internal tensions made it very difficult for stability to be maintained in the Balkans. When the Turkish Empire began to weaken, the various minorities and groups realised that there was a prospect of change, and possibly of independence.

In order to reinforce their own sense of security, each of the three surrounding great powers – Austria-Hungary, Russia and the Ottoman Empire – were interested in the

KEY TERM

Orthodox Church The Orthodox Church broke with the Roman Catholic Church over the issue of whether priests could marry. It therefore gave Christians in Eastern Europe an identity which was different from both the Muslims and the Roman Catholic Austrians.

The decline of Turkey in Europe, 1812–1914.

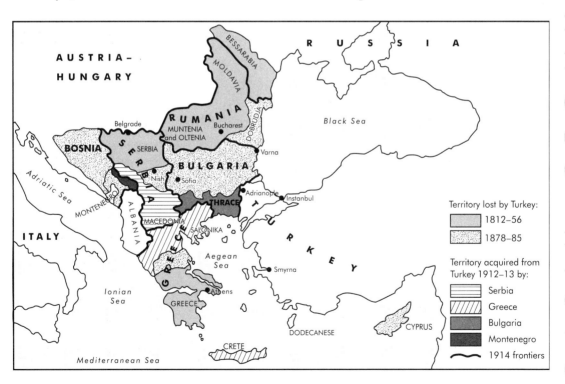

Balkans. Certainly the Balkans were in a key position, providing access to the Mediterranean. Austria-Hungary wanted to prevent the formation of a large Slav state in the Balkans, and so was keen to expand into and control areas on its borders, especially after being sidelined by the unification of Italy and defeated to the north by Prussia. The Russians wanted to expand to the south to gain clear access to the Mediterranean, which in effect meant control of the Bosphorus and Dardanelles. Russia's key aim, in this respect, was defensive – it wanted to exclude the fleets of the other great powers from the Black Sea.

AUSTRIAN EXPANSION INTO THE BALKANS BEFORE 1870

The Austrian emperors saw it as their historic mission to defeat the Turks. And, in an age of territorial expansion, the natural area for Austrian expansion was over the land border with the Ottoman Empire. Just as British soldiers could build careers by making conquests in India, Austrian generals could hope to win fame by adding more territory to the empire at the expense of Turkey.

By 1699 the Austrians had recovered Hungary from the Turks. During the eighteenth century Austria only made small gains from Turkey because it was busy fighting Prussia in several wars in northern and western Europe. After 1866, when Austria was finally defeated by Prussia, the Hungarians were made partners with Austria in a **Dual Monarchy**, Austria-Hungary. The Hungarians then became very aggressive towards the other nationalities within the Austrian Empire, such as the Croats and Slovenes, wanting to demonstrate that the Dual Monarchy was a reality and that they had to be treated as equal to the Austrians. For example, they enforced the use of Hungarian in schools just as previously everyone had had to recognise German as the official language. This increased the desire of people like the Serbs to leave the Austrian Empire.

Italian unification 1871. Italian unification in 1871 had an important impact on the politics of the Balkans. Until the 1860s Austria had dominated northern Italy. However, the

KEY THEME

Dual Monarchy The Dual Monarchy, created by the *Ausgleich* (literally, the 'settlement'), describes the Austrian Empire from 1867 when the Hungarians were given equal status with the Austrians. It enabled the Hungarians to have self-government, with a joint monarchy, army and foreign ministry. In the period prior to 1914, the Austrians often found it difficult to secure Hungarian agreement to extra armament spending. The special status of the Hungarians led other nationalities, such as the Czechs, to demand equal recognition.

unification of Italy ended Austrian imperial ambitions south of the Alps, just as German unification closed off hopes in the north. For Austria the Balkans were the last available area of imperial expansion.

RUSSIAN EXPANSION INTO THE BALKANS BEFORE 1870

Russia's borders in western Europe had effectively been fixed in 1793 when Austria, Prussia and Russia agreed to partition Poland. At the end of the Napoleonic wars in 1815 the Congress of Vienna reinstated this 1793 division of Poland, consistent with its policy of restoring Europe to its pre-war condition as far as possible.

During the eighteenth century Russia had gradually pushed the Turks back to the Black Sea in a series of campaigns on its south-eastern frontier. In 1783 Russia annexed the Crimea. The Russian Empire had expanded to meet the Austrian Empire in 1699 but in 1812 Russia took the Black Sea port of Odessa and the surrounding region. After the capture of Odessa it was clear that the two powers would meet before they reached Constantinople as both were trying to control the western shores of the Black Sea. Ironically, before 1850 Russia had been a powerful ally of Austria, and in 1848 Russian troops had saved the Emperor from **revolution**. However, Austria chose to remain neutral in 1854 whilst France and Britain joined Turkey in attacking Russia in the Crimea. The Russians felt betrayed by Austria and this led to deterioration in relations between the two empires. It also marked a turning point in their attitudes to the Balkans, since they would now openly rival each other for Balkan spoils as Turkey became increasingly weaker.

The British feared that Russia's aim was to reach the Mediterranean, which would enable it to have a 'warm-water' port all year round and unrestricted access to world trade. Russian power would then stretch into the Mediterranean and cut off the British trade route to India. The Austrians feared that any extension of Russian power would lead to the growth of Serbia and to the break-up of Austria's multinational empire (as Serbs and others sought

KEY THEME

1848 revolutions In 1848 revolutions took place in many European countries. The ideal behind the revolutions was liberalism. The liberals wanted to replace their monarchies with governments based upon written constitutions. In Austria, the Emperor Franz Josef came to the throne and, supported by Russia, was able to restore the monarchy's position. In Prussia the crown retained control but agreed to a written constitution.

Punch cartoon of 1908 entitled 'The Balkan cauldron'.

to join together in their ethnic groups to create independent states). Given the tensions explained above it is not surprising that the Balkans were to be politically unstable for the fifty years leading to the eve of the First World War.

WAR IN THE BALKANS 1875–8

The extent of the tension in this period can most clearly be seen in the events of 1875–87. In July 1875 a rebellion broke out in Herzegovina, and then in Bosnia, against Turkish rule. The Serbs supported the insurrection, mainly because they hoped to gain the two provinces for themselves. Russia was sympathetic to the Serbs because they supported **Pan-Slavism**, and because they thought this would further their own ambitions in the region. For example, Prince Milan, the Serbian leader, had been encouraged by Count Nikolai Ignatiev, Russia's diplomat in Constantinople.

In 1876 the revolt spread to Bulgaria, and Montenegro and Serbia declared war on Turkey. On 2 July 1876 a Serbian army of 125,000 poorly-trained peasants advanced out of its principality to challenge Ottoman power. The Serbs were supported by 500 Russian volunteers led by General Chernayev. However, the Turks had been improving their army. After three months of his rule the new Sultan, Abdul Hamid II (1876–1909), was able to celebrate a victory over the Serbs on 1 September 1876 at Alexinatz.

Despite its victory, the ruthless methods used by the Turks to suppress the opposition led to international condemnation. During the Bulgarian revolt the Turkish forces massacred over 12,000 inhabitants, which provoked the Russians to the verge of war. Russian pressure on the Sultan followed and led him to make peace with the Serbs and to restore their limited powers of self-government. The Grand Vizier (chief minister) of the Ottoman Empire also announced a new constitution, which suggested the possibility of reforms; a possibility that encouraged Britain to oppose Russian ambitions. However, **W. E. Gladstone** had stirred up popular opposition to the Turks over their treatment of the Bulgarians. For this reason the British Prime Minister, Lord Beaconsfield (**Benjamin Disraeli**'s new title), could now argue that Turkey must be given time to make any internal change effective. Russia's response was to invade the Ottoman Empire on 24 April 1877.

The Russo-Turkish War, 1877–8
Russia was hoping for a quick victory which the other great powers would accept. The Russians advanced south from the mouth of the River Danube to the fortress of Plevna. Here the Turkish garrison fought courageously and only on 9 December 1877 did Plevna surrender. The other great powers had been hoping for a Turkish victory. Now they began to worry as the Russian army advanced and defeated the Turks at the Shipka Pass (10 December 1877). The Russian army then continued through the province of Eastern Rumelia before entering the city of

KEY PEOPLE

William Ewart Gladstone (1809–98) At that time, W.E. Gladstone was in retirement. However, as the formal Liberal leader and Prime Minister from 1868 to 1874 he was still a powerful political figure. His pamphlet on the Bulgarian atrocities aroused the concern of the then middle-class electorate and began to reinvigorate the Liberal Party. This process was completed by Gladstone's Midlothian Campaign of 1879, which laid the basis for the Liberal victory in the 1880 general election and Gladstone's own return to the party leadership and the premiership.

Benjamin Disraeli (1804–81) British statesman and Conservative Prime Minister. Led the Conservatives to victory in 1874, their first success since 1841. A middle-class man who was picked to lead the party because of his speaking skills in Parliament, Disraeli is famous for his view of the Conservative Party as classless – 'One Nation'. Promoted popular imperialism, famously through purchasing the Suez Canal shares and asking Parliament's approval afterwards. Took a peerage in 1876 as Lord Beaconsfield and subsequently lost the general election of 1880 at a time when the economy was in recession.

Adrianople on 20 January 1878. The Russian army was now in a position to attack Constantinople and bring down the Ottoman Empire.

Austria was faced with seeing its rival beat it in the race to the Mediterranean, and therefore appealed to Germany for help. Also with interests in the outcome of the war, the British government threatened military action if Russia broke the **Black Sea Clauses** of the Treaty of Paris of 1856, which had ended the Crimean War (though these were cancelled in 1871). In January 1878 the British government, encouraged by Queen Victoria, prepared to send the Royal Navy to Constantinople in support of the Turks. However, the fleet was recalled as reports came back from Constantinople that the city had not been attacked. Instead, in February 1878 the Royal Navy was ordered through the Dardanelles. At this point war seemed imminent between Britain and Russia, which sparked an outburst of '**Jingoism**' in Britain.

The Treaty of San Stefano, March 1878. Before Britain could intervene, Russia and Turkey came to terms. Their treaty was humiliating for the Turks, who were forced to agree to the following conditions:

• Serbia, Romania and Montenegro were to become independent.
• Bulgaria was to become an autonomous province under an elected prince and was to be occupied for two years by Russian troops. Russia wanted to create a 'Big Bulgaria' in the hope that it would therefore be a grateful ally of Russia. Russia proposed that Bulgaria would receive the whole of Eastern Rumelia and further territory along the Black Sea coast. In addition, Russia wanted Bulgaria to include the province around Nish on the eastern Serb borders. The British objected to this plan because it would give Russia effective control of the Black Sea almost up to Constantinople. The resignation of the pro-Russian Lord Derby as Foreign Secretary made war seem more likely since he was replaced by Lord Salisbury, who took a more aggressive approach. Faced with the strong possibility of war with Britain, the Russians agreed to an international congress in Berlin.

The Balkans after the Treaty of San Stefano, March 1878.

Map labels: River Danube, AUSTRIA – HUNGARY, RUSSIA, BESSARABIA, ROMANIA, BOSNIA, DOBRUDJA, HERZEGOVINA, SERBIA, Nish, ANNEXED, River Danube, MONTE-NEGRO, Adriatic Sea, BULGARIA, Black Sea, Constantinople, DARDANELLES, Mediterranean Sea, Aegean Sea, TURKEY, GREECE, Turkish Empire, CRETE, N

KEY TERMS

'Big Bulgaria' The Russians had wanted to create a 'Big Bulgaria' which included Eastern Rumelia. However, the other powers believed that if they agreed to this then Bulgaria would simply be a Russian client state. By persuading Russia to back down the other powers inadvertently sealed the disappointment of the Bulgarian nationalists, who were left with a much smaller country.

The Congress of Berlin, June to July 1878. At the Congress in Berlin the great powers wanted to limit Russia's territorial gains. The idea of a **'Big Bulgaria'** was blocked. However, the following points of agreement were made, largely owing to the diplomatic skills of Bismarck:

- Eastern Rumelia was made into a self-governing province of Turkey and was eventually joined to Bulgaria in 1885 (see below).
- The Bulgarians annexed the Dobrudja region, which gave them control of more of the Black Sea coastline.
- Serbia gained the whole area around Nish.
- The main power to make gains was Austria-Hungary, which was to occupy (but not formally to annex)

What were the long-term tensions in the Balkans and why did they lead to war?   19

Bosnia-Herzegovina. Austria was also to occupy the Sanjak of Novibazar which bordered Serbia and Montenegro. Thus Austria-Hungary had done very well for a power that had not conquered anyone, whereas Russia had gained very little from its successful campaign.

- The British desire to block Russian expansion was appeased by the transfer of Cyprus from Turkey to Britain. This gave Britain a naval base from which to shield the approaches to the Suez Canal. Disraeli had bought a controlling interest in the canal in 1875 on behalf of the government, and now he could use Cyprus to show the public that this was another British triumph.

Russia could feel justifiably bitter at the way in which the other powers robbed it of its gains. This was to make it even more sensitive about its prestige in 1914, and lead to serious consequences. Russia was not prepared to risk any further loss of prestige in 1914 so it backed Serbia despite the risk of a general European war.

WHAT LED TO THE END OF TURKISH CONTROL IN THE BALKANS?

Bulgarian unification 1885. Despite Russia's disappointment at the results of the Congress of Berlin, the Russians were pleased in 1879 when Prince Alexander of **Battenberg** was made Prince of Bulgaria. He was an officer in the Russian army and the nephew of Tsar Alexander II's wife. Also, Britain accepted him, as he was related to and liked by both Queen Victoria and her daughter the Crown Princess of Germany. In 1885 Prince Alexander decided to take advantage of a revolt in Eastern Rumelia, and declared himself prince of a united Bulgaria that included Eastern Rumelia. Such actions roused Serbia into attacking Bulgaria in November 1885, although the Serbians were defeated at the battles of Slivnitza and Pirot. The Russians were affronted by this victory: they wanted to be seen as the power upon whom Bulgaria relied. They were also unhappy at seeing their client, Serbia, defeated. Prince Alexander's actions made it seem as if he, a German, had achieved what Russia had not been able to achieve at the Congress of Berlin: a 'Big Bulgaria'. Again, therefore, the Russians were seen to have been humiliated in the Balkans.

The Russo-Japanese War 1905. Although this was fought much later and outside the Balkans, its impact was to have important consequences for the balance of power in that region. Russia was concerned to increase its interest in the Balkans but it also wanted to expand eastwards. This was partly encouraged by the opening of the completed **Trans-Siberian Railway** in 1903. Whilst this war might have eventually led to conflict with the other powers, it was in a much less sensitive area. Britain and France agreed to remain neutral in the war, thereby showing that alliances in the Pacific did not automatically lead to war, unlike those in Europe in 1914. Russia's defeat by Japan both on land and at sea, where the Russians lost two fleets, seriously undermined the Tsar's regime, and ultimately increased Russian sensitivity over its position in the Balkans.

Why was there a Bosnian crisis in 1908–9? The Sultan of Turkey depended upon the army to prevent Turkey's enemies trying to break up his empire. Some army officers, however, began to realise that in order to survive the Ottoman Empire must undergo political reform. In July 1908 the Sultan, who resented his dependence upon the army, decided to strike against military conspirators and sent General Semsi Pasha to Macedonia to root out rebel leaders. However, Semsi Pasha was assassinated in broad daylight and this led to several army garrisons declaring support for the rebels. The Sultan's power collapsed rapidly and the **Young Turks**, as the conspirators were known, came to power. They were committed to reforming Turkey, initially by the introduction of a democratic constitution.

On 5 October 1908 Prince Ferdinand of Bulgaria, Alexander's successor, proclaimed the country's full independence with himself as tsar. He therefore laid down a challenge to Turkey, as the title of tsar meant he was rejecting all Turkish authority over the area. (Turkey's nominal authority over parts of Ferdinand's new kingdom such as Eastern Rumelia had been agreed as part of the overall compromise at the Congress of Berlin in 1878.)

On the same day, 5 October 1908, Austria-Hungary announced that it was annexing Bosnia-Herzegovina. There were two main reasons why Austria-Hungary wanted to **annex** Bosnia-Herzegovina. The first was an attempt to take advantage of Russia's willingness to compromise in order to gain access to the Dardanelles. The second reason was to have something with which to celebrate **Emperor Franz Josef**'s Golden Jubilee. The fact that he had initially come to the throne in 1848 with Russian military backing would have only further annoyed the Russians. Ultimately, this move was seen as a challenge to Turkey and also to Serbia and to Russia.

Greater Serbia Austria's annexation of Bosnia-Herzegovina blocked the Serb concept of a 'Greater Serbia'. To achieve a Greater Serbia the Serbs would now have to attack Austria-Hungary. In 1909 the Black Hand terrorist group was formed to pursue the goal of a Greater Serbia – five years later Gavrilo Princip, a member of the Black Hand, was to assassinate Archduke Franz Ferdinand in pursuit of this ideal.

- For Serb nationalists the idea of a **Greater Serbia** stretching to the Adriatic was a powerful one. To be truly independent it was vital to secure Bosnia-Herzegovina which lay between Serbia and the sea.
- To Russia, Austria's move seemed not only aggressive but also deceitful. The Russian Foreign Minister A. P. Isvolsky had initially agreed to the Austrian plans in return for the Russian right to sail the Black Sea fleet through the Dardanelles. While Isvolsky was visiting the European capitals seeking further support for Russia's aims, Austria acted. In the end, the Russians gained no support and Austria had outwitted it. When Isvolsky's initial agreement leaked into the Russian press he was forced to resign.

Having been humiliated in 1908 and frustrated in 1878 Russia was determined not to fail to give Serbia its full backing in 1914. One of the fundamental reasons why war broke out in 1914 was that each one of the great powers felt it could not risk backing down again.

THE BALKAN WARS 1912–3

The First Balkan War, 1912–3. The tension in the Balkans was not confined to the great powers. As has already been seen, there were bitter ethnic conflicts in the region and considerable rivalry between the smaller Balkan states. This rivalry was to spill over into war and was to increase further the possibility of war between the great powers. In 1912 war broke out with Bulgaria, Serbia, Montenegro and Greece uniting against Turkey. The reasons for this war were many.

- In 1885 Bulgaria had defeated Serbia. This minor war meant that both sides then concentrated on building up their armies and on developing modern weapons to fight the next war, which both felt was inevitable.
- The Balkan arms race was fuelled by loans from the great powers. Bulgaria purchased weapons from both France and Germany. In 1906 Serbia owed France 300 million francs but it received a loan of 95 million francs

in return for an exclusive contract with the French firm Schneider-Creusot to supply the Serbs with artillery.

- In 1903 **King Alexander of Serbia was assassinated**, partly because he maintained close ties with Austria. This set Serbian politicians upon a collision course with Austria, encouraging those who wanted a 'Greater Serbia' which would include Bosnia-Herzegovina.
- The bitter disagreement between Austria and Russia in 1908–9 opened the way for the small Balkan countries to challenge Turkey, as it was clear that Austria-Hungary and Russia would not co-operate to save Turkey.
- Opportunity for the small Balkan powers came in the wake of the Libyan War of 1912. In this war Italy defeated Turkey and won control over Libya, Tripoli and the Dodecanese Islands. This defeat for the Ottoman Empire served to emphasise the extent of its weakness.
- Even though they had competing claims on Turkish territory the Greeks, Serbs, Montenegrins and Bulgarians had formed a military alliance in March 1912 – the Balkan League – to attack Turkey.

The Balkan League declared war on Turkey in October 1912 and advanced to within 32 km of Istanbul (Constantinople). Its aim was to force the Ottoman Empire to hand over Macedonia so that members could divide it among themselves; the League quickly secured a complete victory. Under the Treaty of London, signed in May 1913, the First Balkan War officially ended. Turkish rule on the mainland of Europe was reduced to a small part of eastern Thrace.

The Second Balkan War, June to July 1913. The Treaty of London, while recognising the effective removal of Turkish influence from Balkan affairs, did not deal with, let alone solve, the consequences within the Balkan states of Turkey's departure. As a result Serbia and Greece formed an alliance against Bulgaria. The reasons for this were as follows:

- Serbia had failed to fulfil its ambitions to reach the Adriatic.

The assassination of King Alexander The assassination of King Alexander of Serbia by a military conspiracy, and his replacement by Peter I, increased the influence of the army in Serbian politics as Peter I knew what had happened to his predecessor. Serbia switched to buying French weapons, instead of German ones, as deliveries would not be stopped in the event of a war with Austria-Hungary. Rearmament was accelerated, leading to the Balkan wars.

- Serbia was also offended by Bulgaria's unwillingness to give it more of Macedonia.
- Greek ambitions to reunite Thrace with the rest of Greece remained unfulfilled.

Greece and Serbia now fought successfully against Bulgaria. At the Treaty of Bucharest in August 1913 Serbia gained control of part of Macedonia whilst Greece won areas in Thrace. Meanwhile the Romanians took advantage of the situation, seizing the Dobrudja and therefore gaining access to the Black Sea.

It was possible that the First Balkan War might have triggered a wider conflict. Austria-Hungary, in particular, was concerned about whether Serbia would try to seize Bosnia-Herzegovina. That the situation was settled without involving the great powers owed a lot to Anglo-German co-operation in restraining their allies' demands. However, this co-operation did not undermine their commitment to their allies; Britain remained committed to the Entente with France (1904) and Germany still recognised Austria-Hungary as its only reliable ally:

- Prince Lichnowsky, the German ambassador in London, was told not to support Russian demands even if Russia was prepared to make considerable concessions. He was instructed that solutions must be found 'without undermining the solidarity of our relationship with Austria'.
- The British Foreign Secretary, Sir Edward Grey, noted in May 1913 that it was an important time to keep close to both France and Russia.

What were the effects of the Balkan Wars? The Balkan Wars were to have a profound impact not only on the strategic planning of the great powers, but also on their belief that the decisive moment was approaching when war would be a less risky option than peace.

- Like Turkey, Austria-Hungary was a multinational empire. Turkish authority in the Balkans had collapsed. Faced by a victorious Serbia, **General Conrad von Hötzendorf** (referred to from now on as Conrad), the

Austrian Chief of Staff, recommended to the Emperor again that the best course of action was to strike against Serbia before it grew any stronger.

- In February 1913, **Helmuth Moltke**, the German Chief of Staff, wrote to Conrad to say that sooner or later there must be a war between the Germans and the Slavs but that the first move must come from the Slavs. This would give the other great powers (France, Russia and Great Britain) less justification to intervene.

By July 1914 the assassination of Archduke Franz Ferdinand was to give Conrad his best argument for a strike against Serbia, and by then Moltke favoured war as he considered Germany more ready for war in 1914 than its potential enemies. The Emperor had refrained from a pre-emptive strike against Serbia in 1913, but in 1914 he could use the assassination to justify action. Conrad advised him strongly that the assassination at Sarajevo was the opportunity they had been waiting for.

CONCLUSION

The Balkans were a politically unstable region where new national governments were emerging to replace those of the multinational Ottoman Empire.

- Russia's policy of sponsoring new Slav states was in direct conflict with Austria-Hungary's determination to maintain its empire and add to it where possible.
- The Balkans were the area in which Austria-Hungary wanted to extend its empire whilst other powers looked to Africa.
- After their defeat in Japan in 1905 the Russians turned their attention back the Balkans. Until at least 1907 Russian expansion was opposed by Britain. This contributed to a sense of failure on the part of the Russians. Under increasing pressure at home, Tsar Nicholas II felt all the more keenly the need to maintain Russian prestige abroad. Therefore in 1914 Serbia could rely upon Russian backing even at the cost of war. Nicholas II may have believed that war would unite his empire behind him – fatefully, this was not the only

miscalculation made during the July crisis of 1914 following the assassination of Archduke Franz Ferdinand.

SUMMARY QUESTIONS

1 Why was the decline of Ottoman power such a cause for concern to both Austria-Hungary and Russia?

2 What was Great Britain's interest in the 'Eastern Question'?

3 Why did Russia feel humiliated in the Balkans by the end of 1913?

4 Why was Serbia to grow between 1870 and the end of 1913?

CHAPTER 3

Which were the important colonial rivalries, c.1890–1914?

In the period up to 1914 the major European powers were establishing colonial empires. Much of this activity was centred upon Africa and is commonly called the **Scramble for Africa**. Because the great powers were competing for colonies there was a growth in nationalism, and this contributed to the popular enthusiasm for war in 1914. Before 1900 the most intense rivalries seemed to be between Britain and France on the one hand, and Britain and Russia on the other. Since these three countries ended up fighting as allies it is easy to believe that colonial rivalries played little part in causing the First World War. However, other rivalries, such as those between Germany and Britain and between Russia and Austria-Hungary (explained in the previous chapter), were crucial factors in the build-up to war.

THE RIVALRY BETWEEN AUSTRIA AND RUSSIA IN THE BALKANS

We have seen that this rivalry was important because the Balkans were the area where war eventually broke out, and both Russia and Austria had territorial ambitions in the Balkans. Other European powers had territorial ambitions in Africa. The situations were not identical, as Austria and Russia preferred annexation to colonisation, and defending one's own territory was a crucial factor in Europe. The **Mürzstag Agreement** between Austria and Russia in 1903 eased the Balkan tension between them, for it provided for the maintenance of the **status quo**.

However, this balance was destroyed when Austria-Hungary decided to annex Bosnia-Herzegovina in 1908. The Mursteg Agreement had been signed when Russia had completed the Trans-Siberian Railway (1903) and was thinking about developing its empire eastwards on the

KEY TERMS

Scramble for Africa is the term given to the actions of European powers between 1880 and 1914 when they tried to establish and increase their rule in Africa by promoting colonies. It was described as a race, since the various powers were competing with each other for land and dominance.

Mürzstag Agreement 1903 Russia and Austria-Hungary signed this agreement to maintain the status quo in Macedonia. However, it included a clause permitting a review leading to changes in administrative boundaries. Greece, Serbia and Bulgaria interpreted this clause as allowing the future division of Macedonia.

Status quo is a Latin phrase used to describe a situation which remains the same. So an agreement to maintain the *status quo* means agreeing not to make any changes. Sometimes an agreement refers to the *status quo ante* which means the situation as it was before an event, such as before a war.

Pacific coast rather than in the south towards the Mediterranean. By 1908 Russia had lost its war against Japan (in 1905) and its attention was again turned towards the Balkans.

Acquiring Bosnia-Herzegovina extended Austria-Hungary's control of the Adriatic coast. This reminded the other great powers that Austria-Hungary had to be considered as a key power in the Mediterranean. Also, German support for this annexation may have indirectly led to war since Britain took any naval threat to the Mediterranean very seriously. Though there was no formal naval agreement in the Anglo-French Entente, from 1904 onwards the main role of the **Royal Navy** was cancelling out the new Imperial German Navy whilst the **French Navy** secured the Mediterranean from Austrian interference. Both countries would then impose a blockade upon the central powers.

The 'promises' made to Italy by Britain and France, such as support for gains from Austria e.g. along the Adriatic coast, were designed before 1914 to secure Italy's neutrality, at the least. If Italy stayed neutral then this would further swing the balance of naval power in the Mediterranean towards the Entente. After 1906 Italy saw Austria as its main naval rival.

THE RIVALRY BETWEEN BRITAIN AND FRANCE

Background. Britain and France had been colonial rivals since the eighteenth century. The British had triumphed over the French in India and Canada; the French had then helped the Americans to throw the British out of their 13 American colonies south of Canada. By the late nineteenth century the two countries were also rivals in Africa and Asia. This rivalry hindered Britain and France becoming allies in opposition to Germany.

Africa. The concession the French desired most from Britain was to end its occupation of Egypt (Britain had abolished dual control of Egypt with France in 1882). France resented the way Britain had ousted French power in Egypt. But with the increasing pressures on the Ottoman Empire from Russia and the Austrian Empire (see

KEY THEME

Anglo-French naval co-operation To cancel the threat from the new Imperial German Navy, the Royal Navy withdrew ships from the Mediterranean. The British Home Fleet was concentrated in the English Channel, whilst the Grand Fleet was based at Scapa Flow to guard the North Sea. After July 1912, the French therefore switched battleships form their Channel Fleet to their Mediterranean Fleet based at Toulon in order to guard the Mediterranean. This increased the pressure on Great Britain to fulfil 'its commitments' to France in 1914 since the French fleet was not in the right place to defend the Channel.

Chapter 2), the British did not want to abandon Egypt. If the British maintained control of Egypt they would continue to protect the Suez Canal and the short route to India, even if the Russians reached Constantinople.

The British had occupied Egypt after 1882 because the **Khedive** was unable to suppress the anti-western rebellion led by the **Mahdi**. In effect, Britain had taken a slice of the Ottoman Empire. Like all the great powers Britain found it easier to find reasons to justify its own occupation of Egypt than to agree with similar moves by others. However, the broad geographical bands were now established – France from west to east Africa and Britain from north to south. Eventually they were to meet in the middle, at Fashoda on the Nile's upper reaches.

Africa in 1914, showing European possessions.

Lord Salisbury
(1830–1903) Initially Conservative Prime Minister in 1885 following the Liberal Party split over Home Rule. He went on to win the general elections of 1886, 1895 and 1900. During this period he resisted Home Rule for Ireland and maintained a foreign policy of 'splendid isolation' (no formal alliances). Despite his victories at the polls, he deeply distrusted democracy and the impact it would have upon Britain's foreign policy. He shared Gladstone's dislike of imperial expansion but recognised its popularity.

Joseph Chamberlain
(1834–1914) Famous as a radical politician from Birmingham where he made a fortune as a screw manufacturer. Serving under Gladstone as President of the Board of Trade from 1880, he split with Gladstone over the issue of Home Rule. From 1891 he was the leader of the Liberal Unionists and took office under Lord Salisbury in 1895 as Colonial Secretary. In 1903 he resigned from the government so that he could campaign for tariff reform.

The attitude of the British government under **Lord Salisbury** towards France was cautious. However, the Colonial Secretary, **Joseph Chamberlain**, was keen to oppose the French and in 1896 organised the formation of the West Africa Frontier Force, a colonial force of African troops and British officers. This was designed to keep the French back from the hinterland of the Gold Coast, Lagos and the Niger territories, which they were threatening from their North African territories. A French advance into this hinterland would threaten British coastal territories and create rival trade routes. Also, if the French occupied the territory inland from the British then trade would flow northwards and make the British colonies less profitable, as had happened with the Gambia and Sierra Leone. Chamberlain was prepared to risk war with France, as he was keen to establish an alliance with Germany. However, in 1896–7 Germany embarked upon its plan to build a modern navy and an alliance with Germany became increasingly unlikely.

Fashoda. Even the pro-French Salisbury was forced to be firm in 1898 when the Fashoda incident occurred. In 1895 the British had declared that they would regard French interference in the Nile Valley as an unfriendly action. But to encourage the British to negotiate over Egypt a French expedition under Captain Marchand was sent to Fashoda on the Upper Nile. In September 1898 Marchand was met by a substantial British force under General Sir Herbert Kitchener (created Earl Kitchener in 1902), and the French were heavily outnumbered. On 2 November 1898 the French government ordered Marchand to withdraw and war was averted. Public opinion in both countries favoured war. Salisbury himself might have been prepared to make minor concessions but opinion in Parliament and the country was against this. As a result of Fashoda Britain found itself more solidly established in the Nile and even less likely to abandon Egypt.

The French had expected Russian support over Egypt. However, France had recently failed to support Russia in its claims on Port Arthur in Asia so Russia now failed to support France in Africa.

The Fashoda incident left a legacy of bitterness between Britain and France. However, relations between the two countries did improve, mainly because of the work of the French Foreign Minister Theophile Delcassé. As a result of Russia's inconstancy as an ally he wanted to improve relations with Britain, and areas of agreement between Britain and France did emerge.

- On 15 January 1896 the British and the French signed an agreement over Siam (modern Thailand). The French agreed to respect the independence of Siam, and the British surrendered their protectorate over the upper Mekong River in what is modern Vietnam. Lord Salisbury felt that this was an easy way to achieve better relations with the French as he regarded the upper Mekong as worthless.
- **The Boxer Rebellion.** There was co-operation in China in 1900 when western powers, among them the French and the British, joined forces to protect their interests and prop up the Chinese government from the attacks of nationalists, known as the Boxers, in the district of Peking.
- **The Anglo-French Entente.** In 1904 Delcassé concluded secret negotiations with the British. The basis of the deal was that France would accept British control of Egypt if Britain would accept French control over **Morocco**. Morocco became a favourite French cause partly because its rivals for influence here were the Germans. The disposition of the French and British navies was also decided, in that the French navy would cover the Mediterranean whilst the Royal Navy would concentrate more of its forces in the Channel.

WHAT WAS THE RIVALRY BETWEEN FRANCE AND GERMANY?

Introduction. The issue of Alsace-Lorraine (revanchism, see Chapter 1) declined after 1900 but the French debate over conscription in 1912 again emphasised Germany as the main enemy. France had undergone major political traumas during the period of the **Dreyfus affair** and the continuing debate about the role of the Catholic Church.

Morocco was an independent sultanate in a strategically important position which was at this time rapidly collapsing into anarchy.

The Dreyfus affair The Dreyfus affair caused deep controversy in France between 1894 and 1906. Major Dreyfus was a Jewish officer of the French Army General Staff. He was accused of betraying secrets to the Germans. The General Staff was dominated by Catholics, many of whom hated Jews and who assumed that it was Dreyfus who was responsible for the leaks, refusing to consider evidence pointing towards the real culprit. Dreyfus was imprisoned, and was only rehabilitated after a campaign in which the famous French writer Zola was forced into exile for having lent his support. The Dreyfus case exposed deep divisions in French society. Success in Morocco promised to reunite Frenchmen in a common opposition to the Germans.

The Law of the Separation of the Church and State (1905) had formally ended the role of Catholicism as the official church, but the decision by the Pope to declare Joan of Arc a saint (1909) was seen as confirming God's approval of French nationalism.

Morocco. In 1905 the Germans attempted to limit the extension of French influence in Morocco. After Britain's triumph in Egypt, Morocco represented France's last hope of adding to its African Empire. From the German point of view the moment seemed opportune: the French government had angered the French army over its response to the Dreyfus affair, and Japan had just defeated France's ally, Russia. Wilhelm II visited Tangier and made a strongly-worded speech in which he supported maintaining both the Ottoman Empire's and Germany's interests in Morocco. This stance was initially successful: the French Foreign Minister Delcassé was forced to resign and Germany won its demand for an international congress.

The Germans were disappointed, however, when the congress met at Algeciras in 1906. The congress recognised that Morocco was a place of international concern but, thanks to British support, also agreed that France had the main role. Germany's defeat at the congress made its leaders even more conscious that Austria was Germany's only ally. Reliance upon Austria was exactly the situation Bismarck had tried so hard to avoid. Not surprisingly, after 1906 French influence in Morocco continued to expand. Another Franco-German war scare in 1908 led to the French and Germans signing an economic co-operation and equality of opportunity agreement, although French influence continued to dominate. For example, the Union des Mines Marocaines (the main Moroccan mining company) was funded up to 80 per cent by French capital compared to 20 per cent from Germany.

Second Moroccan crisis 1911. The Franco-German Agreement of 1909 precluded either power from military intervention in Morocco, but recognised that France had 'special political interests' there. In April 1911 the French government sent a military expedition to the Moroccan capital, Fez. The official reason given was that the troops were to assist the Sultan in suppressing rebels and to protect the lives of French civilians there. The real reason was to establish a French protectorate over Morocco. Not unreasonably the Germans declared that France was breaking the 1909 agreement.

On 1 July 1911 the German gunboat *Panther* arrived in Agadir. This move made the kind of powerful statement the Germans had envisaged they would want to make when they started to build up their navy. On 4 July the British cabinet told Germany that Britain should be involved in any solution to the crisis. Although the British cabinet recognised the crisis had largely been caused by the French, and British interests in Morocco were actually very small, the Chancellor of the Exchequer David Lloyd George made a speech on 21 July emphasising Britain's vital interest in an 'equitable stability' in Morocco. This was seen as a clear warning to Germany that Britain would back its French ally. By referring to 'stability' Lloyd George was showing that Britain wanted to maintain the current balance in Morocco, i.e. leave France to dominate. 'Equitable' meant some hope of Germany receiving minor concessions to make the situation a little fairer.

The crisis was actually ended by Germany and France – Germany withdrew the *Panther* and effectively backed down at the Paris conference later that year.

- Germany gave France a free hand in Morocco.
- The Germans had initially said they wanted the whole of the French Congo in return for recognising the French protectorate over Morocco. In September 1911 the Germans agreed to the French Protectorate and in return received two strips of territory in the French Congo.

What was the significance of the Moroccan crises?
- The crises had a profound impact upon Britain because for the first time the cabinet had considered going to war to preserve France. In the wake of the first Moroccan crisis, the British government authorised Anglo-French staff talks. Co-operation between Britain and France was also emphasised in 1912 when the French were able to

establish a protectorate over Morocco with British backing. In this way, aggressive German policy was encouraging British and French co-operation.
- The rivalry between France and Germany was emphasised.

The Moroccan crises thus considerably shaped the alliances facing each other in the July crisis of 1914.

WHAT CAUSED RIVALRY BETWEEN BRITAIN AND RUSSIA?

After 1905, France was keen to see a closer understanding between Britain and Russia. The two main areas of conflict between them were the Mediterranean (see also Chapter 2) and the Middle East, but Britain also feared Russian expansion overland into India.

- Britain had been opposed to Russia for a long time. The educated middle classes in England saw Russia as a barbaric and backward country, which threatened British interests in the Mediterranean and India. However, between 1870 and 1912 there was a gradual shift in British foreign policy with the recognition that the threat to British interests now came from Germany. After 1900 the balance of naval power shifted as the German navy was visibly developed and the weaknesses of the Russian navy were exposed (both the Russian Pacific and Baltic fleets were destroyed in the Pacific by Japan during the Russo-Japanese war).
- Britain feared Russian expansion overland into India, and on 31 August 1907, Russia and Britain signed an agreement covering Persia, Afghanistan and Tibet. This in effect limited the two powers' influence in Persia to those provinces closest to their other territories, and cleared away the possibility of a Russo-British conflict outside the Balkans.
- As Britain moved closer to France after 1908 the implication was that British opposition to Russian aims would soften.

WHAT CAUSED THE RIVALRY BETWEEN BRITAIN AND GERMANY?

Introduction. Since Britain had the largest empire in the world any desire of Germany to become a colonial power was seen to challenge the British position. Indeed, **Admiral Alfred von Tirpitz**'s proposal to build a naval fleet was intended to deter Britain (see Chapter 5 on the arms race) and also to enable Germany to create a colonial empire. It was therefore a factor in encouraging colonial rivalry.

However, rivalry between Britain and Germany was not inevitable. There were occasions when the two countries managed to settle their main confrontations.

- **Africa.** Here British and German ambitions were largely settled by an agreement over the future of the Portuguese Empire. The international Hague Convention on the rules of war was signed on 30 August 1898. On the same day the British and the Germans signed a secret convention to divide up the Portuguese Empire if the Portuguese government failed to pay its debts. The secret agreement gave Germany the promise of territory in Luanda and Northern Angola.
- **The Near and Middle East.** Britain was very interested in Persia (now Iran). Oil, which was found in Persia, was an increasingly important commodity for the propulsion of ships and cars. The proposed Berlin to Baghdad railway threatened to increase German influence in the Middle East. Despite this, the British government did not object to the Germans building such a railway and in 1903 encouraged British banks to help finance the stretch of line from Konia to Basra. However, public opinion in Britain was against the idea. Eventually on 15 June 1914 the British and German governments signed a convention whereby the Germans agreed to support the election of two British directors to the Berlin to Baghdad Railway Company (on the condition that those chosen were acceptable to the British government) and also to terminate the line at Basra rather than continuing to the Persian Gulf. In return Britain agreed not to build a competing railway nor to object to the Berlin to Baghdad Railway

Admiral Alfred von Tirpitz (1849–1930) Influential admiral and politician responsible for the policy of *Flottenpolitik* – the building of a German navy to rival Britain's Royal Navy, and the Navy Laws of 1898 and 1900, which set out the plans for naval expansion. He convinced the Reichstag to agree to his plans, with the help of powerful lobbying by the Navy League, and hoped that Germany's challenge to Britain would make them seek an alliance with Germany. In fact, however, Britain sought a closer alliance with France.

Company buying shares in the Ottoman River Navigation Company.

It is of course impossible to say that these agreements would have prevented any colonial disputes causing a future war with Germany. However, it would appear that colonial rivalries on their own were unlikely to lead to a major conflict in the foreseeable future.

CONCLUSION

There were two main colonial conflicts which contributed towards the build-up to the First World War.

- **France and Germany.** In Morocco, France and Germany renewed the clash which had been dominating Europe since the French Revolution. A cleverer German approach might have been to encourage the French ambitions in North Africa. This would have provided France with something to think about other than the lost provinces of Alsace-Lorraine.
- **Austria and Russia.** For the Russians and the Austrians the Balkans came to take on a symbolic importance as well as a strategic one. Their ambitions led them into a struggle which was to topple the ruling dynasties of both Russia (the Romanovs) and Austria (the Hapsburgs).

SUMMARY QUESTIONS

1 Explain the rivalry between Russia and Austria-Hungary c. 1890–1913.

2 Why were France and Great Britain colonial rivals before 1904?

3 How did the rivalry between France and Germany change between 1871 and 1913?

4 Did colonial rivalries change international relations between 1890 and 1913?

CHAPTER 4

What were the internal pressures for war among the great powers?

It is important to remember that when the leaders of the great powers decided to declare war in 1914 they were all influenced by events at home. In 1914 **hereditary monarchs** ruled most of Europe; the only genuine republic to declare war in 1914 was France. In the years before the First World War each of the European powers faced problems at home. In the case of Austria-Hungary and Germany, as well as their rival, Russia, these pressures made war seem more attractive to their rulers. War was seen as a unifying force which would encourage discontented groups to focus upon a common enemy. Monarchs saw themselves as national symbols and they believed that fighting a war would increase national loyalties and therefore make their dynasties more secure. At first it seemed that the crowned heads of Europe were going to be proved right as jubilant crowds filled the streets in August 1914 and a wave of patriotism swept through their countries. The fact that by 1918 emperors were a thing of the past should not obscure the importance of their role in 1914.

WHAT WERE THE ECONOMIC AND POLITICAL EFFECTS OF THE NAVAL PROGRAMME IN GERMANY?

From 1897 onwards Germany embarked on an ambitious shipbuilding programme, *Flottenpolitik*. The aim of such a programme was to build a battle fleet capable of challenging the Royal Navy, and which would enable Germany to pursue its colonial ambitions. The German Minister of Marine, Admiral Alfred von Tirpitz, believed that this fleet would deter Britain from intervening in a future European war. The British response was to outbuild Germany. This decision led both countries into a naval 'arms race' with important consequences for the German and British economies – after 1906 the financial costs were especially heavy. Coupled with increased shipbuilding

A Dreadnought battleship.

another policy emerged, that of *Weltpolitik*. This was a further militarist policy which was aimed at imperial expansion and military dominance.

- The new Dreadnought design for battleships for the Royal Navy was launched in 1906. The key point about a Dreadnought battleship was that it was armed with big guns to deliver a broadside which could sink an enemy ship. With steam turbine engines it could also move at approximately 30 knots. Because of her armament the original *Dreadnought* was held to have made previous vessels obsolete and therefore her launch triggered a naval arms race. The battleship was eventually made obsolete by the development of the aircraft carrier. Dreadnoughts cost Britain £1 million each. The result was that Britain spent £13.8 million in 1890 and £47.4 million in 1914.
- German naval spending rose from £4.6 million in 1890 to £22.4 million in 1914.
- By 1908 the cost of the German naval programme was equal to 23.7 per cent of government expenditure. By 1914 Germany's overall expenditure on the navy was equal to 4.6 per cent of its national income compared to 3.4 per cent for Britain.

One important reason why the German **Kaiser Wilhelm II** and his government were prepared to undertake these costs was that spending on the navy helped to unite Germany politically. Conservative politicians such as

KEY PERSON

Kaiser Wilhelm II Even as Kaiser (Emperor) of Germany, Wilhelm II was a particularly immature man. From 1901 he was driven by jealousy of his uncle, King Edward VII of Great Britain, and the desire to outshine Britain. In his youth he had been encouraged to be anti-British by his grandfather Wilhelm I and by Bismarck. Both these men held very different views from Wilhelm's father Frederick (Kaiser for three months in 1888), who was married to Victoria, the eldest daughter of Queen Victoria of Great Britain.

Johannes von Miquel (1828–1901), who became Deputy Prime Minister of Prussia in 1897, put forward the idea of **Sammlungspolitik**. This spending was also supported by pressure from the Navy League, which was founded by Admiral von Tirpitz and funded by industrialists to popularise the importance of seapower as an instrument of national power. (Over 1 million people eventually joined the Navy League.) The importance of the naval race in driving a wedge between Britain and Germany is difficult to overestimate.

The introduction of tariffs (taxes on imported goods) in Germany had raised the cost of food and this increased worker demands for higher wages. The building of ships led to government contracts for steel and other engineering products, which not only helped manufacturers meet the cost of higher wages, but were also very profitable. The Navy League's efforts as a pressure group helped to stop any questions about government expenditure from subsequently being raised in the Reichstag. The navy also provided opportunities for the middle classes: the army was dominated by the landed gentry (**Junkers**) and so the navy gave the middle classes a chance to pursue a military career. **Admiral Karl Dönitz**, who became Reich President when Hitler died in 1945, was one of the middle-class boys who entered the Imperial German Navy on the eve of the First World War.

Demands of the army. The huge increase in expenditure on the navy led to other problems for Germany, since, unlike Britain, it also needed an army able to fight on a continental scale. Fears that the naval race had led to neglect of the army surfaced after 1910. In the face of Russian and French rearmament **General Erich von Ludendorff** asked for large increases for the army in 1912 and 1913. The result was a rise in the cost of the army from £40.8 million in 1910 to £88.4 million in 1914. This massive increase had to be funded partly from the imposition of higher taxes.

The tariffs imposed by Bismarck led to rising prices and fuelled support for the German Socialist party (the SPD). Although it was increasingly less revolutionary in its

**Admiral Karl Dönitz
(left) and
General Erich von
Ludendorff (right).**

and the subsequent Allied advances Ludendorff was dismissed and fled to Sweden. After the war he became involved in extreme right-wing politics and marched with Hitler in the Munich Putsch of 1923.

outlook it retained its official Marxist ideology, and was loathed and feared by the Kaiser and senior officials. On several occasions the Kaiser discussed launching a right-wing coup to abolish the Reichstag and cut off the SPD from political power. But the SPD's success in becoming the largest party in the Reichstag in 1912 meant that the conservative military were now dependent upon their political enemies.

War in 1914 offered the Kaiser and the military the opportunity to unite the country before they were forced to make real political changes.

WHAT WERE THE PRESSURES IN GREAT BRITAIN?

Great Britain underwent a long period of social change and relative economic decline before the First World War.

Economic problems. In 1879 there was an agricultural depression due to the impact of American exports competing with and replacing British goods sold in Europe. In 1878 the Germans decided to protect their farmers by introducing tariffs (taxes). The British political parties feared being labelled as the party of the 'dear loaf' so they retained the policy of free trade. Britain had followed this policy since 1846, which meant that goods were allowed to enter Britain without the imposition of tariffs. The idea was that if raw materials were not taxed on entry then the costs of manufacturing to British industry would be low. Until the end of the 1850s this policy had worked well as British industry led the world. However, British agriculture and industry faced increasing competition towards the end of the century. One of the main industrial competitors was Germany, for example in building railway engines, and this fact increased the tension between the two countries further.

The Conservative leader, Benjamin Disraeli, committed the Conservative Party to free trade in 1872 in order to win the next general election. Free trade was one of the basic policies of the Liberal Party so the issue did not arise again until 1905. In December 1905 the Liberals won by a landslide because the Conservatives were divided over the question of whether to reintroduce tariffs to finance domestic social reforms and colonial developments. The issue then remained settled until after the First World War, when the post-war depression resurrected the argument for protection (putting taxes on imported goods).

Home Rule. Great Britain also faced major problems in Ireland. Since 1886 there had been various attempts by Liberal governments to introduce **Home Rule**.

- Following two general elections in 1910 over the budget crisis, the powers of the House of Lords were reduced by the Parliament Act of 1911. The most important immediate result was that if the Liberals passed a Home Rule Bill with Irish **Nationalist** support, the House of Lords could now only delay it rather than defeat it outright.
- Protestant Ulster began openly arming to resist Home Rule and in 1912 militant **Unionists** signed the Solemn League and Covenant. Some signed in blood to demonstrate their commitment.
- The British government proved to be much more effective in stopping arms reaching the Nationalists

(who supported Home Rule) than they were in preventing arms reaching the Unionists. The police and the army in Ulster allowed the Unionists to import arms without interference.

• In the spring of 1914 it was rumoured that the government was about to send troops to Ulster to stop the Unionist Ulster Volunteer Force (UVF) from openly drilling and training. At the main cavalry barracks at the Curragh in Dublin, many officers received the news with alarm. Though many were politically conservative and anti-Catholic, they supported the Unionists, but faced the difficulty that they could be court-martialled if they disobeyed an order. In the end they declared they would prefer to be dismissed if ordered to Ulster to stop the UVF. This rebellion became known as the 'Curragh Mutiny'.

A determined government might have felt obliged to enforce military discipline but in the face of what was in fact a mutiny by members of the English Protestant ruling class, the government backed down. The Curragh Mutiny demonstrated that the Liberal government lacked the will to enforce political control over the army. In any case, war in 1914 allowed the Liberals to postpone the problems of Home Rule.

HOW DID PRESSURE BUILD UP IN THE RUSSIAN EMPIRE?

Introduction. In 1913 **Tsar Nicholas II** had celebrated 300 years of Romanov rule. The official outpourings of support for the Tsar did not necessarily represent the feelings of the people, particularly of the workers in the cities and the peasants in many regions. The Tsar, however, may have been lulled into a false sense of security. He appears to have believed that the Russian people loved their Tsar, apart from a few agitators who were causing trouble, especially in the growing industrial centres. On the surface, the Tsarist regime in 1914 was secure. However, there were weaknesses that were to have an important impact on the regime's policy towards war.

KEY PERSON

Tsar Nicholas II (Tsar 1894–1917) Nicholas was a weak ruler dominated by a strong sense of inadequacy engendered by his father's all-too-honest assessment of his abilities. Obstinately against change, he failed to back Stolypin's reforms (1906–11) which many believe was the last opportunity to avoid revolution. This weakness influenced his decision to declare war in 1914 and become Commander-in-Chief in 1915, which ensured that defeat would lead to revolution. Nicholas and his family were shot by the Bolsheviks in July 1918 during the civil war (1918–22).

Tsar Nicholas II blesses his troops, 1914.

Fear of political reform. The Tsar's government still lived in the shadow of the 1905 Revolution when the Tsar's brother-in-law, the Grand Duke Sergei, had been blown up in his carriage, and when the Tsar had been forced to concede the '**October Manifesto**', which included the creation of a Duma (parliament). After 1905 the Tsar had steadily eroded the rights of the Duma, causing frustration amongst the middle classes. The Tsar thereby demonstrated that he could not be trusted to carry out reform from above, and this only increased the pressure for reform from below. War in 1914, in this respect, constituted an opportunity to unite the country against a common enemy.

Land. At the heart of the discontent with the Tsar's rule was the issue of the peasants and the land (see Chapter 1). Perhaps due to an element of personal dislike, the Tsar had failed to support **Pyotr Stolypin** in his attempts to introduce reforms, and Stolypin's land reforms, known by the saying 'Bet on the Strong', had failed to attract more than a minority of peasants. Responsibility for carrying out the reforms had been given to the hated Land Captains (minor nobles who forced peasants to obey regulations), and many peasants were intimidated by other peasants, who resented their desire to leave the commune (mir). By the time Stolypin was assassinated by a police agent in 1911 he had seen the Tsar reject most of his ideas.

Industrial unrest. The Lena massacre of 1912 in which around 200 gold miners died came early in two years of

The October Manifesto 1905 Faced by middle-class support for the revolutionary demands of peasant and urban protestors, Nicholas II granted the October Manifesto which created a Duma (parliament) for the first time. However, as Leon Trotsky recognised, Nicholas II retained the right to amend the constitution. Unwilling to accept criticism, Nicholas II tried to manipulate the franchise to obtain a more pliable Duma. Nicholas II's abdication in 1917 was necessary because Nicholas's actions since 1905 showed that he would never accept the role of a constitutional monarch.

**Pyotr Stolypin
(1862–1911)** Russian
reformer and prime minister
(1906–11) who tried to
overhaul Russian agriculture.
He was assassinated in 1911.
Stolypin sought to preserve
the tsarist state but realised
this could not be achieved
without social and economic
reform. He tackled
agricultural backwardness in
Russia by encouraging
peasants to set up as
independent farmers away
from the traditional
communes. Hated by
revolutionaries for his
repressive measures and by
reactionaries for trying to
change Russia, Stolypin could
only have survived if he had
the full backing of the Tsar.
Nicholas II refused to back
many of the reforms,
believing that there was a
loyal peasant Russia to whom
he could turn.

Jean Jaurès (1859–1914)
One of a group of French
intellectuals who wanted to
unite the divided elements in
French socialism. In 1890
Jaurès painted a picture of a
socialist society that would
bring order, liberty and
goodness.

Paris Commune established
a regime opposed to ending
the war with Germany and
based on egalitarian, socialist
and democratic principles.

industrial unrest. This unrest was partly because of the
growing number of large firms and the failure of factory
inspectors to enforce minimum safety standards. By 1914
the Bolsheviks had gained control of all the biggest trade
unions in Moscow and St Petersburg, and in the first six
months of 1914 around 1.4 million workers went on
strike. Nicholas II now felt that it was his final chance to
rally 'traditional' peasant Russia – a Russia unspoilt by
socialist agitation.

To fight or not to fight? The Tsar was aware of the
dangers of an unsuccessful military campaign. In February
1914 Minister P.D. Dunrovo warned the Tsar that any
disasters would be blamed upon the government, and that
a defeated army would be unable to control popular
discontent. However, in July 1914 Sergei Sazonov advised
the Tsar that not declaring war would lead to revolution.
And on Sunday 2 August 1914, as the crowds outside the
Winter Palace knelt before him singing the national
anthem, Nicholas believed there would be an outburst of
patriotism as there had been in 1812 in the war against
Napoleon.

WHY WAS THERE UNREST IN FRANCE?

France too faced industrial unrest. In 1912 a strike by
French railway workers only came to an end when the
government threatened to conscript them all into the
army. If conscripted they faced death if the strike
continued, in that they could then be court-martialled for
disobeying an order and executed. The rise of the socialist
parties and their leader **Jean Jaurès** worried the French
establishment.

France had a tradition of revolution. In February 1848,
revolution took place just weeks after the publication of
the Communist Manifesto. Written by Karl Marx and
Friedrich Engels, this document contained the famous call
to the workers to throw off their chains. The liberal
revolution of 1848, however, did not bring the working
classes to power. In 1871 revolution returned to Paris and
led to the establishment of the **Paris Commune**, a regime

opposed to ending the war with Germany and based on egalitarian, socialist and democratic principles. The Commune was brutally suppressed with considerable bloodshed. In 1914 the fear of a return to revolution was in the minds of many French conservatives.

A right-wing fanatic assassinated Jean Jaurès on the eve of mobilisation. Railways played a key part in mobilisation and conservatives feared that Jaurès would call the railway workers out on strike to prevent war.

The arms race. France was also finding the arms race a heavy burden. France was spending 4.8 per cent of its national income on defence in 1914 which was a higher figure than for either Germany or Great Britain. Between 1910 and 1914 French defence spending rose by just under 10 per cent. Over the same period Germany had increased its spending by over 60 per cent. Given the high burden France was placing upon its economy it would be best for France if war came sooner rather than later. The French were concerned that their national **birth rate** was below that of Germany: each year there would be more young German men than French men reaching military age. After a long and bitter debate France had, in 1913, extended compulsory military service to three years (the Three Year Law) in order to increase the size of the army. Many French politicians did not feel able to extend the length of conscription beyond three years. To many Frenchmen, therefore, time was not on France's side.

WHAT WERE THE DOMESTIC PROBLEMS IN AUSTRIA-HUNGARY?

The serious ethnic divisions in the Austro-Hungarian Empire have already been explained. However, it is still important to point out that one of the greatest threats to the stability of the Empire was the growth of nationalism. It was the desire of some of the nationalities within the Empire to have their independence that led many in government to conclude that force should be used to crush them. Above all it was the threat of Serbian nationalism

The build-up of armies, 1900–14.

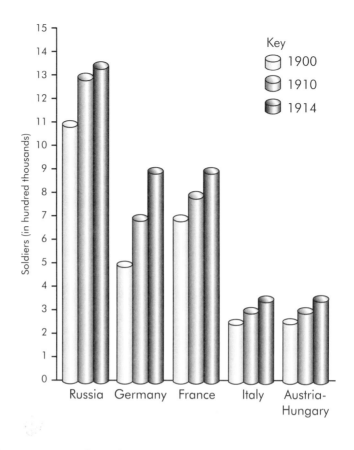

that was most feared. However, these were not the only domestic problems faced by the Emperor Franz Josef II.

Economic weaknesses. By 1914 Austria-Hungary was spending 6.1 per cent of its national income on armaments (compared to Germany's expenditure of 4.6 per cent and Britain's 3.4 per cent). Only Russia was spending a higher proportion of its income on the arms race. Between 1910 and 1914, Austria-Hungary had more than doubled its defence spending from £17.4 million to £36.4 million. As the war was to prove, Austria-Hungary lacked the necessary economic base for modern warfare. Alone amongst the great powers its **coal production** failed to rise between 1910 and 1914.

The decline of the Emperor. The court of Emperor Franz Josef epitomised the decay at the heart of the empire. Archaic court etiquette excluded the wife of his heir, the Archduke Franz Ferdinand, from court because of her lowly birth, and the Emperor openly maintained a mistress despite his Catholicism. His reign since 1848 had been one of almost continual decline, and in 1866 Austria had been replaced by Prussia as the leading power in Germany (see Chapter 1). This had forced Austria to concede power to the Hungarians. It also meant that Austria-Hungary was particularly concerned to maintain its empire in south-east Europe and to resist any threats of independence or expansion from Serbia. The Archduke Franz Ferdinand was believed to favour reforms which would create a **tripartite** or even a **four-pillar monarchy** to embrace the various nationalities in the empire. These views were opposed by the ageing Emperor.

KEY TERMS

Tripartite or four-pillar monarchy Converting the Dual Monarchy to either a tripartite or four-pillar model would have involved granting autonomy to either or both of the Czechs and southern ('Yugo') Slavs.

CONCLUSION

In 1914 all the major European powers faced problems at home. German policies were heavily influenced by the need to avoid further concessions to the socialists in order to finance the arms race. In Great Britain there was a strong possibility of civil unrest in Ireland, and Austria-Hungary was on the brink of losing its status as a great power. The same fate awaited Russia and France if they did not mobilise when the others did. All in all, domestic problems did not lead to war in 1914 but they increased the sense that if war was inevitable, then it was better if it came sooner rather than later.

SUMMARY QUESTIONS

1 What were the pressures within Germany which encouraged a policy of war? How real were the pressures?

2 For what domestic reasons did Austria-Hungary feel it was necessary to go to war in 1914?

3 Which themes would you use to explain why countries across Europe felt that war in 1914 would solve their domestic difficulties?

CHAPTER 5

What was the importance of the alliance system and the arms race, 1870–1913?

The alliance system that had developed as part of European diplomacy between 1882 and 1913 had a major impact upon the military plans of the great powers, and both were to have considerable importance in 1914.

WHAT WAS GERMANY'S POSITION?

Bismarck's success in winning three wars and then creating the German Reich (Empire) under Prussian leadership in 1871 completely altered the balance of power in Europe:

- Bismarck had taken Schleswig-Holstein in 1864, jointly with Austria.
- He then led Prussia into war with Austria. Having defeated Austria at the Battle of Sadowa (1866), Prussia gained freedom from Austrian interference in Schleswig-Holstein and established control in northern Germany. Bismarck was therefore able to establish the North German Confederation in 1867.
- In July 1870 Bismarck provoked Napoleon III of France into declaring war against Prussia. Victory at Sedan a month later meant Bismarck could bring the southern German states into a united Germany.

Naturally, European statesmen wondered if this really marked the limits of German ambitions.

Bismarck remained Chancellor until 1890 (when he was forced out of power by Kaiser Wilhelm II) thus effectively controlling German foreign policy from 1870 to 1890. Although there was no major European war in this period, Bismarck's diplomacy did not create a stable and peaceful Europe, and his successors inherited a number of diplomatic problems.

Otto von Bismarck in military uniform, 1894.

The Triple Alliance, 1882. In 1879 Germany formally allied with Austria in the Dual Alliance. In 1882, Bismarck signed an alliance with Italy and Austria-Hungary known as the Triple Alliance. This followed Bismarck's belief that in a Europe of five great powers, Germany should always be in an alliance with two other powers. Italy was not yet one of the great powers but as Britain was not allied to anyone this left only Russia as a possible ally for France. These were the main features of the Triple Alliance:

- The Germans and Italians were each promised support by the other powers if the French attacked them.
- Article III promised support in the event of an attack by two great powers. Germany and Austria-Hungary benefited most from this – Bismarck was anticipating a possible Russo-French alliance.
- Article IV referred to any threat by another 'non-signatory' power which created a situation in which Germany, Austria or Italy felt obliged to fight. This might have referred to a possible war between Italy and Britain in the Mediterranean, but everyone understood it to mean a conflict between Austria and Russia. In these circumstances the other signatories to the treaty promised, if not involved, to remain neutral. Therefore in 1914, when the Austrian government declared war on Serbia, Germany could have remained neutral – but it chose to support Austria-Hungary.

Reinsurance Treaty with Russia, 1887. To prevent Russia allying with France, Bismarck negotiated a treaty with Russia in 1887 known as the **Reinsurance Treaty**, which lasted for three years. In 1890 Bismarck did his best to make his resignation look like a dispute over whether or not to renew the Reinsurance Treaty. However, Bismarck was deceiving people:

- Even in 1887, when the Tsar was visiting Berlin to agree the Reinsurance Treaty, Bismarck was making ill-judged economic moves against Russia. He encouraged the German press to attack recent Russian attempts to limit foreign ownership of Russian land and, crucially, Bismarck instructed the **Reichsbank** to refuse further loans to Russia.

Portrait of Kaiser Wilhelm II as Field Marshal. This is an idealised portrait of an insecure man which disguises his withered arm.

Reichsbank This is the name of the German national bank, equivalent to the Bank of England. Russian loans were offered on the German market but needed Reichsbank support to be successful in attracting investors.

Realpolitik was Bismarck's term for doing what suited one's country best, regardless of sentimental ties or previous alliances or agreements.

- The Russians signed the Reinsurance Treaty but as we have seen it offered no help to Russia if it clashed with Austria-Hungary.
- By the time the Treaty was due for renewal in 1890 French loans were providing the money needed by Russia. Also, Bismarck was by then in difficulties with Kaiser Wilhelm II, who insisted upon his right to see ministers without Bismarck. Bismarck felt obliged to resign since it was clear that the Kaiser would not allow him to dominate their relationship as he had dominated Wilhelm I. The decision to let the Reinsurance Treaty lapse was convenient: it made it look as if Bismarck was resigning on an issue of principle. Ironically, after 1914 people thought Bismarck looked wise to have wanted to carry on with the Reinsurance Treaty.

Bismarck's successor, General Georg von Caprivi, tried to improve relations with Russia by easing tariffs. However, this upset the influential Junkers who helped to push Caprivi from office in 1894. It can thus be seen that economic reasons played a significant part in deciding who made an alliance with whom.

Bismarck and Austria. Bismarck had linked Germany to Austria, which was the weaker of the two eastern European powers (the other being Russia). The most significant result of this diplomatically was that he prompted an alliance between France and Russia. On ideological grounds the two countries were at opposite ends of the political spectrum: France was a democracy whilst Russia was run by the Tsar as an autocracy (autocracy means rule by one person). However, Bismarck could hardly argue that no one could have expected France and Russia to form an alliance. Bismarck was famous for his belief in *Realpolitik* and should have realised that he was pushing France and Russia together.

Princess Victoria Born 1840, the first child of Queen Victoria and Prince Albert, married in 1858 to Frederick, Prince of Russia, who became Emperor for three months in 1888. Her liberal convictions brought her into constant conflict with Bismarck.

Bismarck might have been more open to pursuing an alliance with Britain had his power struggle with Wilhelm's mother, **Victoria**, not meant domestic issues clouded his foreign policy. Throughout his reign Wilhelm I had sought an understanding with Austria, but had been restrained by Bismarck until Prussia was clearly the dominant power. Bismarck's admirers might argue that, as the political mastermind behind German unification, he would have had the authority to rein back the army in 1914 but he had played a major part in creating the alliance with a weak power, Austria, which would drag Germany into a war on two fronts which it could not win. So Bismarck must accept at least some responsibility for the events of 1914. His successors lacked Bismarck's prestige and so the army was increasingly dominant after 1890.

Bismarck and Britain. It could be said that by encouraging Wilhelm II to be anti-British Bismarck left behind a time bomb waiting to explode.

Bismarck had been opposed to the liberal views of Wilhelm II's father, Crown Prince Frederick, who succeeded as Kaiser Frederick III in 1888. The Crown Prince and his wife, Victoria, favoured a more liberal system of government, similar to that in Britain, but Frederick was dying of cancer by the time he reached the throne. If he had lived as long as his father or his son, then the history of Germany and Europe might have been very different. Both Kaiser Wilhelm I and Bismarck encouraged the future Wilhelm II to oppose his father. After 1890, this policy left a young man ruling Germany without any stable guidance and who resented British supremacy.

In 1908 Wilhelm II visited Britain and gave an interview to the *Daily Telegraph* newspaper. In the interview Wilhelm announced that while he and the best elements in Germany were favourable towards Britain, the same could not be said for the bulk of German opinion. He also claimed that his ideas had helped win the **Boer War** for Britain. Not only was this untrue but British opinion was even more outraged because Wilhelm had publicly supported the Boers during the war. Wilhelm expected the Chancellor, **Bernhard von Bülow**, to accept the blame for this diplomatic blunder because Bülow had failed to read the draft of the proposed article when the *Daily Telegraph* had sent it to Germany for approval. Bülow felt the Kaiser should have accepted the blame for being so stupid as to make such a comment. Bülow's account to the German parliament officially absolved the Kaiser, but left few in any real doubt that their Emperor had been very foolish.

Punch cartoon of 1 February 1896. 'Fidgety Wilhelm's' impetuosity is shown to threaten the stability of Europe.

THE STORY OF FIDGETY WILHELM.

(*Up-to date Version of "Struwwelpeter."*)

"LET ME SEE IF WILHELM CAN
BE A LITTLE GENTLEMAN;
LET ME SEE IF HE IS ABLE
TO SIT STILL FOR ONCE AT TABLE!"

"BUT FIDGETY WILL
HE WON'T SIT STILL,"

JUST LIKE ANY BUCKING HORSE,
"WILHELM! WE ARE GETTING CROSS!"

THE BRITISH GUARANTEE TO BELGIUM

In London on 19 April 1839 Britain and the other great powers signed the Treaty of London, which recognised the creation of Belgium. Having fought for independence from Holland, this new state was officially recognised by all the relevant powers, including the King of Prussia.

Article 7 of the Treaty of London said Belgium would 'form an independent and perpetually neutral state'. Britain could therefore allege in 1914 that Germany had broken the Treaty of London by invading Belgium. Although the treaty made no provision for enforcement, Germany's breach of the agreement could be used to justify Britain's declaration of war.

The Treaty of London provided Britain with a 'just cause' for war that the informal Entente with France did not provide (see Chapter 3). This does not mean that Britain went to war because of Belgium. The British decision to fight was more fully based upon its desire to prevent France being defeated, and also because it feared Germany as a competitor and felt it necessary to protect it's world position.

THE FRANCO-RUSSIAN ALLIANCE

Bismarck's decision to cut off loans to Russia in 1887 encouraged the French to build economic links with this potential ally. Led by the Credit Lyonnais, French banks began to fill the gap left by the German banks. To encourage the Russians to stop dithering about an alliance, in 1891 the French government persuaded Rothschilds Bank in Paris to turn down a loan to Russia. This coincided with news from Italy of a Mediterranean secret agreement between Britain and Austria made in 1887 (see Section 1), which also helped to persuade the Russians to negotiate. We should also bear in mind that the countries of the Triple Alliance tried to persuade Britain to join them, though Britain was reluctant to enter into formal military alliances. In these circumstances, France and Russia entered into a treaty of alliance in 1893. Russia's ratification of the treaty in 1894 followed the fall of Chancellor Caprivi in Germany (see page 51). He had lost the support of the Junkers because he had reduced tariffs on the import of Russian horses and grain. With Caprivi's departure it was clear to the Russians that those in Germany who favoured an understanding with Russia did not have the Kaiser's support.

On 27 December 1893 the Russians signed a military convention with France. The convention was to remain in force as long as the Triple Alliance. There were many important clauses in the convention.

- The first clause bound each of the parties to support the other if attacked by Germany or Austria. Strictly speaking, therefore, France did not have to back Russia in 1914, since neither Germany nor Austria were the first to mobilise: Russia was.

- The Russian decision in 1914 to support Serbia did not come under clause 1. The trigger for war in 1914 was based on clause 2. This clause said:

In case the forces of the Triple Alliance (Germany, Austria and Italy), or of one of the powers composing it, should mobilise, France and Russia, at the first news of the event and without the necessity of any previous concert (meeting), shall mobilise immediately and simultaneously the whole of their forces and shall move them as close as possible to their frontiers.

By allowing this clause to dictate its actions in 1914, even though Russia was not directly threatened, France chose war not peace.

The clause was even more vital in its impact in Germany upon Count von Schlieffen (see Chapter 1) and his successor Count von Moltke. Schlieffen guessed the content of these clauses correctly. However, he believed, mistakenly, that it was possible for Germany to win even if fighting on two fronts. If he had been clear that it was now essential to prevent a war with Russia, then German politicians might have opposed Admiral von Tirpitz's attempt to deter Britain by building a battle fleet, which had two negative consequences:

- The first was to push Britain into an informal agreement with France.
- The second was the diversion of resources away from the army. This slowed up its development so that it lost the advantage it enjoyed in 1894 and, by 1914, its lead over France and Russia.

KEY TERM

'Blank Cheque' Moltke promised Austria that Germany would back Austria against Serbia even at the cost of war with Russia. Since the Schlieffen Plan required an attack on France to precede an attack on Russia, Moltke was allowing Austria to start a *European* war.

By 1914 it was therefore Moltke's belief that this was the German army's last chance to fight and win, which led the Kaiser to give the **'Blank Cheque'** (full support) to Austria. With this assurance Austria took Europe into the war. News of Russian mobilisation was the signal for the Schlieffen Plan to be implemented, including the attack on France through Belgium.

HOW DECISIVE A FACTOR IN THE LEAD UP TO WAR WERE THE ARMS RACE AND MILITARY PLANS?

The military plans that each country developed, and the arms race to be in the strongest position to fulfil these plans, were as significant a cause of war as the existence of the alliances. The most famous plan was the German Schlieffen Plan but it is important to remember that each country had a **mobilisation** plan. In 1914, some of the decisions made by rulers and military leaders were influenced by their views of the arms race – the position they believed their country held in the arms race and where they thought their country would be in future years.

The Anglo-German naval race

One of the most significant aspects of the arms race was the naval competition between Great Britain and Germany. It is seen as significant in that it may explain why Britain decided to form an alliance with France. It is also the case that this naval race helped to set an **anti-German tone** in the British popular press, and popular feeling about Germany being Britain's rival helped to set the context for the declaration of war in 1914.

- **The Naval Laws.** In 1897, Admiral von Tirpitz was put in control of German naval policy by Kaiser Wilhelm II. Tirpitz was one of three key appointments in 1897 (the others were Bernhard von Bülow as State Secretary of the Foreign Office and Johannes von Miquel as Vice-President of Prussia) who wanted to see Germany expand and create an empire. Tirpitz believed that if Germany was to gain 'her place in the sun' then it must have a navy which would deter Great Britain from challenging its plans. The Kaiser agreed, and in 1897 the Reichstag passed the first Naval Law. Subsequent Naval Laws in 1890 and later years further increased the money available to build new ships. As the greatest naval power in the world Britain was bound to be alarmed.

- **Dreadnoughts.** The growth of German naval power threatened British supremacy and prevented otherwise pro-German Britons like **Houston Stewart Chamberlain** from supporting an alliance between

KEY TERM

Mobilisation Term used by military planners to describe the process by which peacetime forces were increased to wartime levels by the recall of reservists to join the army. The plans also included details of how the armies were to be transported to the front.

KEY THEME

Anti-German sentiment
Lord Northcliffe's *Daily Mail* used William Le Queux's *Invasion of 1910* to stir up fears of a German invasion. Also, between August 1911 and August 1914 ten 'suspected' German spies were arrested and six were jailed, fuelling popular anti-German feelings.

KEY PERSON

Houston Stewart Chamberlain English-born writer who became a naturalised German in 1916. He believed in the ideas of Aryan supremacy and so, like Hitler, thought that Britain and Germany should be natural allies. His emphasis upon Aryan supremacy encouraged Wilhelm II's anti-Slavism and anti-Semitism. (Aryan supremacy was the belief that Aryans – Caucasians not of Jewish descent, with blond hair and blue eyes – formed a superior race.)

Britain and Germany. In this sense the arms race contributed to the British eventually declaring war on Germany. The event which spurred this rivalry was the decision by the British Admiral Lord Fisher to adopt the new Dreadnought design for battleships for the Royal Navy. *Dreadnought* was launched in 1906 and gave her name to all the ships of this type. With their combination of armour, heavy guns and speed they marked a revolution in ship design and made all previous battleships obsolete. This had the effect of re-starting the naval race, but since Britain's large fleet of pre-Dreadnought battleships was now redundant, Britain was very conscious of how numerically small its lead was.

The naval race quickly became intense. Britain kept announcing that it had twice as many ships as Germany, and popular slogans like '**we want eight** and we won't wait' showed how much the arms race was in the public eye – in this case responding to a decision by the Germans to build four new Dreadnoughts in one year. The naval race thereby ensured that Britain was in the opposing camp to Germany in 1914.

The Schlieffen Plan

Germany's strength was primarily dependent upon its army and this influenced its decisions in 1914. German military strategy was based on the Schlieffen Plan, which was drawn up under Count von Schlieffen, who was Chief of the German General Staff from 1891 until 1906. Its aim was to solve the strategic dilemma created by the Franco-Russian alliance. Schlieffen believed that Germany could not hope to win a long war on two fronts against Russia and France combined, and he therefore proposed the following:

- Germany would strike first against France with the maximum possible force.
- The right wing of the army would actually sweep down into north-western France and capture Paris by advancing from the west ('the right hook').
- To allow him to capture Paris, Schlieffen planned that other armies would not swing so far to the west, but would turn eastwards to attack the French army in the rear as it advanced into Alsace-Lorraine. This element

KEY THEME

'We want eight!' On coming into office in 1906, the Liberal government had intended to reduce naval spending. However, when it became clear that Admiral von Tirpitz was placing advanced orders to accelerate German Dreadnought production to four ships per year in 1907-8, public pressure demanded that eight British Dreadnoughts be built.

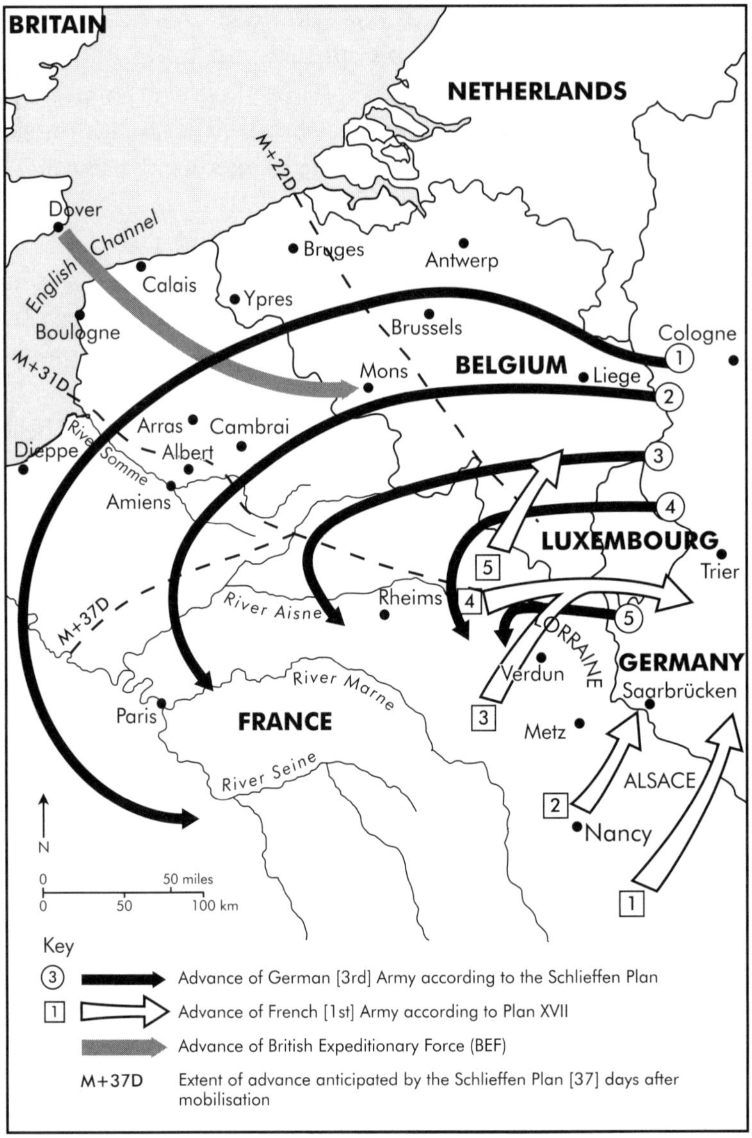
BRITAIN
NETHERLANDS
Dover
English Channel
Calais
Boulogne
Bruges
Antwerp
Ypres
Brussels
Cologne
BELGIUM
Mons
Liege
M+22D
M+31D
Arras
Cambrai
Albert
Dieppe
River Somme
Amiens
LUXEMBOURG
Trier
River Aisne
Rheims
LORRAINE
GERMANY
Verdun
Saarbrücken
M+37D
River Marne
Paris
FRANCE
Metz
ALSACE
River Seine
Nancy
N
0 50 miles
0 50 100 km
Key
Advance of German [3rd] Army according to the Schlieffen Plan
Advance of French [1st] Army according to Plan XVII
Advance of British Expeditionary Force (BEF)
M+37D Extent of advance anticipated by the Schlieffen Plan [37] days after mobilisation

Map showing Schlieffen Plan, French Plan XVII and route of British Expeditionary Forces, 1914.

was sometimes called 'the revolving door', as the French advance (Plan XVII) would actually push them further into the trap.

- In any war with France, Schlieffen was prepared to let the French reach a little way into Germany in order to get the bulk of the French army away from Paris. This was likely as the French Plan XVII involved re-conquering Alsace-Lorraine as soon as war began. Schlieffen therefore devised a plan which used only a small part of the German army to resist the French advance.

HEINEMANN ADVANCED HISTORY

KEY TERM

The German General Staff
The officers who made the plans for war should war break out. Other countries modelled their general staffs on that of the Germans. Because of the awe in which the General Staff was held after the successful wars of unification (1864, 1866 and 1870) they were able to influence politicians very heavily both before 1914 and, crucially, in the July crisis of 1914.

• Schlieffen assumed that Russia would be slower to mobilise and that this would give Germany the opportunity to defeat France before having to grapple with the huge military resources of Russia. The **German General Staff** thus watched developments in both countries very carefully.

What were the threats to the effectiveness of the Schlieffen Plan? Since the Schlieffen Plan required a rapid victory over France, any increase in French forces worried the German General Staff. Similarly, improvements in the equipment of the Russian armed forces and, crucially, the speed with which they could mobilise, also threatened the effectiveness of the Schlieffen Plan. Developments in 1913–4 were of particular concern to the German military high command.

• **France.** In August 1913 the French government succeeded in passing a law extending French military service from two to three years (the Three Year Law). Not only did this mean that men would be better trained, it also doubled the number of fully trained conscripts serving in the army at any one time. Naturally, the Germans feared that this would mean that France could mobilise faster and would therefore have more men available to prevent a rapid German victory. What the Germans did not accept was that they had inadvertently persuaded the French to make this move when General von Ludendorff had obtained agreement to a 30 per cent increase in the size of the German army in 1912. Ludendorff's original request was so large that even Moltke, the Chief of the General Staff, thought it was unrealistic and reduced it; but further increases were planned for 1914. One of the reasons why Ludendorff was pushing for such dramatic increases was the increased budget being allocated to the Russian army.
• **Russia.** In 1908 the Russian army began to benefit from the so-called 'Little Programme', which provided several billion roubles per year to be spent on the army in addition to its normal budget. The announcement in early 1914 of a 'Great Programme' to develop the Russian army further, served only to convince military leaders like Moltke that waging war in 1914 gave

Germany its best chance of victory, as its opponents were certain to grow stronger in future. A further factor about Russia that worried the Germans was their railways: because the French were desperate to ensure that the Russians came to their aid as quickly as possible, the French government arranged loans to Russia specifically to finance the development of strategic railways which would carry Russian troops towards the border with Germany.

To meet the threat posed by a faster Russian mobilisation the Germans believed they would need more troops, hence they increased their army and therefore so did the French. This aspect of the arms race made a major contribution to the decision to declare war in 1914.

The significance of military plans

The Schlieffen Plan. The influence of the Schlieffen Plan on the decisions made in the July crisis in 1914 was considerable. The plan itself was based on certain assumptions: if these assumptions were mistaken, the plan would be less effective.

- **Speed of mobilisation.** The plan was based upon there being a 40-day delay between German mobilisation and the arrival of significant Russian forces on the border of East Prussia. However, the Russian 'Little Programme' and French investment in Russian railways had reduced this gap by at least three days by 1914. Moltke was therefore afraid that there would not be time to defeat France before the Russians arrived. When Wilhelm II asked Moltke on 1 August 1914 to delay the western deployment he consequently refused, saying he could not be responsible for the chaos which would result and because he feared that this would make the whole plan fail.
- **Unbalancing the plan.** Moltke knew that in amending the plan he had not followed Schlieffen's famous advice to **'keep the right strong'** when allocating the new forces created since 1912. The news of Russian mobilisation therefore panicked him into insisting on German mobilisation (**'war by timetable'**) despite the news of Britain's opposition.

'Keep the right strong' Schlieffen knew that it was vital that Germany's two most northerly armies must be kept strong if they were to reach Paris quickly. When the German army was expanded after 1912 most of the additional forces were allocated to the 'left' to blunt the anticipated French offensive. Moltke lacked the strong nerves required to carry out the high-risk Schlieffen Plan.

'War by timetable' This phrase was coined by the historian A.J.P. Taylor to emphasise how events in 1914 were influenced by the belief that to mobilise first was essential.

- **The Military Travel Plan.** A key part of German mobilisation was the Military Travel Plan. This plan was based upon the railways delivering the armies to the various fronts. The plan was reviewed each year and especially in light of the increases in German forces. All trains were scheduled to run at a common speed in order to maximise the number of trains that could be run. Every year after 1 April, when the war plan was updated, the railways section would test segments of the plan. Also, ghost stations were built near the border in readiness for the arrival of troop trains.

- The announcement of the Russian 'Great Programme' in 1914 was taken to indicate that the gap between German and Russian mobilisation would be even shorter in 1915. This reinforced the view reached at the **Crown Council** in 1912 – that the summer of 1914 was the most opportune moment for Germany to wage war – and therefore reinforced Moltke's view that 1914 represented Germany's 'last chance' to win.

- **Invading through Belgium.** Another important impact of the Schlieffen Plan was the decision to invade Belgium. The original plan had involved invading Holland too, but this had been blocked because the Dutch were seen as friendly to Germany. The deciding factor for the German high command was the quality of the Belgian railway system. Belgium had the densest railway network and therefore would provide the capacity for Germany to move troops through the country once resistance was overcome. However, the decision to invade Belgium also gave Britain a reason to declare war (see page 53).

- **Potential weaknesses of the Triple Alliance.** The pressure on the German General Staff to act decisively was increased by their belief that the Italians would not honour the Triple Alliance. Italy's naval and army developments after 1908 were based on **anti-Austrian popular opinion** which influenced members of the Italian parliament. The Germans also had doubts about Austrian strength. Even in 1914, with the Austrian army descending upon Serbia, the Germans could not be sure how effective the Austrian army would be in holding back the Russian army. The state of Germany's allies in

1914 only served to increase the pressure felt by Moltke that no time must be lost.

- **Potential weaknesses of the plan.** In the backs of the minds of the German generals must also have been the knowledge that, during the annual autumn staff exercise in 1904, Schlieffen had demonstrated how to defeat his own plan. In this elaborate wargame senior officers played the parts of both the Germans and the French. Just as those acting as the French were about to admit defeat, Schlieffen demonstrated that by transferring all their reserves to their left wing they could block the German 'right hook'. The fear of the German high command was that if the Schlieffen Plan was not implemented rapidly, the opportunity would increase for the French to recognise the solution and to transfer their resources to the left flank. (This actually happened in August 1914 when the French managed to halt the German advance.)

Plan XVII. The French General Staff also had a plan. This plan was called **Plan XVII** and was based on the idea of all-out attack, '*offensive a l'outrance*'. The French General Staff believed they had lost the war of 1870 because they had remained immobile: this time they would attack. Because the German army was larger the French therefore put the maximum pressure on Russia to mobilise rapidly and completely when the crisis came in 1914.

The Russian plan. Like the Germans, the Russians faced a war on two fronts. For the French a rapid Russian advance into East Prussia was vital, but Austria was Russia's most likely enemy because of the tensions between them in the Balkans. The tension between these two objectives was reflected in the way in which Russian military spending was divided. The cavalry faction led by Grand Duke Nicholas wanted to make the drive into Austrian Galicia the focus of operations. The 'reformist' wing led by War Minister General Vladimir Sukhomlinov put more emphasis on invading Prussia.

In the crisis of 1914 the difficulties of implementing only part of the plan, by mobilising against Austria only, led to pressure on the Tsar to agree to full mobilisation. When

KEY TERM

Plan XVII The central thrust of this plan was to seize Alsace-Lorraine as quickly as possible and invade Germany. A subsidiary force, including the British, would be stationed on the Franco-Belgium border in case of a German flank attack.

the Tsar was persuaded to order general mobilisation on 30 July the Germans followed suit. Here the Russian and German plans interacted; since the Schlicffen Plan assumed a certain headstart over Russia the Germans had to mobilise immediately or change their entire plan on the eve of war.

The main focus of this section has been on German plans as these were crucial to the outcome of the crisis: they led to Moltke's insistence on mobilisation. The French and Russian plans sought to deal with the anticipated German moves. The British plan to deliver 100,000 men to guard the left flank of the French Army was to have far greater significance in August–November 1914 than the planners foresaw. The Austrian plan to crush Serbia before turning to face Russia was significant, in that like the Germans the Austrians felt the need to start as quickly as possible. As a result, they moved to bombard Belgrade which triggered Russian and therefore German mobilisation.

CONCLUSION

Did alliances cause the war that broke out in 1914? They may have been significant, but other factors must also be considered.

- Germany went to war in 1914 despite the knowledge that its Austrian ally was the weakest of the great powers and that Italy was likely to remain neutral.
- Alliances did, however, escalate the scale of conflict that broke out in 1914.
- Moltke lacked the technical skill to alter the Schlieffen Plan either before 1914 or when it became obvious that the British army would be sent to France. Even though Moltke knew how critical any delay was on the Western Front he urged the Kaiser on, even in the face of Belgian defiance and British involvement.
- Alliances influenced the composition of the two sides in 1914 but not the decision to gamble on war.

What was the major significance of the military plans?

- The Schlieffen Plan guaranteed that a war between Austria and Russia would become a general European war if Germany decided to fulfil its alliance with Austria. If Germany mobilised to support Austria-Hungary then, following the Schlieffen Plan, Germany would first attack France. Russia's decision to back Serbia combined with the Russian General Staff's fear of the chaos of partial mobilisation provided the trigger for Germany to order full mobilisation.
- French fear of German mobilisation led them to maximise the pressure on Russia to mobilise fully. This helped to create the situation in which Moltke felt he must advise Wilhelm II to order mobilisation.
- Moltke's obsession with the timetable, assumed in the Schlieffen Plan, reflected the view expressed at the War Council in December 1912. This view was that, because of Russian rearmament, Germany should fight Russia sooner rather than later.
- As the arms race intensified in 1913 so the arguments for avoiding war weakened and the pressure on the Schlieffen timetable became greater.

The War Council's decision to accept an opportunity to go to war in 1914 was crucial to the outcome of the July crisis of 1914.

SUMMARY QUESTIONS

1 How important was the pre-war arms race in leading to war in 1914?

2 Did the Alliance systems lead to war in 1914?

3 Why did Germany commit itself to an alliance with Austria-Hungary?

CHAPTER 6

How did Sarajevo lead to war?

The assassination of the Austrian Archduke Franz Ferdinand in Sarajevo on 28 June 1914 triggered a chain of events that led to the start of a world war by 4 August 1914. The decisions which linked the two events cover all the major European capitals. For much of the period few people realised how serious the situation was. The politicians assumed that war, if it came, would be short and, of course, that they would win.

FROM SARAJEVO TO AUSTRIA'S ULTIMATUM TO SERBIA

The Austrian Archduke Franz Ferdinand was heir to the throne of the Austro-Hungarian Empire. This empire consisted of the many people that Austria had conquered in its wars with the Turks over the previous 400 years. The most recent territory it had formally acquired was Bosnia-Herzegovina in 1908. The 2 December 1908 also marked the Diamond Jubilee of the ageing Emperor Franz Josef who had come to the throne in 1848. Although Franz Ferdinand was heir to the throne, he was not popular with the Emperor because he was seen as a supporter of reforms that would give more influence to other nationalities within the empire. After their defeat by Prussia in 1866 the ruling Austrians had been forced to share power with the Hungarians, but the Hungarians were very harsh on the Slavs they ruled and this increased tension in areas like Bosnia-Herzegovina.

The assassination

Archduke Franz Ferdinand's wife, Sophie, was not a noble by birth so she was treated as unimportant at the protocol-ridden Imperial court in Vienna. However, when she accompanied the Archduke in his capacity as an army commander she had to be accorded proper respect appropriate to his rank. The Archduke therefore decided to visit Sarajevo in Bosnia on his wedding anniversary so that they could have a day together, even though 28 June was also a special day for Serbians, as it was the anniversary of a great battle, the **Battle of Kossovo**, against the Turks.

In the morning, one of a group of Serbian terrorists belonging to the secret **Black Hand** organisation threw a bomb at the Archduke's car. Reacting quickly, the Archduke deflected the missile into the road behind the car. The bomb exploded causing injuries to the people in the car behind. The Archduke therefore arrived for lunch with the local governor enraged by the lapse in security and threatening to cancel the rest of the visit. However, he decided to continue but wanted to visit the injured in hospital. It appears that the driver did not realise that there had been a change of plan and set off on the planned route before being told to go to the hospital. Whilst the driver was putting the car into reverse it was stationary and **Gavrilo Princip**, a student member of the Black Hand, was able to approach. Princip shot the Archduchess and the Archduke who died minutes later. Pictures of the day show the Achduke's car driving along streets without troops lining the streets or a large military escort. Security was so lax that there has been speculation that the officer in charge bore a grudge against the Archduke over lack of promotion or possibly because of his plans to reform the empire.

Reactions to the assassination

Austria-Hungary's response. The Emperor Franz Josef felt that the other monarchies in Europe would be very sympathetic towards any retaliatory action Austria-Hungary might take. However, Gavrilo Princip had been arrested at the scene so the actual assassin had already been caught. The question really was how far should Austria-Hungary go in pursuing those in Serbia who were indirectly responsible because they had tolerated the Black Hand or had connived at allowing them across the border?

- **The 'hawks'.** The Austrian Chief of Staff, Conrad von Hötzendorf, called for the immediate mobilisation of the army against Serbia. Conrad had previously argued that

Austria-Hungary should launch a pre-emptive strike against Serbia in order to prevent a later war when Serbia and Russia would be stronger. Conrad's confidence proved to be justified because one of the few successes of the Austro-Hungarian army during the First World War was the defeat of Serbia. However, his attitude contributed to the willingness to risk war. Another key adviser was Count Berchtold. He had been an opponent of war, so his decision to advise the Emperor, on 30 June 1914, to go to war was crucial in influencing Franz Josef. Count Berchtold had also been a close friend of Archduke Franz Ferdinand.

- **The 'doves'.** The Hungarian Prime Minister, Count Stephen Tisza, argued that the empire already contained enough Serbs and therefore there was no point in attacking Serbia to acquire territory. Therefore Tisza opposed Berchtold and Hötzendorf. Tisza feared that defeat would destroy the special position of the Hungarians whilst victory would restore the prestige and power of the court in Vienna.

The overriding issue was what response Russia would make to any action against Serbia. Russia shared both a Slavonic heritage and the **Orthodox** faith with the Serbs. In its attempts to push its power into the Balkans, Russia thereby posed as the champion of all Slavs in the face of Muslim Turkey and Catholic Austria.

Russia's attitude. In 1908 Austria-Hungary had annexed Bosnia-Herzegovina. The then Russian Foreign Minister, A. P. Isvolsky, had been forced to resign when it became known that he was prepared to accept the Austrian takeover in return for Austrian support over Russian access to the Black Sea. (The Austrians had subsequently double-crossed Russia in 1908.) Russia had been defeated by Japan in 1905 and had felt humiliated when Austria took advantage of its weakness. To confirm its position, Austria-Hungary had used its alliance with Germany to threaten Russia with war in 1908 and in 1913 (**the 1913 crisis**). In 1914 the Austrian leaders decided to see if they could repeat their success in forcing Russia to stand aside.

KEY TERM

Orthodox This is the term used for those who belong to the Eastern Orthodox Church which split from the (Western) Catholic Church in the eleventh century. After the fall of Constantinople in 1453 to the Turks, the Orthodox Patriarch of Moscow became the de facto head of the Orthodox Church. (The Catholic Church is headed by the Pope in Rome.)

KEY THEME

The 1913 crisis The Peace of London of 30 May 1913, which brought to an end the Balkan Wars, followed Austria-Hungary's mobilisation in December 1912. The Emperor had also restored Conrad to his post as Chief-of-Staff – a clear signal to the Serbs, given his public support of war. In 1913, Russia backed down from supporting Serbia and so an independent Albania was created, thereby denying Serbia an Adriatic port. The impact of this crisis was catastrophic in 1914, as Russia feared backing down again whilst Austria-Hungary hoped that it would.

Austria seeks German support. Following the Archduke's funeral, a letter was sent by the Austrian Emperor to the Kaiser with a memorandum from Berchtold seeking German support. The Kaiser assured Count Hoyas of full German support when they met on the afternoon of 5 July. Count Hoyas favoured war and was Berchtold's Chief of Cabinet. The Kaiser told his Chancellor, Theobald von Bethmann Hollweg, to assure the Emperor of Austria that Germany would not desert it in these difficult times. This was in effect the 'Blank Cheque' that Austria needed to offset the risk of Russian intervention. The official German response supporting Austria-Hungary was given on 6 July.

On 7 July the Austrian council of ministers met to discuss the German reply. Tisza maintained his arguments against war but the majority decided in favour of taking action against Serbia. This view was then reported to the Emperor who was, as usual, spending the summer at the resort of Bad Ischl. The Austrians were also told on 7 July by Bethmann Hollweg that he regarded war against Serbia as Austria's 'best and most radical solution' to its problems.

Both the German and Austrian governments had originally taken the view that the sooner action was taken the less likely Russia was to intervene. The Tsar's uncle Grand Duke Sergei had been blown up by terrorists in 1905 and his grandfather had been assassinated in 1881. The Austrians hoped therefore that Russia would not wish to be seen to support terrorism. However, the longer the Austrians took to act the more it would seem like a repeat of 1908 with Austria seeking to outmanoeuvre Russia.

The difficulty for the Germans was that having given the Austrians full support with the 'Blank Cheque' they had no way of putting a time limit on it. To back down would expose the limits of German support for Austria. By 1914 Austria was Germany's only ally as it was clear to the German General Staff that Italy would not honour its commitment to support Germany. Having created a situation where Germany had only one ally, the German government was obliged to support that ally. However, it must be remembered that both Bethmann Hollweg and Moltke preferred war in 1914 to war in future years.

THE AUSTRIAN ULTIMATUM

KEY TERM

Ultimatum An ultimatum is a series of points that need to be met. If they are not met then action will be taken.

Having managed to overcome Count Tisza's reservations about dealing with Serbia, by nominally accepting his condition that war should not be an attempt to annex Serbian territory, the Austrian council of ministers were able to prepare a formidable **ultimatum** to Serbia between 14 and 19 July. This ultimatum was important because if Austria was to act the ultimatum had to be made unacceptable to Serbia.

- The suppression of anti-Austrian propaganda and the tightening of border controls were reasonable demands. There were also reasonable suspicions that nationalists in the Serb police had turned a blind eye to the passage across the border of terrorists like Gavrilo Princip.
- The purging of anti-Austrian officers and officials as well as the arrest of those the Austrians suspected of aiding Princip was a harder demand for the Serbs to accept.
- A further demand for the suppression of the Black Hand was probably beyond the powers of the Serb government. The key stumbling block was the Austrian demand that Serbia permit Austrian officials to take part in the Serb investigation into the assassination. Such a demand effectively meant that the Austrians could not trust the Serbs to do the job. This offended Serbia's sovereignty and was designed to ensure rejection and therefore war.

Since the Austrians were keen to move whilst the French President and Prime Minister were at sea returning from Russia (see Chapter 7), they not only delayed sending the ultimatum but also gave the Serbs only 48 hours to reply.

FROM THE REJECTION OF THE AUSTRIAN ULTIMATUM TO WAR

Upon receiving the ultimatum, the Serbs were inclined to accept it with only minor adjustments, but changed their minds to a less pliable response when they heard on 25 July that Russia's mood was fiercely pro-Serbian. However, they did send a conciliatory response that met most of the

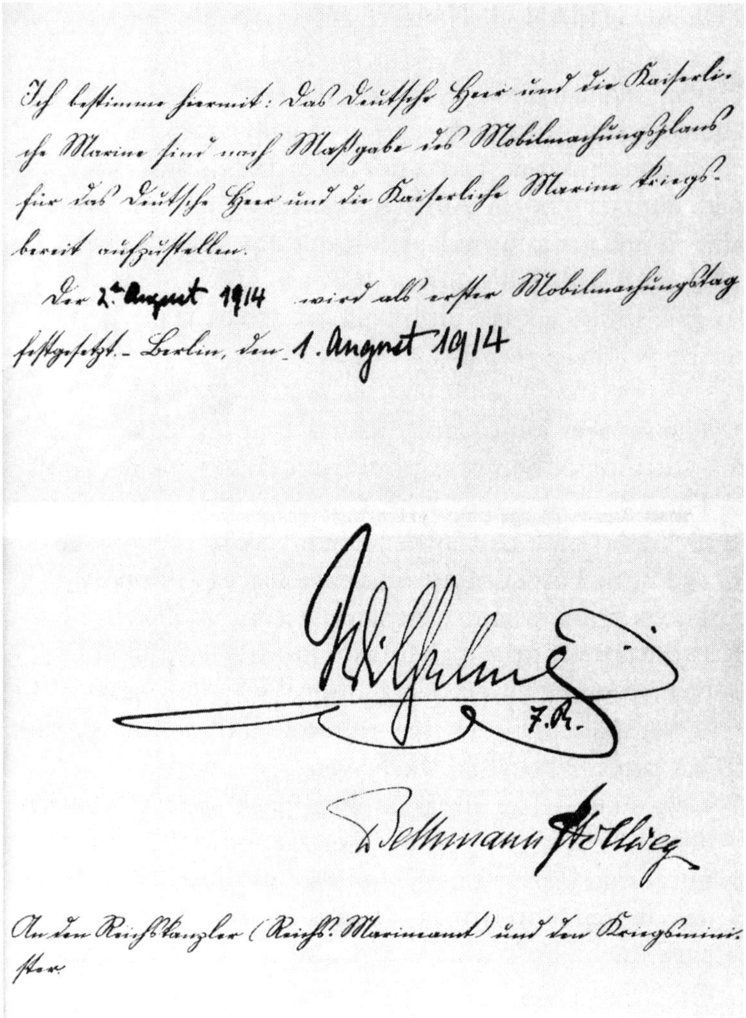
Ich bestimme hiermit: Das Deutsche Heer und die Kaiserliche Marine sind nach Maßgabe des Mobilmachungsplans für das Deutsche Heer und die Kaiserliche Marine kriegsbereit aufzustellen.

Der 2. August 1914 wird als erster Mobilmachungstag festgesetzt. – Berlin, den 1. August 1914

Wilhelm I.R.

v. Bethmann Hollweg

An den Reichskanzler (Reichsmarineamt) und den Kriegsminister.

German mobilisation order, 1914.

Austrian requests but refused the demand for Austrian police to enter Serbia. The Serb reply even struck the Germans as reasonable. If the Austrians had not wanted war then this was the opportunity to negotiate a settlement.

Having received the Serbian reply, the Austrian Foreign Minister, Count Berchtold, went to see the Emperor at Bad Ischl on 26 July. Berchtold had favoured war from the beginning and it was his close friend, Count Hoyas, who had taken the Emperor's letter to the Kaiser and returned with the 'Blank Cheque'. As well as reporting on the ultimatum, Berchtold told the Emperor that the Serbs had fired on Austro-Hungarian soldiers at Korvin. This story was untrue but it helped to ensure that the Emperor signed the mobilisation order.

Mobilisation. The mobilisation of any one power immediately raised the stakes. If the other powers did not respond then they would fall behind in the race against the timetable created by their military plans. Mobilisation involving mass armies could not be hidden. Therefore when the mobilisation notices were published in Austria-Hungary on 27 July all the other powers would know as soon as their embassies or other informers could contact them.

KEY POINTS

Moltke's role On 29 July Moltke told the Kaiser 'we shall never hit again so well as we do now'.

The role of Bethmann Hollweg Berchtold, the Austrian Foreign Minister, famously asked Conrad 'who was in charge in Berlin?' The military had supported a 'Blank Cheque' being given to Austria-Hungary. Bethmann Hollweg was not actually able to reverse this position. This was shown when later on the 30 July he agreed to a 'military state of emergency' which was the next step towards full mobilisation. Bethmann Hollweg accepted the main thrust of the military argument that war was more likely to be successful in 1914 than later. At the end of the July crisis he concentrated upon making sure Germans backed their government's decision for war.

- On 28 July Austria declared war on Serbia and Austrian shells landed on Belgrade, the Serbian capital.
- On the evening of 28 July, **Moltke** sent **Bethmann Hollweg** a secret memorandum saying that Germany's military options were now reduced to war or future decline in the face of stronger enemies. In effect Moltke was saying that war was now inevitable and that all that remained to decide was the timing. Both men had viewed the July crisis as an opportunity to launch a war at a favourable time for Germany. They were now on the brink of that goal.
- The Russians had discussed partial mobilisation on 24 July. On 28 July in St Petersburg the Tsar proclaimed

General Helmuth von Moltke.

German Chancellor Theobold von Bethmann Hollweg.

How did Sarajevo lead to war? 71

the 'Period Preparatory to War', which gave all the advantages of starting general mobilisation of the Russian army, but without using the word. Initially Russian 'mobilisation' was directed only at Austria-Hungary and therefore in support of Serbia.

- On 29 July Moltke thus urged the Kaiser to order German mobilisation. Moltke was afraid of Russia getting ahead and therefore reducing the time available to defeat France according to the Schlieffen Plan.

- On 30 July, Sergei Sazonov, the Russian Foreign Minister (see Chapter 7) persuaded the Tsar to order a full mobilisation of Russian forces. He even used such arguments as full mobilisation was written into the agreement with France in 1894. This agreement promised that Russia and France would mobilise if one of the central powers did, but since France had not yet mobilised this was a weak argument. French warnings not to provoke mobilisation by Germany were too late to affect events that were being driven by the Russian response to Austria-Hungary. Since the French cabinet had nevertheless decided to stand behind its alliance with Russia such warnings were, in any case, of limited impact.

- France's armies were ordered to cover its eastern border but not to approach within 10 km of the border. The French government did not wish the French or British public to gain the impression that it was the aggressor. The French commander **General Joseph Joffre** was unhappy about this restriction on his preparations but felt obliged to obey.

- On 30 July, Bethmann Hollweg received news from the German Embassy in London that Britain would not remain neutral. Having failed to limit the war even to the continent this was the moment for him to urge the Kaiser to hold back. Instead he urged the Austrians to settle for occupying Belgrade whilst Serbia fulfilled the terms of the ultimatum. Moltke, also, would not hold back and sent a telegram to Conrad urging him to continue mobilising and assuring him that Germany would mobilise.

- On 31 July news reached Berlin from their embassy staff in Moscow that Russian mobilisation notices were being published. Bethmann Hollweg was delighted with this news since it allowed him to tell the Socialists in the

General Joseph Joffre (1852–1931) Joffre built his reputation in France's colonial wars in Indo-China and Africa. Having served as Director of Engineers since 1905, he was made Chief of Staff in 1911. He was the author of the French Plan XVII, which France used in 1914. His greatest success was the Battle of the Marne, 6 September 1914, which saved Paris. Subsequent failure and heavy losses, and an unwillingness to accept political direction, led to his effective dismissal in December 1916. He received promotion to Marshal of France but had no further influence on the conduct of the war.

Reichstag that Russia had forced Germany to mobilise. Moltke was now able to get the Kaiser to sign the decree that a 'threatening state of war' existed. This was another stage laid down in the Schlieffen Plan for bringing Germany's peacetime army up to wartime strength.

- Whilst technically the final stage of actual mobilisation was not ordered until 1 August, the German plan had already been set in motion. On the afternoon of 1 August 1914 France and Germany both issued their mobilisation decrees. The continent of Europe was now at war.

- On 3 August the British government was informed that Belgium intended to reject Germany's demand that its armies be permitted to cross Belgian territory to reach France. This provided Great Britain with a legal reason to support France against Germany. In 1839 Britain had signed the Treaty of London in which it promised to maintain the independence of the newly created state of Belgium. Fulfilling Britain's obligation to Belgium was therefore given as the reason for Britain's declaration of war against Germany on 4 August 1914. Since the British Dominions (Australia, Canada, New Zealand and South Africa) declared their support for Britain, the world was now at war.

CONCLUSION

- **A Balkan war.** The assassination of the Archduke Franz Ferdinand led to a European war because it created a situation in which Austria thought it could strike a blow against Serbia. Austria saw Serbia as a mortal enemy.
- **A European war.** By seeking and receiving German support Austria increased the possibility of a European war. Germany's leaders preferred war in 1914 to one at a later date and therefore urged Austria-Hungary on. Russia, like Austria-Hungary, felt that its future status as a great power was at stake and therefore did not believe it could refuse the challenge. Given the proposals of the Schlieffen Plan, Russian mobilisation led to Germany's attack on France. Moltke, Hötzendorf and Bethmann Hollweg all believed war was inevitable. They therefore chose to fight in 1914 when they believed they could

still win. Given that they wanted war and Russia felt unable to back down again, war was almost inevitable after 5 July when Austria received Germany's 'Blank Cheque'.

- **A world war.** Since the Schlieffen Plan involved invading Belgium the British were provided with a legal reason for fulfilling their unwritten obligations to France.

SUMMARY QUESTIONS

1 Why did Russia fight in 1914 having chosen not to risk war in earlier crises?

2 Did war in 1914 result from muddled responses by the great powers?

3 'A bluff that backfired.' Is this a convincing assessment of why the assassination of the Archduke led to war?

CHAPTER 7

Which country was most to blame for the outbreak of war in 1914?

Treaty of Versailles and war guilt Article 231 of the treaty stated that Germany was guilty of starting the war. This idea of German guilt was initially only contested in Germany. However, Lenin's publication of Tsarist treaties helped to expose the degree to which the other powers had also tried to make sure they were in a strong position if war broke out.

The impact of Fritz Fischer Many Germans felt very bitter that a German historian should put the blame for the war back on Germany. There has been some criticism that Fischer was giving too much weight to the war aims drawn up by the Germans in September 1914 – that is, after the war started. The difficulty for Fischer's opponents was countering the extensive research which Fischer, and later his supporters, had carried out in the official archives.

'Old Contemptibles' It was the small size of the British army that led the Kaiser to describe the British forces as 'a contemptibly little army'. The British soldiers thereby gave themselves the nickname the 'Old Contemptibles'.

In 1919 the **Treaty of Versailles** expressed the view of the winners: the principal loser, Germany, had caused the war. During the British election campaign of 1918, phrases such as 'Hang the Kaiser' were popular. Then, in 1961, the German historian **Fritz Fischer** rocked the German historical establishment by publishing his book *Grasping after World Power,* in which he argued that in 1914 Germany had declared war in a bid to become a world power. However, it is important to look at the contribution of all of the great powers before attempting to reach a conclusion.

WHAT WAS BRITAIN'S ROLE?

It is customary to see Britain's role as a passive one, and the most common criticism of Britain is that had it made its position clear, then the other powers would have held back. The difficulty with this view is twofold.

- The Entente between Britain and France was well known and therefore the Central Powers (Germany and Austria-Hungary) could only, at best, hope for British neutrality.
- Secondly, the expectation was that this would be a short war in which the relatively small British forces, the **'Old Contemptibles'**, would not prove significant.

The role of Sir Edward Grey. The role of Sir Edward Grey, the British Foreign Secretary, is of real importance in assessing Britain's response to the mounting European crisis.

- He is criticised for being too slow to react to the crisis and therefore of only intervening when it was too late.

- Grey's attempts to halt the slide into war on 1 August only exposed the inflexibility of German planning. Moltke refused to alter the military timetable and thereby limited the Kaiser's ability to compromise even if he had continued to have doubts.

- In August 1914 Grey was considering whether British neutrality could be traded for a limitation of war to the Eastern Front. If the Germans did not violate Belgian neutrality, and if Britain could prevent France from supporting Russia, then the Balkan war would not engulf the whole of Europe. However, Grey was overtaken by events.

- Grey may also have been influenced by the Russo-Japanese war (1905). Since Britain was allied to Japan and France to Russia, Britain had been able to remain neutral by keeping France out of the conflict. It would seem that Grey was looking for a similar way out again. However, in 1914, unlike 1905, France felt its vital interests were at stake so it issued the order for general mobilisation at 3.40 p.m. on 1 August 1914, which effectively ended any possibility of Grey being able to limit the war to eastern Europe.

The significance of the Entente. Since 1904 the British and French Entente had led to an informal British commitment to land a force of 100,000 men in France in the event of a German attack. Faced by the reality of German mobilisation and correctly anticipating that the initial attack would be on France, the French government asked the British to honour the **commitment** which the French felt was real, albeit unwritten. Unlike the German 'Blank Cheque' to Austria the Entente could not be used to support a case for starting a war, but it did, however, point towards this possibility. In *The Pity of War* (2000), Niall Ferguson sees Grey as anti-German, so although the commitment was not binding, he argues that Grey treated it as the desirable outcome.

In 1914 Britain honoured its commitments. Those who had argued against any form of alliance were proved correct. Even if **splendid isolation** was not always 'splendid' it gave more room to manoeuvre and avoided

The role of Poincaré Some historians have argued that the French President Raymond Poincaré was a warmonger. After the war the legend developed of 'Poincaré la Guerre', but this was a product of German and left-wing propaganda. However, he was from Lorraine and had seen his country invaded by the Germans when he was ten years old so he was likely to be less than sympathetic to Germany.

The Military Convention 1892 The main area of discussion over the convention was the measures either country should take if the other was threatened with aggression. The convention revolved around France and Russia trying to meet the 'necessities of a defensive war'. It is debatable whether Russia backing Serbia in a contest with Austria-Hungary was really a defensive war. The key clause of the convention read: 'If Russia is attacked by Germany, or by Austria supported by Germany, France shall employ all her available forces to fight Germany'. German conservative opposition to Chancellor Caprivi's (1890–94) attempts to improve trade relations with Russia heightened Russian fears of conflict with Germany. Since France too feared Germany, Russia and France came to see each other as potential allies.

the ties that any formal alliances with France would have created by 1914.

WHAT PART DID THE FRENCH PLAY IN PRECIPITATING WAR?

France's decision to mobilise on 1 August ended any possibility of a compromise or a limited war. Germany's decision to mobilise was an automatic one, especially given Moltke's belief that 1914 was Germany's last chance to win a European war on two fronts. Moltke told the Kaiser that it was too late to change the Schlieffen Plan, but it was his failure to develop alternative plans that brought Germany to this impasse. The role of the French in encouraging war revolves around the actions of a small number of important and influential individuals.

- **President Poincaré's visit to Russia.** The French contribution to the outbreak of war in 1914 needs to be considered in relation to their encouragement of Russia. One of the aspects of July 1914 which is sometimes overlooked is the visit of the **French President Raymond Poincaré** and Prime Minister Réné Viviani to St Petersburg from 20 to 22 July 1914. It is often pointed out that the sea passage back made it difficult for a peace conference to be organised. However, the French politicians left Russia only two days before the Russian council of ministers reached the decision to back any Serb rejection of the Austrian ultimatum. It is thus most unlikely that the Russians did not discuss the possibility of war with their close allies.
- **The role of the French Ambassador to Russia.** On 24 July, before the council of ministers met in the afternoon, the Russian Foreign Minister, Sergei Sazonov met with the French Ambassador, Maurice Paleologue. Paleologue urged Sazonov to take a tough line in support of Serbia and promised full French backing. France, through Paléologue, was therefore making it clear that it would fulfil the terms of the **Military Convention of 1892** even though it could be argued that these circumstances did not exactly fit those outlined in the convention. So Russia made important

decisions in July 1914 in the knowledge that its ally was prepared to go to war. The council decided to back any Serbian rejection of the ultimatum, justified by loss of sovereignty.

- **The role of the French War Minister.** On 27 July the French War Minister, M. Messimy, sent a message to the Russians urging them to invade East Prussia as soon as possible in the event of war. This was the latest in a series of belligerent statements from Paris urging Russia to adopt a hard line. France, therefore, was guilty of encouraging Russia to push Europe to the brink of war.
- **The weakness of the pro-German lobby.** It must also be remembered that Joseph Caillaux, the most pro-German member of the French government, had been forced to resign after his wife was charged with shooting the editor of *Le Figaro* newspaper in March 1914. Her trial, which ended with her acquittal on 28 July, distracted most of France, including the politicians, from the growing crisis in the Balkans.

AND THE RUSSIANS…

As in France, the decision in Russia to go to war was taken by a small group of influential leaders.

- **The Russian council of ministers meeting 24 July 1914.** At the Russian council of ministers on 24 July the Russian Foreign Minister Sergei **Sazonov** argued that Russia could not afford to be seen to be as weak, as it had appeared at the Congress of Berlin in 1878 or after Austria-Hungary's annexation of Bosnia-Herzegovina in 1908. He was supported in this view by the influential Minister of Agriculture, A. V. Krivoshein. He argued that although Russia did not want war it might happen anyway if it did not make a firm stand. Clearly then the risk of war was fully appreciated but the view of the meeting was that Germany was behind the Austrian ultimatum and that war might be forced on Russia.
- **Russian support for Serbia.** Sazonov conveyed the council of ministers' support for Serbia to the Serbs via their ambassador. It is likely that this support went some

KEY THEME

Sazonov's view At the meeting Sazonov said, 'Germany had looked upon our concessions [in 1878] as so many proofs of our weakness and far from having prevented our neighbours from using aggressive methods, we had encouraged them'.

way to encouraging the Serbian cabinet to reject point 6 of the Austrian ultimatum, which required the Austrian police to be allowed into Serbia. Since Vienna was looking for an excuse for war the Serb response moved Europe closer to war.

- **Russian preparations for mobilisation.** Following the council of ministers the Russian armed forces moved into the 'period preparatory to war'. By making the preparations for mobilisation Russia put the German General Staff under acute pressure. The Schlieffen Plan required the maximum available time between German mobilisation and the arrival of Russian forces in East Prussia. On 29 July Germany warned Russia that if it did not cease preparations for war then Germany would mobilise. As each side stepped nearer the abyss so the other felt obliged not to be left behind.

- **General mobilisation.** The most crucial decision by the Russians therefore was **Nicholas II's order for general mobilisation** on 30 July. Despite the advice of some of his ministers, the Tsar accepted the views of Sazonov and Krivoshein that the Central Powers wanted war and that a partial mobilisation would only make Russia vulnerable to German attack. Given the requirements of the Schlieffen Plan this step led Germany to mobilise.

KEY THEME

Nicholas II and mobilisation Nicholas was notoriously indecisive. However, he felt strong enough to ignore pleas from his cousin, the Kaiser, that they might deal with the problem 'within the family'. Perhaps the official outpouring of support had unduly impressed Nicholas II during the Romanov's 300-year-anniversary celebrations in 1913. Nicholas II, who had frequently demonstrated poor judgement, now made another fatal error.

Russia's decision to defend Serbian independence put it and Austria-Hungary on a collision course. Defeated in 1905 and outwitted in 1908, Russia believed its status as a great power would be fatally undermined if it were not prepared to fight. Having received strong French support, Russia felt able to risk war. Russia, correctly, assumed that Germany would back Austria so it entered the conflict with no illusions. To that extent it was guilty of helping to cause the First World War.

HOW CRUCIAL WERE THE ACTIONS OF AUSTRIA-HUNGARY?

Austria-Hungary made a crucial decision when it decided to respond to the assassination of Franz Ferdinand as it did. The royal courts of Europe could hardly be unsympathetic to Austria in its loss. However, Austria's

decision to point the finger at Serbia as the state
sponsoring the Black Hand terrorist group was too
provocative to the Russians to allow them to stand aside.

The Austro-Hungarians wanted a war. Austria-Hungary
was fully aware of the risk of war. Since it had appeared to
triumph over Russia in 1908 when it annexed Bosnia-
Herzegovina, Austria-Hungary understood that it was
putting Russia in a corner by threatening Serbia. This is
also suggested by the request to Germany for support.
Austria-Hungary thus no doubt understood the risks, but
with the German 'Blank Cheque' it carried on regardless.

Attitude towards the Serbs. Confident of German support,
Austria-Hungary rejected the Serbian response to its
ultimatum. Most European leaders believed the Serbs had
responded as positively as possible, given that the Austrian
demand to conduct an investigation in Serbia was likely to
be rejected and that the Serbs had only 48 hours to
consider it. By rejecting the Serbian response the Austrians
clearly demonstrated that they were determined to go to
war. As Count Tisza, the Hungarian Prime Minister, put it
to the German Ambassador to Vienna, Austria-Hungary
'must take an energetic decision to show its power of
survival'. Having decided that Austria-Hungary needed to
fight, the leaders of Austria-Hungary rejected every
opportunity to pull back from the brink. By opening a
bombardment on the Serb capital, Belgrade, on 28 July,
the Austrians helped to push Russia into full mobilisation
with all the consequences which followed.

Austrian attitude towards protecting the Empire. The
German soldier and scholar Karl von Clausewitz, in his
famous book *On War* (1822), wrote that war was simply
the pursuit of political goals by other means. In 1914
Austria-Hungary made the decision that its central goal of
maintaining its multinational empire could best be
achieved by war. Austria-Hungary went to war in the hope
that popular patriotism would bind together the
centrifugal pressures that existed by 1914." Without
Austria-Hungary's desire for war in 1914 there would not
have been a general war in Europe that summer."

Austria-Hungary has therefore to bear a significant share in the responsibility for the First World War.

HOW INFLUENTIAL WERE THE GERMAN LEADERS?

It was the Schlieffen Plan which linked the conflict in eastern Europe to the conflict in the west, and thereby turned war between Serbia and Austria into a general European war. The plan had been completed in 1905 and was not developed or replaced under Moltke; as he once confided to a friend, his uncle (Moltke the Elder) was awarded the Order of the Red Eagle for conquering France whilst he (Moltke the Younger) got his for organising a parade. Lacking his uncle's skill, Moltke the Younger insisted upon following the Schlieffen Plan rigidly even when the Kaiser began to have doubts.

The elder Moltke was famous for creating the Prussian General Staff but his campaigns demonstrate how brilliantly he improvised to cope with the reality of war. In this sense the Kaiser was right when he told the younger Moltke in 1914 that his uncle would never have told him (the Kaiser) that the plan could not be altered. H. H. Herwig (*The First World War*, 1997) argues cogently that in the final crisis of July 1914 the Kaiser was marginalised, as he was later to be during the war. By 1914 Moltke and the Prussian military leadership had come to be dominated by the Schlieffen Plan. They therefore became reactive. Each decision was driven by the fear of falling behind the timetable. This does not mean Germany was not to blame for war in 1914.

Moltke's obsession with the timetable reflected the view expressed at the War Council, held by the Kaiser in December 1912, that Russian rearmament meant that Germany should fight Russia sooner rather than later. The arms race had intensified in 1913 so the arguments for avoiding war weakened as the pressure on the Schlieffen timetable became greater.

In his book, *Moltke, Schlieffen and Prussian War Planning* (1991), Arden Bucholz has shown that Moltke was a fatalist who believed that war was inevitable. Lacking the skill to rewrite German plans he and the other German leaders seized upon the assassination of Archduke Franz Ferdinand as the ideal opportunity. They were therefore prepared to give Austria-Hungary German military support even if this led to war. Given that neither Austria-Hungary nor Germany believed that Russia would be able to back down, Germany's leaders were triggering a war. This supports Fischer's thesis that in 1914 Germany made a deliberate bid to deal a knock-out blow. In 1913 the Kaiser's ministers had only been able to obtain further increases of money and men in the army at the cost of an inheritance tax which hit the Junker aristocracy. The SPD (Socialist Party) had become the largest party in the Reichstag in 1912 and it was clear that any further increases in military expenditure would only be possible at the cost of higher taxes on the wealthy. The naval race, resulting from **Flottenpolitik**, had led Germany into mounting debt since 1908. German leaders faced the dilemma that to prolong the arms race would lead to increasingly difficult problems with the Reichstag, and also that Russian and French rearmament was reducing their competitive advantage (see Chapter 5).

The German ruling elite lacked the policies necessary to solve either the domestic or the military problems they faced, so they chose to fight. The elite (the Kaiser, Junker aristocracy, top industrialists) refused to concede political reform so they had no answer to the apparent threat of the **SPD**. Without a war the elite could not secure the money to develop the army further without significant political concessions. Therefore, Fischer was correct to see 1914 as a 'bid for world power', but the timing reflects the primacy of military policy. The German elite was therefore guilty of helping to cause the First World War.

CONCLUSION

Germany sought war in 1914 and therefore was guilty of helping to cause the First World War. However, such a simple statement ignores the fact that it was Austrian desperation to maintain their failing status which provided

KEY TERMS

Flottenpolitik The policy of using the fleet to solve domestic problems. The empire supported by the fleet would appease the middle classes whilst the employment created would help to appease the working classes. The political term for this attempt to create a wide alliance of interests in support of the traditional German ruling class was *Sammlungspolitik*. The deepening political 'crisis' after 1912 made the failure of these policies very clear.

SPD The German Social Democratic Party (SPD) was founded in 1869 by Karl Liebknecht, a dedicated follower of Marx and a revolutionary. Committed to the Marxist tenets of class conflict and the necessity of overthrowing the existing system, the party was also prepared to work within the system to achieve short-term reforms in education, working conditions, and the suffrage. Despite Bismarck's Anti-Socialist Law, the SPD steadily gained seats in the Reichstag, and after Bismarck's fall was able to campaign openly.

An Austrian propaganda picture of 1914. Wilhelm II is pointing toward the map of France.

Germany with the means to pursue its ambition for a European war. Buoyed by the 'Blank Cheque' from Germany the Austrian shells landing on Belgrade ensured a European conflagration.

France encouraged Russia in its belief that its status as a great power was at stake. The Russians refused to back down as they had in 1908. Since neither side blinked, the result was war. Britain was slow to react but was not a major factor in the calculations of the continental powers. Britain had perhaps helped to create a Europe of two armed camps and to frustrate German ambitions, but it did nothing to start a war in Europe in 1914.

HISTORIOGRAPHY: THE DEBATE OVER THE ORIGINS OF THE FIRST WORLD WAR

Introduction

The slaughter and destruction of the First World War fuelled an intense debate on why it occurred. This historiographical (the writing of history) debate has to be assessed in the same way that all evidence has to be assessed: the views of historians need to be evaluated rather than simply rehearsed as a list of facts.

The Versailles phase

The Treaty of Versailles not only contained the famous Article 231 or 'war guilt' clause but it also blamed the Kaiser:

> *The Allied and Associated Powers publicly arraign William II of Hohenzollern, former German Emperor, for a supreme offence against international morality and the sanctity of treaties.*

This not only reflected the 'Hang the Kaiser' mood of the 1918 general election in Britain but also US President Wilson's requirement in 1918 that peace could only be negotiated when the Kaiser had abdicated. Even though Sir Edward Grey was one of those who agreed with this approach we cannot see the reports from this period as a serious historical exercise because they were designed to support particular viewpoints.

The secret diplomacy phase

As many of the regimes that led their countries into war had fallen by 1919 it became popular to blame their old ways of diplomacy. Blaming them had begun in 1918, with President Wilson's **Fourteen Points**, which called for 'open covenants of peace, openly arrived at … no private undertakings'. This view, that secret diplomacy was to blame, was given historical weight by G. Lowes Dickinson in 1926 when he published *The International Anarchy, 1904–14*. Dickinson was able to put forward his case because, following the revolutions in their countries, the secret treaties of Russia and Germany had been published. The German government believed that the publication of these documents would help to prove that Germany was

KEY TERM

The Fourteen Points The Fourteen Points were very significant because they provided an apparently fair basis for peace. The Germans later felt that the British and, especially, the French had been much harsher in practice. For example, the British only agreed to negotiate on the basis of the Fourteen Points if freedom of the seas did not apply, so the British naval blockade was maintained. However, the German government was informed of this and other reservations and qualifications prior to an agreement.

not alone in causing the First World War. By 1927, the German government had published 39 volumes of diplomatic documents entitled *The High Policy of the European Cabinets* and in 1930 the Austrian government published eight volumes of diplomatic material. Ironically, Britain published relevant material only from 1926 to 1938 whilst the French began publication only in 1930 and did not complete the series until 1953. So 'secret diplomacy' was used mainly by Germany and Russia to distance themselves from pre-revolution governments.

One major difficulty with the idea that secret diplomacy led to war is the extent to which each side successfully anticipated the intentions of the other. For example, Schlieffen correctly divined the probable military clauses of the Franco-Russian treaty whilst the French asked Britain to operate on their left flank in case of a German sweep through Belgium. The Germans also correctly estimated that the Italians would not support them in 1914 despite their alliance.

Diplomatic history. The publication of these documents was not accompanied by the publication of relevant domestic policy material, which continued to be undisclosed and classified. Therefore the conclusions of historians such as P. Renouvin in France (*The Immediate Origins of the War*, 1927) who blamed Germany, and the German historian A. von Wegerer (*Der Ausbruch des Weltkrieges*, 1939) who blamed Russia and Britain, were based solely upon a reading of the diplomatic documents.

Another historian who blamed Germany was the American B. E. Schmitt, who published *The Coming of the War, 1914* in 1928. In appraising the work of Schmitt and other US historians it is important to remember their perspective. Despite President Wilson's call for openness he was seen by many Americans (such as William Jennings Bryan, the Secretary of State) to have been quite devious. Wilson had allowed the British to impose a blockade from 4 August 1914 but then complained when Germany tried to break it using U-boats. Wilson's own underhand methods thus led Americans to emphasise the role of secret diplomacy. If secret diplomacy was to blame then it was good that the new mass electorates created by the changes in 1918 would increase the political importance of those who previously had only had the role of being sacrificed on the battlefield. Public opinion was very receptive to this view since it suggested that the new mass electorates which had been created in 1918–9 would prove superior to the social elite who had steered Europe to catastrophe. There was no proof that mass electorates would be better, but they themselves were happy to believe they would be. It is a truism that with hindsight the old elite would not have started the war either if they had known the outcome.

The Hitler phase

The advent of the Second World War in 1939 overtook the completion of the Italian L. Albertini's magisterial study, *The Origins of the War of 1914,* which was eventually published in 1942–3. This book argued that the German government bore considerable blame for the outbreak of war. Not only did the war delay the book reaching a wider audience, for example it only appeared in English in 1957, it also seemed to make the debate about the origins of the First World War academic. Hitler's invasion of Poland, despite British and French guarantees to Poland in 1939, seemed to confirm the popular view that German militarism had started the First World War. To many people it seemed obvious that, as each successive German regime had invaded other countries, then the Second World War proved that it had been correct to blame Germany for the outbreak of war in 1914.

Prussian militarism. At the Nuremberg Trials in 1946 the German military leadership was put on trial. The high command of the German Armed Forces, the OKW (Oberkommando der Wehrmacht), was identified as a guilty organisation which had planned and carried out aggressive war. This approach reflected the view that the Prussian General Staff had caused the First World War and that its successors, recreated by Hitler in defiance of the Treaty of Versailles, had started the Second. The absence of Prussia from the provinces (*Länder*) of the new Federal Republic of Germany thus symbolised a break from the past influences of **Prussian militarism**.

The Cold War. In the context of the Cold War, west European historians began to emphasise the positive view

KEY THEME

Prussian militarism The victories of Frederick the Great, most notably in the Seven Years War (1756–63), established the military reputation of Prussia. Although later dented by Napoleon, this reputation was restored after 1807 by Scharnhorst, Gneisenau, Boyen and Clausewitz. Their reforms led to Prussia's success at Waterloo. Subsequently, Moltke the Elder's brilliance restored Prussia to being the standard against which all other western armies were judged.

that the majority of Germans had never been Nazis or Prussians, and the origins of the First World War thereby became obscured in the debate about the '*Sonderweg*' or 'special path' which Germany's development had taken. It was into this increasingly comfortable world that the 'academic hand grenade' of Fritz Fischer's work exploded, though the Sonderweg debate did not really come to the fore until almost a decade later.

The Fischer Era

Fischer. The work of a German historian, Fritz Fischer's *Griff nach der Weltmacht* (1961) was sensational because it showed how much territory Germany wanted to annex and suggested that there was a continuity between German aims in 1914 and the aims of Hitler. Some of Fischer's critics said Fischer was also suggesting that Germany had deliberately gone to war in 1914. This latter view was only really developed in *Krieg der Illusionen* published in 1969, where Fischer stressed that Germany wanted to become a world power. After these titles were published in translation as *Germany's Aims in the First World War* (1972) and *War of Illusions* (1974) the Fischer controversy spread much further. Bitter rows developed between Fischer and his followers, and the rest of the academic establishment in Germany. The debate about Germany's war aims centred upon its desire to annex both Belgium and more territory to the east, the latter intention providing the link with Hitler's desire for *Lebensraum* ('living space'). The main criticism of Fischer is that Chancellor von Bethmann Hollweg drew up the list of war aims *after* the war began and when it was becoming clear that the Schlieffen Plan had failed, indicating that Germany had not formulated ambitions for domination prior to the First World War. However, the German title of Fischer's first book could be translated as *Grasping after World Power*: Fischer therefore highlighted the basic motivation, which was for Germany to become a world power.

The role of Chancellor von Bülow, Admiral von Tirpitz and the Kaiser in pursuing a world policy (***Weltpolitik***) has been well documented and so this argument has to be accepted. The debate itself begins with the agreement that there was a policy from 1897 onwards to make Germany a great power; views differ on how to integrate the decisions of July 1914 into this framework. In 1965, I. Geiss (*Juli 1914. Die europäische Krise und der Ausbruch des Ersten Weltkrieges*) broadly supported Fischer's views. The main debate put forward by G. Ritter (*Der Erste Weltkrieg. Studien zum deutschen Geschichtsbild*, 1964) to counter support for Fischer is that such a view ignores the degree to which other powers were also prepared to risk war in order to achieve their aims. Ritter thus argued that the First World War was not entirely down to Germany, and appeared concerned to avoid Germany being thus blamed. Chapter 7 has reflected this by seeking to assess the contribution made by each country. L. C. F. Turner (*Origins of the First World War*, 1967), too, argued that Geiss ignored the critical issue of Russia's decision to mobilise. This argument assumed that if Russia had maintained its original decision to mobilise only along the German and Austro-Hungarian borders then war would not have started. This blurred the national responsibility issue into the debate over German motives. E. Zechlin (*Kriegsausbruch 1914 und Kriegszielproblem in der internationalen Politik*, 1972) adopted Fischer's view that Germany was prepared to risk war but distinguished between acceptance of the inevitable and actively seeking war to further its foreign policy aims. A. Bucholz's evidence, backed by H. H. Herwig, suggested that Germany went beyond merely being prepared to risk war. The central question remains why Germany opted for war in 1914 – this is the **primacy debate**.

The primacy debate. The great German historian Ranke laid down the premise that Germany was primarily inspired by foreign policy objectives (*Primat der Aussenpolitik*). However, in Fischer's *War of Illusions*, and subsequent works by Geiss for example, greater weight was given to the domestic pressures which led to the decision to declare war. This argument is referred to as the *Primat der Innenpolitik* and centres upon the crisis in the German government (and the governments of other states) as old established elites were threatened by social and economic change. American historians such as Arno Mayer in *The Persistence of the Old Regime* (1981) reflect this view. Mayer saw the war as a last bid by the old ruling classes to retain their supremacy. In this respect, the rise of the SPD in Germany to be the largest political party by 1912 is seen as

Primacy debate Historians recognise that the German government's decisions in July 1914 cannot be attributed to a single (monocausal) reason. Therefore, the debate has centred upon when foreign or domestic policy is the prime or main reason for the German government's actions.

a key indicator. It can be argued that Bethmann Hollweg's attempts to forge a domestic consensus once he believed war to be inevitable also supports this view.

The military debate. In attacking Fischer's work, Ritter postulated that the Chancellor, Bethmann Hollweg and the generals should not be treated as the same. This may be true after 1914 but it is still very unclear how different their views were before the July crisis. As V. R. Berghahn argued, in *Germany and the Approach of War in 1914* (1973), it may be the case that only when no option remained did Bethmann Hollweg attempt to unite the country behind war. A. Bucholz's study *Moltke, Schlieffen and Prussian War Planning* (1991) demonstrated the active role played by the General Staff in seeking war in July 1914. Ironically, despite the General Staff's reputation across Europe, Bucholz's research shows that it was the rigidity of German planning that drove Germany to war and in addition the inadequacy of Moltke. Based on his actions during the campaign of 1870–1 it is possible to postulate that the elder Moltke would have responded to Russia's partial mobilisation with an innovative recasting of the Schlieffen Plan. Kaiser Wilhelm II was right to tell Moltke his uncle would never have failed to provide alternatives, but then the Kaiser failed to draw the obvious conclusion that to accept Moltke's advice was to invite failure. H. H. Herwig echoes this view of the central role played by Moltke, in particular in 1914, in *The First World War* (1997).

Synthesis

Germany's 'grasping after world power', as Fischer suggests, is the context in which Germany's challenge to the other powers must be seen. J. Joll in *The Origins of the First World War* (2nd edition, 1992) and David Stevenson in *Armaments and the Coming of War* (1999) both set the conflict in a **Social Darwinist** context which provided an intellectual framework for the challenge which Fischer outlines. The view of Moltke and other generals, that the summer of 1914 was the last favourable opportunity to strike against Germany's opponents, fits this Social Darwinist framework. However, the fear of the Junker elite – from which the officer corps was drawn – that the socialist triumphs in the 1912 elections to the Reichstag marked the beginning of the end, and that the 1913 budget debate proved this, strengthened the argument for the primacy of domestic politics. Nevertheless, Britain's opposition to Germany, created by the naval race, was a product of the primacy of foreign policy.

Having assessed the situation from a Fischer perspective – that is, focusing upon Germany – it is important to balance this by adopting Ritter's point about the other powers. The Austrians wanted war in 1914 but pursued this option secure in the knowledge of German military support. Fischer was right to entitle his second work *War of Illusions*. Conrad and Moltke believed they could save their respective sovereigns and their empires by unleashing their military might at the right time. Neither Wilhelm II nor Franz Josef was prepared to sponsor a **'revolution from above'** and so they signed the mobilisation orders. In the absence of internal reform they had to try to validate their regimes through war, but this time there could be no retreat from the brink because Russia too believed there was no alternative.

CONCLUSION

It is fashionable to ascribe great events to great movements. The reality, however, is that, in 1914, several men came to believe that war was inevitable; Moltke insisted that the time for war had come. It could therefore be better to abandon the idea of the primacy of foreign policy and that of the primacy of domestic policy, and to recognise that, by July 1914, we are dealing with the primacy of military policy.

SUMMARY QUESTIONS

1 Was Germany responsible for the outbreak of war in 1914?

2 Was Fischer correct to assert that war was the result of German ambitions?

3 'War was not inevitable after the Archduke died; it was the decisions of the powers that made it so.' Discuss.

4 'The primacy of military policy.' Is this a valid assessment of why Europe descended into war in 1914?

CHAPTER 8

What were the diplomatic consequences of the war?

Many of the major figures in 1914 were anticipating a short war similar to the Franco-Prussian war of 1870–1. When the guns fell silent after 11 a.m. on 11 November 1918, Europe was a very different place from the one which had gone to war in 1914. The three empires of Germany, Russia and Austria-Hungary were effectively destroyed by the war, although Germany itself was not to lose some of its land until after the **Treaty of Versailles** had been negotiated by the victorious powers.

WHAT WAS THE IMPACT OF THE RUSSIAN REVOLUTION?

The Russian Revolution. One of the most significant consequences of the war was the Russian 'October Revolution' in 1917. Even before the war ended the Bolshevik Revolution in Russia had created a major break in diplomatic relations. The original March 1917 revolution, which forced Tsar Nicholas II to abdicate, had actually bound Russia more closely to Britain and France. As both these countries were democracies they believed that Russia would be more efficient now that it had a democratic government. However, the Provisional Government (which ruled Russia from the abdication of the Tsar in March 1917 until replaced by the Bolsheviks in November 1917) proved too weak in dealing with the Bolsheviks and made the fundamental mistake of continuing the war. Keen to see Russia continue fighting, its allies gave Russia more loans. However, when the Bolsheviks seized power in November 1917 **Lenin** knew that he must end the war. Although it took several months of negotiations before the Treaty of Brest Litovsk was signed, the Germans were able to begin transferring troops to the Western Front. Although the German offensive of March 1918 eventually failed, the British and French bitterly resented being let down by Russia. This practical

KEY EVENT

The Treaty of Versailles
The key terms were:
- War guilt was Germany's alone
- German General Staff to be abolished
- Demilitarised zone in the Rhineland
- Allied army of occupation for 15 years (including phased withdrawal)
- Reparations were to be paid, *later set at £6600 million*
- Alsace-Lorraine to be returned to France
- High seas fleet to be surrendered to Britain, and Germany forbidden to have U-boats
- Army reduced to 100,000 with no conscription, tanks or aeroplanes
- Territory to be lost to Belgium, Denmark and Poland; Saar coalfields to France for 15 years.

KEY PERSON

Vladimir Ilyich Lenin (1870–1924) Russian revolutionary leader and Marxist philosopher, who came from a middle-class background. Lenin ruled Russia from 1917 to 1924, by which time it had been renamed the Soviet Union.

point needs to be remembered as well as the ideological differences developing with the growth of communism.

The result of Russia's diplomatic isolation. Even if a democratic Russia had been defeated it would probably still have been represented at Versailles and treated well. Evidence to support this can be drawn from the treatment of Romania. Romania had only joined the Entente powers in 1916 and was rapidly defeated but was rewarded at the expense of Hungary. Lenin's decision to establish **communism** and his refusal to pay Russia's debts effectively left Russia isolated. This created an unusual situation in European diplomatic circles.

Communism A political theory advocating a society in which all property is publicly owned, derived from the ideas of Karl Marx, a German socialist and philosopher. Marx believed that a communist world would emerge from the ruins of capitalism. He therefore did not set a date for the revolution, but saw it as inevitable.

- Since the time of Peter the Great (1672–1725) Russian actions had affected the other great powers.
- In 1793 Russia had joined Austria and Prussia in dividing Poland.
- At the end of the main phase of the Napoleonic wars in 1814 Russian forces had played a major part in the Allied victory and had even marched into Paris. At Vienna in 1814 and 1815 Russia had also played a key role in settling the new map of Europe.
- After 1815 it was Russia which provided the main force to prevent revolution in Europe and this was clearly demonstrated in 1848–9 when Russian troops saved the Austrian monarchy.

Therefore, Versailles was the first major redrawing of the European map without Russia since 1815.

THE IMPACT ON FRANCE

Of the major powers, the one most directly affected by the absence of Russia was France. In the 1890s France had turned to Russia for support in the face of the new united Germany. The rapid mobilisation of the Russian forces in 1914, especially those whose objective was to invade East Prussia, had helped to save France from defeat. Therefore in 1919 the French were very aware that they now faced Germany on their own. The **French search for security** in the absence of Russia could be said to be the single most influential impact of the war on international relations.

French priorities It is important to see the continuity of French policy between 1870 and 1940. The overriding objective of French diplomacy was to find security in Europe in the face of what they perceived to be a very real threat from Germany.

Perfide Albion Despite being allies during the First World War, there was still a history of mistrust between Britain and France. The French could point to the fact that the British had frustrated the ambitions of Louis XIV in the seventeenth century and then Napoleon at the turn of the nineteenth century. Even more recently, Britain had remained neutral during the Franco-Prussian war, and had prevented French domination of Egypt during the late nineteenth century.

Geddes Committee Cabinet committee established under Sir Eric Geddes to recommend how Britain could reduce defence expenditure. It had been decided to try to return to the gold standard as soon as possible, which meant that the British government needed to balance its budget. Defence cuts by Britain only made French insecurity worse.

Palestine Under the League of Nations' authority, Britain governed what is today Israel and Jordan (France had responsibility for Syria and Lebanon).

Evacuating the army of occupation The Treaty of Versailles provided for the British and French occupation zones in the Rhineland to be evacuated in three stages over 15 years.

Without Russia as an ally and with the US Senate refusing to ratify the Treaty of Versailles, France felt vulnerable. Historians have tended to claim that France therefore wanted to punish Germany as severely as possible, though this view has been recently challenged.

How good were relations between Britain and France?

The most obvious and reliable supporter of France appeared to be Britain. In 1914 the French found themselves supported by their oldest rival, who fought alongside them throughout the war. However, after the war the French had serious reservations about relying on the British as their main ally.

- One problems was that the French still viewed Britain as **'Perfide Albion'** (untrustworthy Britain).
- Although detailed military talks had taken place between Britain and France after 1905 the British had never formally signed a treaty promising to help France.
- For the French there was also the issue that British forces were small by continental standards. Russia had rapidly mobilised over 600,000 men to help France in 1914, compared with Britain's initial 80,000.
- Once the war was over Britain demobilised rapidly and the **Geddes Committee** recommended further cuts in defence expenditure. From a French perspective this was hardly encouraging, especially as Britain's responsibilities had expanded to include such trouble spots as **Palestine**, which would require British troops. With the British army thus stretched to cover colonial commitments, Britain was even more keen to avoid continental involvement. Indeed, it welcomed the provision in the Young Plan of 1929 which said that Britain and France would **evacuate their army of occupation** in Germany five years earlier than agreed at Versailles.
- For France, which prided itself on its military heritage, the lessons of 1914–8 were uncomfortable. France had made enormous sacrifices and eventually been victorious under the command of Marshal Foch. However, it had been the French army which had mutinied in 1917 and the British Army which had made the biggest gains in the final months of 1918.

(From left to right)
David Lloyd George,
Georges Clemenceau
and Woodrow Wilson
at Versailles, 1919.

How did Franco-American relations develop?

Since the French alliance with Britain was sometimes
strained they naturally looked elsewhere. Their first choice
was the United States. In April 1917 the United States had
entered the war, and the availability of fresh US troops had
bolstered Entente morale during the difficulties of 1917.
Although American manpower was still more potential
than real, they had played an important role in blunting
the German offensives at the Marne in 1918. So President
Wilson now came to Versailles with real authority. Part of
the reason why France was anxious to secure reparations
was that the United States wanted France to pay its debts
to the United States.

The French and Americans at Versailles. The relationship
between France and the United States became defined by
what happened during the negotiations at Versailles.

- **Treatment of Germany.** The French government had wanted to break Germany up in order to weaken the country in the future. As A. Adamthwaite shows in *Grandeur and Misery* (1995), one of the French government's proposals was to create an independent Rhineland. This area bordered France and it had only belonged to Prussia since 1815. The area was also Catholic so the French hoped it would be prepared to side with France against the rest of northern Germany, which was strongly Protestant. Via a US and British guarantee of maintaining French security on France's eastern frontier, the British and Americans were able to persuade the French to accept a **demilitarised** Rhineland instead. (Though the US guarantee was contingent on the Senate accepting the commitment, and ultimately collapsed.)

- **The League of Nations.** In the negotiations at Versailles the French were under pressure to accept President Wilson's idea of a League of Nations. The League was intended to offer a form of **collective security**. After Lenin had published some of the secret treaties made by Russia before 1914, it was popularly believed that treaties with secret clauses had helped to bring about the First World War. In this environment, the French were persuaded to accept a League of Nations backed by the United States. Therefore they were bitterly disappointed when President Wilson failed to persuade the US Senate to **ratify** the Treaty and the United States did not join the League.

France and eastern Europe

With Russia sidelined, and its attempts to break up Germany restricted, France looked to eastern Europe to provide a counterweight to Germany.

- **Poland. Poland** was re-created from lands previously ruled by Russia, Germany and Austria. France decided to go further than this by giving military aid to the Poles in their war with Russia (1920–1). The result was that France gained an ally against Germany. Given the bitterness between Germany and Poland the Poles were likely to side with France anyway. The French support of Poland in 1920–1 also helped to make Stalin

---

KEY TERMS

Demilitarised This means that although the Rhineland remained part of Germany, no German troops were allowed into the area. The idea was to prevent the Germans from launching a surprise attack against France.

Collective security is the term used to describe a system by which countries are protected by a general agreement rather than by making their own individual alliances.

Ratify Under the US constitution the Senate must agree to a treaty which has been negotiated by the President. The process of approving the treaty is called ratification.

KEY AREA

Poland Poland was awarded access to the Baltic through German territory. This left 1 million Germans living in Poland and was clearly in breach of the principle of national self-determination. Such obvious injustices fuelled parties like the Nazis.

suspicious about French aims in 1939. Stalin turned to Hitler instead.

- **Czechoslovakia.** France also sought an alliance with the newly created Czechoslovakia. Czechoslovakia proved to be a reasonably strong democracy and it had the famous Skoda armaments works to supply its military needs. However, like Poland, it was separated from France by Germany so the two countries could only assist each other by attacking Germany. Ultimately, when France, influenced by Marshal Pétain and the memory of the losses suffered in 1914–8, decided to build the **Maginot Line** in the 1930s, it became obvious that the French were unwilling to help their allies. Poland and Czechoslovakia would never be saved by a French army which took shelter behind the Maginot Line and waited for a German attack.

The French referred to their allies in eastern Europe as 'the Little Entente'. This name emphasised that the French did not feel that they were as secure as they had been before 1914 with Russia and Britain as their allies.

BRITAIN, FRANCE AND AUSTRIA

French insecurity was also shown in the way that they dealt with Austria. Despite the principles of **self-determination** and **particularism**, the Austrians, who spoke German, were forbidden by the Treaty of Versailles to join with Germany. This union was known as the Anschluss. French opposition to the Anschluss continued and had a devastating impact upon Austria's banking system in 1931 during the Depression when France used economic sanctions to stop an Austro-German plan to create an Austro-German Customs Union. The French regarded this as the backdoor to the Anschluss. Great Britain played a key role in restoring the Austrian economy after 1919 but in the 1930s Britain became less helpful: during the early 1930s the British Foreign Office became convinced that Austria could not survive and so did little to help. The British Board of Trade refused to give favourable trade opportunities to Austrian wood or hats and so the Austrian economy continued to suffer.

KEY TERMS

Maginot Line A system of concrete fortifications designed to stop a German invasion of north-east France. It proved useless in 1940 as the German tanks easily outflanked it and it was not continued along the Franco-Belgian border.

Self-determination
Concept of peoples with the same language grouping together, put forward by President Wilson in his Fourteen Points in 1918 and accepted by Britain and France. The promise of self-determination encouraged the break up of Austria-Hungary but created expectations which were mutually incompatible in many cases. For example, giving the Sudetenland to Czechoslovakia gave the latter a defensible border but upset the Germans living in that region.

Particularism This describes the desire to maintain local identities. For example, many Bavarians considered uniting with Austria (they had much in common being mainly Catholic and rural), though Bavarian nationalists wanted a separate Bavaria as they distrusted the socialists and Protestants in the north of Germany. (In the end Bavaria remained part of Germany.)

THE ALLIES AND ITALY

The other power interested in the fate of Austria was Italy. At Versailles, Italy's leader, Vittorio Orlando, was part of the 'Big Four' (the others being Wilson, Clemenceau and Lloyd George), but most commentators felt that he had little influence on the decisions reached by the USA, France and Britain, even before political problems led to his departure from Paris. The problem of Dalmatia reflects the whole issue for Italy. Lord Hankey in *The Supreme Control at the Paris Peace Conference* (1961) describes how Italian ambitions to gain Dalmatia were blocked on principle by the 'Big Three'. Italy was bound to feel aggrieved when Poland was treated generously whereas Italy was not. Having joined the Entente in 1915 Italy enjoyed good relations with the winning powers but was to become increasingly disillusioned at its small rewards after three years of fighting.

GERMANY AND RUSSIA

The isolation of Germany and Russia led to one of the most unexpected treaties when the two countries signed the Treaty of Rapallo in 1922. France was especially angry since it argued that if Germany could trade with Russia then it could afford to pay more reparations to France. The treaty went beyond trade and implicitly confirmed the military co-operation between Germany and the Soviets that had already been taking place from 1920 onwards. The Treaty of Rapallo thus enabled Germany to begin to get around the restrictions of the Treaty of Versailles. Under the treaty Germany would train Russian tank and submarine crews. This would enable Germany to keep its experienced servicemen in practice despite the ban imposed by Versailles.

CONCLUSION

- **The supremacy of France.** The immediate diplomatic impact of the war was to leave France as the strongest power in continental Europe. However, France's position was due to the effective withdrawal of Russia from European affairs and the humbling of Germany, as well as the break-up of the Austro-Hungarian Empire. The temporary nature of their supremacy was thus very apparent to the French. As a result they sought security. However, the other powers did not provide this security and France was left to rely upon the newly created states in eastern Europe, especially Poland and Czechoslovakia. In strategic terms this did not make sense once France opted to build the Maginot Line in 1930. France's allies could see that France had abandoned them, for fear of repeating the casualties of 1914–8.

• With the USA opting to turn its back on Europe, but still retaining control of Allied debts, the French were forced to rely on their ancient rival Britain. Britain also recognised that French supremacy was temporary, but was less concerned about a rise in German power, which it saw as inevitable. With Britain's eyes on its empire. France thus sought to achieve its goal of national security by being intransigent in its attitude to its most likely foe. But by being inflexible France failed to take opportunities, such as the proposed Anschluss in 1931 which might have preserved a democratic Germany.

SUMMARY QUESTIONS

1 How significant was the absence of Russia from the traditional political balance of power after 1919?

2 Why was France unable to gain agreement to its desire to punish Germany permanently?

3 What was the impact of the United States's decision not to ratify the Treaty of Versailles?

The human cost of the First World War in millions dead

Germany	over 2.0
Russia	1.65
Romania	0.25
Britain	0.75
British Empire	0.25
France	over 2.0 (including civilians)
Austria-Hungary	1.1

The increase in National Debt 1914–22 in $ millions

Britain	30,811
France	21,266
Italy	5,605
Germany	75

(The figure for Germany shows how far it had benefited from inflation by 1922)

CHAPTER 9

Why were there no major conflicts in the 1920s?

There are a number of reasons that explain the absence of a major war in the 1920s.

- The first point to remember is that Europe had just fought the most exhausting war in its history. For those who actually lived through the war it was the 'war to end all wars'.
- Certainly between 1925 and 1929 peace was reinforced by an economic boom which encouraged an optimistic view of the world. On the other hand the Great Depression of the 1930s helped to create the climate of mutual distrust that was to provide the context in which Europe would go to war again.
- One of the main reasons why there was no major conflict during the 1920s was that no great power was prepared to risk another war. It is also true that during the 1920s diplomacy was in the hands of a number of men who wanted peace. US Secretary of State Frank Kellogg, Foreign Minister of France Aristide Briand, Austen Chamberlain, Foreign Secretary of Britain, and Gustav Stresemann, Foreign Minister of Germany, all worked to ensure Europe settled differences by peaceful means.

THE IMPACT OF VERSAILLES ON GERMANY

The Treaty of Versailles limited the German army to seven divisions totalling 100,000 men. Since Germany was the main loser at Versailles (which it termed the *Schmachfrieden*) this meant that the power with the greatest grievance was effectively too weak to resort to war. Until Versailles was signed this weakness was reinforced by the continuance of the British naval blockade. Once the treaty had been signed, the Allied Control Commission sought to impose the treaty conditions, but there was widespread evasion. A large number of weapons were buried or found their way into the hands of right-wing groups such as the Freikorps (ex-servicemen, who were prepared to fight communists and socialists), and members of U-boat crews were kept together by designating them as physical training instruction teams. However, because no one seriously expected the Germans not to try to cheat, this widespread evasion of the treaty terms on disarmament was unlikely to lead to war. It did contribute to French bitterness, but this was hardly significant after four years of war.

German grievances

Loss of land. Germany, as even most Germans expected, lost the ore-rich areas of **Alsace-Lorraine** which it had won in 1870. The loss of **Posen and West Prussia** to Poland was bitterly resented, partly because the Germans had won the war on the Eastern Front and partly because of a deep racial contempt for the Poles. The ruling elite, in particular, believed the division of **Silesia** was unfair because Polish workers outvoted their bosses in the plebiscite (a form of referendum) organised by the League of Nations and so German-owned industry was lost to Poland. Even Stresemann, generally regarded as a moderate, saw the revision of Germany's eastern frontiers as a long-term goal.

The 'Diktat'. The Versailles Treaty was enshrined in Germany as the 'Diktat' ('dictated peace'). This charge is justified in that, having hammered out a deal amongst themselves, the Allies had no wish to reopen the inevitable compromises by discussing the treaty with the Germans. Whilst the moral strength of the Versailles Treaty was undermined by being forced upon the Germans, this did not lead to a major conflict because the Germans lacked the means to challenge it. Hitler would, however, exploit this reservoir of bitterness after 1933.

The 'stab in the back'. The idea of the 'Diktat' was built upon the foundations laid by General von Ludendorff in 1918 when he fostered the myth of 'the stab in the back'. After the British 46th Division broke through the

Alsace-Lorraine The region's rich supply of iron ore had helped to fuel German industrial development after 1870. The loss of this territory meant that industrialists would have to import their raw materials. This need to import would also pose difficulties for Hitler in the 1930s.

Posen and West Prussia Poland was awarded this area without a vote because the Allies knew the area would vote to remain German. Lord Hankey noted (in *The Supreme Control*, 1963) that the attempted insurrection in Silesia was only to be expected when the treaty terms became known. In a plebiscite on 11 July 1920 the areas called Allenstein and Marienwerder voted to remain German, and became part of East Prussia.

Upper Silesia The plebiscite held on 20 March 1921 resulted in 60 per cent voting to stay in Germany. The Poles then staged an uprising with the support of the French occupation forces. However, the British supported the Germans and helped them form a defence force. On 20 October 1921 the Allied Supreme Council decided to partition the province. The eastern area with most of the important industry went to Poland – 56 per cent of voters there had favoured Poland.

The territorial terms of the Treaty of Versailles, 1919.

Legend:
- ▭ Ceded by Germany 1919
- ▨ Saar: League of Nations control 1919–35
- ▥ Demilitarised Rhineland 1919–36
- ▧ Austro-Hungarian Empire until 1918
- ▨ Plebiscite areas
- ▦ Formerly part of Russian Empire

KEY TERM

The Hindenburg Line This was the last major prepared German defensive position in occupied France. Its capture opened the way for the British army to advance to the German border.

Hindenburg Line on 29 September 1918, Ludendorff knew that there were no more prepared defensive positions between the British Fourth Army and the German border. Ludendorff then recommended the creation of a civilian-led government to seek an armistice – a simple cessation of the fighting. However, Marshal Foch and Field Marshal Haig recognised that they were finally winning and insisted that the Germans surrender 50,000 machine-guns in return for an armistice. **Ludendorff** had only wanted to buy Germany time to regroup; faced with these terms, he wanted to drop the idea of an armistice. However, in the process of creating a civilian government the German high command had been forced to reveal just how weak their military position was and so the civilian-led government of Prince Max of Baden insisted upon making peace.

THE ISSUE OF DISARMAMENT

In 1921 the United States hosted a disarmament conference in Washington. The US Secretary of State, Charles Evans Hughes, put forward specific proposals for disarmament. Included in these proposals were the following.

- For reducing all the major navies in the world the conference proposed a ten-year **naval holiday**. The detail in Hughes's proposals made it difficult for other powers to refuse.
- The conference also agreed to limits on their fleets in the ratio of 5: 5: 3. This meant there would be five major US warships (referred to as 'capital ships') for every five British and three Japanese or French ships. To justify Britain and the United States having more ships it was argued that they were 'two-ocean navies': that is, they operated in both the Atlantic and the Pacific. For the Japanese this was another example of racial discrimination.

Japanese discontent. The Japanese feeling of discontent was further reinforced when Britain ended the Anglo-Japanese alliance at the Washington Conference of 1921–2, under pressure from the US and Australia. US and Australian policy was motivated by a mixture of racism and power politics. Neither country wanted to see Japanese immigration or expansion increase. The United States wanted to expand its influence in the Pacific and therefore wished to detach Japan from its ally. However, Britain's break with Japan did not lead to conflict in the late 1920s because Japanese foreign policy was influenced by moderate leaders.

The outcome of the disarmament conference marked a
major turning point for Britain. Before 1914 Britain had
tried to maintain a **'two-power standard'**, but in
Washington the British were prepared to accept the United
States as equal. Britain was also now in debt to the United
States, which made it hard to disagree, but the cost of war
debt also meant the British government needed to find
ways to save money. Limiting the Royal Navy as part of a
world plan to maintain peace was a politically attractive
way of achieving cuts in government spending. The British
had also been able to intern the **German high seas fleet** in
1919 under the terms of the Versailles Treaty, whereafter it
had scuttled (deliberately sunk) itself after sailing to the
British naval base at Scapa Flow.

REPARATIONS

Article 231 of the Treaty of Versailles is the famous 'war
guilt' clause in which the Allied powers held Germany
solely responsible for the First World War. Since Germany
was held to be guilty it was therefore supposed to
compensate the Allies for the death and destruction which
had been caused. These payments were called **reparations**.

The London reparations commission. In 1919 the Versailles
Treaty specified only that Germany must pay. The amount
was to be decided by a reparations commission, meeting in
London in 1921. Germany was shocked when the figure of
132 billion gold marks was announced in April 1921. In
fact this figure was less than the debt which the German
government had inherited from the Kaiser of 150 billion
marks, but it was politically easier to blame Versailles for
German economic problems. The scale of the payments was
criticised by some economists at the time. The British
economist John Maynard Keynes argued in the pamphlet
The Economic Consequences of the Peace (1919) that the size
of the reparations bill would ultimately damage the
European economy.

The German response. Germany complained that the
burden of reparations was too great and that, in any case, it
had not been responsible for the war. However, given the

economic cost of the war Germany could not resist forcefully, so no major conflict occurred. This weakness was clearly demonstrated in January 1923 when a French and Belgian force occupied the industrial Ruhr on the grounds that Germany had failed to pay part of the reparations due in 1922. Despite the cries of right-wing extremists who advocated armed resistance against the French, the German government, led by Wilhelm Cuno, opted for **passive resistance** only. This meant that the workers refused to work and produce goods whilst under French occupation. The German government printed money to pay the workers, but this only helped to create spiralling **inflation** and economic collapse in Germany.

In truth, the inflation rate in Germany was rising rapidly before the French occupation. However, it was much easier for the German government to blame the French than to blame the Kaiser's ministers for the pre-war arms race or for not taxing Germans more during the war. The end of passive resistance in September 1923, and the issue of the new Rentenmark in November 1923, brought the crisis to a close. The crisis had also led to a re-examination of the reparations and, as the ultimate creditor, the US had nominated businessman Charles Dawes to look into the whole question of payment of reparations.

The Dawes Plan. The Dawes Plan of 1924 was designed to help the German and the European economy by providing US loans. In return the Germans were required to agree to a clear schedule of payments. In the year ending 31 August 1925, Germany only had to pay 200 million marks in reparations whilst receiving an initial loan of 800 million marks. Germany was only due to return to paying the 2500 million marks per year level (decided upon in 1921) in 1928–9. Over the period from 1924 to 1929 it is estimated that Germany received seven times as much in loans as it paid in reparations. This meant that there was plenty of credit available in Germany and the economy stabilised until 1928 when the agricultural sector began to slide into depression. As confidence in the economy was restored it created an illusion of prosperity and extremists such as the Nazis could only persuade 2.6 per cent of the voters to support them in the Reichstag elections of 1928.

Passive resistance By not working, German workers were denying the French the opportunity to take their output, e.g. coal. The main consequence was inflation as the German government printed money to cover the cost of paying the idle workers.

Inflation This is the term given to a rise in the general level of prices. In Germany there was a lot more money but fewer goods available. As goods were in short supply their price rose and hyperinflation took hold. Hyperinflation caused prices to rise rapidly to the point where money was worthless and, for example, people used banknotes instead of wallpaper to paper the wall because it was cheaper. People who owed money could repay it easily, as the value of the marks they had borrowed became almost worthless.

As long as extremists like the Nazis remained upon the fringes of German politics, moderate German politicians would be able to avoid a major conflict abroad. In 1931 Chancellor Brüning tried to achieve an **economic Anschluss** with Austria to strengthen his position against the growing Nazi Party, but this only led to conflict with France.

The Young Plan. The positive atmosphere in Europe after 1924 enabled Gustav Stresemann as German Foreign Minister to persuade the Allies and the United States to undertake another review of reparations. This time the review was chaired by the American banker Owen D. Young. The Young Plan of 1929 reduced the German debt from $33 billion to $9 billion. In return the German government officially accepted the debt for the first time. In addition, the remaining British and French forces occupying the Rhineland were to be withdrawn five years early in 1930.

Given this positive approach to international relations, there was no immediate prospect of any major conflict. However, the impact of the Great Depression which followed the **Wall Street Crash** in October 1929 was to change the context of international relations in the 1930s.

THE IMPORTANCE OF DIPLOMACY

Despite the fact that the Treaty of Versailles encouraged all negotiations to be conducted via the League of Nations the major powers continued to act as they had before 1914. In particular, France was constantly seeking for written assurances from Britain to take the place of the United States after it began to slip into **isolationism**. The Locarno Treaties emerged out of another British attempt to avoid giving a written guarantee to France.

Locarno Treaties
At the heart of European diplomacy in the 1920s were the Locarno Treaties of 1925, whereby Germany agreed to recognise its western borders with France and Belgium as laid down at Versailles.

- This meant the recognition of **Alsace-Lorraine** as French. The treaty therefore offered France reassurance about its most sensitive border.
- The parallel treaty between Belgium and Germany recognised that Eupen and Malmédy would remain Belgian.
- The Rhineland frontiers were unilaterally guaranteed by Britain and Italy (i.e. guaranteed in favour of France).

Although the German Foreign Minister Gustav Stresemann was a nationalist, he was prepared to make these concessions in order to establish a climate of mutual understanding in which he would later be able to raise the issue of Germany's eastern borders.

Reactions to Locarno.
- **In Germany.** Stresemann's approach was criticised by more extreme nationalists. However, Stresemann calculated that the British would probably consider changes in eastern Europe later if they had German assurances regarding Belgium and the Channel coast opposite England.
- **In Britain.** For Britain's Foreign Secretary, Austen Chamberlain, the Locarno Pact was a triumphant step towards persuading the French to start trusting the Germans.
- **In France.** The French Foreign Minister, **Aristide Briand**, took the view that it was important to be realistic. As Briand stated to the foreign affairs committee of the French National Assembly in 1926: 'You must follow the foreign policy that your country's finances, and ability to use force, allow'. In effect France had now got the same guarantee that Belgium had had under the Treaty of London of 1839. Britain had honoured its guarantee to Belgium in 1914 so France could feel that Britain would honour this one too.
- **In Belgium.** For Belgium, Locarno represented a renewal of the British guarantee as well as a welcome reassurance by Germany.

What was the effect of the Locarno Treaties?
- Locarno effectively undermined the Versailles Treaty because the major powers were acknowledging that this

HEINEMANN ADVANCED HISTORY

treaty was more effective, because voluntary, than Germany's signature on the Versailles Treaty.

- Locarno also undermined Versailles because France was seeking security through individual treaties rather than through the collective security of the League of Nations.
- However, the treaty was valuable because Britain had now promised to defend the French borders by acting as guarantor of the treaty.
- In the absence of US ratification of the Treaty of Versailles, France felt justified in seeking alternative guarantees.
- Locarno placed Mussolini beside other major statesmen and it also re-created the role of Italy as one of the 'Big Four' at Versailles – the difference being that Germany had now taken the place of the USA. Treating **Benito Mussolini** on a level with Britain and France gave legitimacy to his **Fascist** regime.

The Kellogg–Briand Pact. The Kellogg–Briand Pact (or Pact of Paris) of 1928 is famous because it outlawed war. Since war followed within a few years and a world war within ten, it has always seemed too idealistic to be taken seriously. In fact the pact was a product of continuing disagreements between France, Britain and the United States over disarmament.

- Aristide Briand, prodded by Professor James Shotwell of the Carnegie Endowment for International Peace, proposed a pact outlawing war in order to try to improve understanding between France and the still isolationist USA.
- The US Secretary of State, Frank Kellogg, wanted to avoid being dragged into France's alliances so he proposed to make the pact open to all countries.
- Lacking any forms of sanctions, the pact depended entirely upon goodwill.

On the same day that the US Senate ratified the Kellogg–Briand Pact, the Senate also voted the money required for the US navy to build 15 new cruisers. The pact was thus always seen as a nice idea but not one to be relied upon. Within two years the French were building

---

KEY PERSON

Benito Mussolini (1883–1945) Italian dictator, and former socialist and journalist, who led the Italian Fascist Party to power in 1922. His attempt to create a Fascist state became a model for both Hitler and Franco of Spain. He was overthrown in 1943 and murdered in 1945.

KEY TERM

Fascist The broad term applied to a number of right-wing regimes that prided themselves on being both nationalist and conservative and trying to offer the ordinary workers an alternative to socialism.

the Maginot Line, preferring concrete gun emplacements to paper treaties.

CONCLUSION

There was no major conflict in the 1920s for the following reasons:

- The European power with the most reason to challenge the situation was Germany but it was both militarily and economically weak. Germany was also too weak to offer a military challenge to the French invasion of the Ruhr in 1923. The response of Britain and the United States to the invasion by France showed that the French lacked support for punishing Germany further.
- France's refusal to disarm led to increasing disagreements between France and its allies. The Kellogg–Briand Pact was a diplomatic fig leaf which fooled none of the major powers. The other powers felt France should be satisfied with the guarantees provided at Locarno.
- Conflict did not occur in the relatively prosperous 1920s but, with the economic depression as their background, the 1930s would see growing tensions lead eventually to war.

SUMMARY QUESTIONS

1 What was the impact of economic factors on international relations in the 1920s?

2 To what extent was the absence of conflict in the 1920s due to the League of Nations?

CHAPTER 10

How successful was the League of Nations?

WHAT WAS THE IMPORTANCE OF THE LEAGUE OF NATIONS?

The aims of the League

The creation of a League of Nations became the focus of US President Woodrow Wilson's efforts at Versailles. The League of Nations was established at Versailles to provide the world with the following:

- Peace through a new form of collective security, meaning that countries should act together to prevent war.
- Co-operation between nations on matters of international concern such as fighting disease, helping refugees, post-war reconstruction, improving living conditions, helping racial minorities, preventing illegal drugs dealing.

What were the weaknesses of the League?

From the start and throughout its lifetime the League suffered from its own **structural weaknesses**.

- Wilson was unable to persuade the US Senate to ratify the Versailles Treaty and so the United States never became a member of the League of Nations.
- The unwillingness of the **great powers** like France to put their faith in the League undermined it even before Hitler forced Europe into war in 1939.
- The exclusion of Germany and Russia confirmed to many that the League was a club for the victors of the First World War.

What successes did the League have in the 1920s?

Most of the League's successes were achieved in dealings with smaller states.

KEY THEMES

The structure of the League Key votes, e.g. on sanctions, were taken by the General Assembly, which contained all the members and was therefore subject to countries negotiating over votes that were due to be taken.

The great powers It was clear from the beginning that Britain and France did not see the League as overriding their status as great powers. Each supported local forces in Silesia to further their own aims, whilst Britain made clear its views on national self-determination by blockading Germany until it sacrificed the Polish Corridor by signing the Treaty of Versailles.

Austria. One of the major successes for the League in the 1920s was the financial reconstruction of Austria. This new state was created under the **Treaty of St. Germain** (1919) when Austria was stripped of its empire. It left Austria and Hungary as independent states. The separation of Austria and Hungary which had taken place by the end of 1918 was recognised, and the two former ruling nationalities now formed ethnically-based states. The **Treaty of Trianon** (1920) was signed between the Allies and Hungary.

- During 1920 and 1921, Austria was largely dependent upon voluntary **foreign aid**. The Red Cross helped to run hospitals whilst the Society of Friends (The Quakers) provided food relief. These organisations sought to care, in particular, for malnourished children as well as many adults. In 1920 Britain supplied Austria with seed potatoes but the problem of food was not the only crisis facing Austria.
- In early 1920 the Austrian krone was trading at £1= Kr 850; by January 1922 it had fallen to £1= Kr 44,000 – in other words, it had fallen in value by approximately 98 per cent in two years. In these circumstances Austrian goods were very cheap for foreigners and so unemployment remained low for some time. In November 1921 two League experts were misled by the low level of unemployment into concluding that the Austrian economy was improving.
- In September 1922 members of the Austrian government went to Geneva (the League headquarters) to ask for help. They met the British minister Lord Balfour and the British had the Austrian problem referred to the League. The British had already made loans to Austria but the French had been less helpful. The League Council then appointed a special committee to conduct the negotiations.
- The result of these negotiations was the agreement for 'The Restoration of Austria' signed in Geneva on 4 October 1922. Under this agreement Britain, France, Italy and Czechoslovakia were the main countries guaranteeing a loan of £26 million to Austria. Security for the loan was to come from Austrian customs duties and the state monopoly on tobacco sales. The Austrians also promised to balance the government's budget in

KEY TERMS

Treaty of St. Germain
Austria was created by the Treaty of St. Germain in 1919. The Allies signed the treaty with Austria which accepted the break-up of the Austro-Hungarian empire, leaving Austria and Hungary as independent states.

Treaty of Trianon
The name of the treaty signed on 4 June 1920 between the victorious powers and Hungary. With the Treaty of St. Germain, it marked the break-up of the Austro-Hungarian empire.

KEY EVENT

Foreign aid given to Austria The scale of the relief is evident in Lord Parmoor's speech to the House of Lords in 1921 when he described how 200,000 meals per day were being provided in Vienna to the destitute.

two years. Nevertheless the French included the requirement that Austria was to accept that there could be no Anschluss for 20 years.

- The League's ability to involve France and Czechoslovakia in a rescue package for Austria was a real success. France had previously been very reluctant to help, and Czechoslovakia was one of the **successor states** with some bitter memories of Austrian rule.

KEY TERM

Successor states Countries formed when Austria-Hungary was broken up. As well as Czechoslovakia this group included Poland and Yugoslavia.

The Åland Islands. The Åland Islands lie in the Baltic Sea and were claimed by both Sweden and the newly independent state of Finland. The Swedish population of the islands was given protected minority status under Finnish rule. Since neither country was large or powerful the League's success (1921) in umpiring the dispute should not be seen as significant. The Minorities Treaty was never accepted by any of the great powers and this actually highlights the weaknesses of the League.

Refugees. The work of the Norwegian explorer Fridtjof Nansen as the League's High Commissioner for Refugees was also important. Many people were stateless at the end of the First World War so the creation of the 'Nansen Passport' gave thousands protection whilst their status was resolved.

The Saar. The League did manage to administer the Saar region for 15 years despite the inevitable tensions created by allocating this German coal-mining area to France. Although the Nazis undoubtedly employed illegal methods to influence voting no one ever doubted that the vote, as agreed at Versailles, to return to Germany in 1935 was a genuine wish of the majority.

Upper Silesia. The League also did well in Danzig and Upper Silesia despite bitter relations between the Poles and the Germans. Upper Silesia (see Chapter 9) presented a particularly difficult problem since the League had to persuade the Poles and Germans to continue to operate it as one economic area after it had been partitioned politically. A 15-year economic agreement was signed in 1922, albeit reluctantly, after strenuous efforts by the League.

Asia Minor. Nansen, the High Commissioner for Refugees, was also successful in persuading the Turks and Greeks to exchange populations (totaling 1.5 million people) at the Lausanne Conference, 24 July 1923. Although the upheaval was hard on the people affected, it reduced tensions in both countries.

Corfu. The League's ability to deal with a major power was tested in 1923 when Mussolini ordered Italian forces to bombard Corfu and sent an ultimatum to Greece. The incident had begun with the murder of the Italian General Tellini whilst he was helping to determine new national borders on behalf of the League. The Greeks appealed to the League supported by the British representative Lord Cecil.

The issue was referred to the Conference of Ambassadors in Geneva, which eventually solved the dispute. Its resolution was complicated by French support for Mussolini; while the French had no intrinsic interest in Corfu, they wished to swap their support for Mussolini on Corfu for his support for them against Germany. The Italian evacuation from Corfu seemed to confirm that small nations were able to protect themselves through the League. In 1923 Mussolini could not afford to defy the League but in the 1930s the situation was to be very different. In retrospect, therefore, Corfu seems to harbour the seeds of the League's future failure.

THE IMPACT OF THE GREAT DEPRESSION

The Great Depression had an enormous influence upon the climate in which international relations were conducted in the 1930s.

- By causing economic chaos the Great Depression increased tensions between countries throughout the world.
- In central Europe this was particularly serious as many of these countries were newly established and lacked the democratic traditions which enabled countries like

Britain and the United States to meet the social challenges of economic depression.

- In Britain, the government decided to extend the period of unemployment pay beyond the two-year period which applied before the Depression. Many Germans who had lost their unemployment pay after two years on the dole turned to Hitler or to communism. In this respect, British taxpayers paid to keep revolution at bay.
- The rise of **xenophobia** made the spirit of compromise and trust encouraged by the League look increasingly unrealistic.

The discussion of Czechoslovakia, Hungary and Germany in the text here reflects the fact that events in Eastern Europe would be central to the drift to war in the 1930s.

Czechoslovakia. There were many minorities that existed within the newly created states, such as Czechoslovakia. After 1930 the Czech Agrarian Party passed laws which stopped the import of Hungarian wheat in order to protect the prices received by Czech farmers. This decision may have protected farmers but had a negative impact on the rest of the country, especially the Slovaks. The Slovaks relied on sales of timber and other products to Hungary, and Hungary could not afford to buy Slovak products without the foreign currency generated by grain sales. The Czech-initiated policy of maintaining the Czechoslovak crown at a high value until 1935 also made it expensive for Germans, and other tourists, to visit the Sudetenland, where there was a substantial population of Germans. Slovak discontent was to be exploited by Hitler in March 1939.

Hungary. Hungary had never been a genuine democracy as the right to vote had been reduced in the 1920s to prevent a left-wing victory. However, the impact of the Depression was to leave Hungary heavily in debt. During the 1920s industrial expansion had been financed through borrowing and the interest on these debts was met through selling grain abroad. The Depression saw grain prices fall and selling abroad became increasingly difficult. Faced with economic crisis, Hungary turned to the Hungarian Fascist party under Gombos since he promised to be tough, like Mussolini.

Germany. Prior to the Depression in 1928 the Nazis only gained 2.6 per cent of the vote compared to 18.3 per cent in 1930 and 37.4 per cent in 1932. The Great Depression therefore played a major role in turning Hitler into a national politician. Hitler's obsession with waging an aggressive campaign to recover the territories lost at Versailles and to secure *Lebensraum* ('living space') in the Ukraine would frustrate the League's efforts to maintain peace. The Great Depression helped to give him that opportunity.

FAILURES OF THE LEAGUE

The general economic prosperity of the 1920s reduced international tensions. The rise of extremists such as Hitler in the 1930s fed off economic discontent.

The Manchurian crisis

The Great Depression also hit Japan. In 1931 and 1932 Japanese rice farmers were badly hit by falling prices for their crops due to a series of bumper harvests. The Japanese government bought up surplus crops but still prices fell. The farmers were also hit by the effects of the Depression in the United States, particularly those who cultivated silk worms to produce silk. The biggest market for their silk was the United States, which was now unable to afford such luxuries.

Powerful right-wing groups in the army were able to take advantage of these economic problems. The officers wanted to pursue an aggressive policy in **Manchuria** and the **Mukden Incident** in 1931 showed how the army could create a crisis which it could then exploit. The Japanese army created the puppet state of Manchukuo – the new name for Manchuria – and installed Pu Yi as its ruler (Pu Yi had been the last Emperor of China before the revolution). The attack proved popular in Japan, and the assassination of Prime Minister Inukai in May 1932 was

Cartoon 'The Doormat' from the *London Evening Standard*, 19 January 1933.

THE DOORMAT.

seen as a move to remove those leaders who were too soft in pursuing Japan's economic interests.

What was the League's response? In response to Japan's attack on China the League set up an enquiry headed by the Englishman Lord Lytton. The commission's report was published in October 1932.

- It rejected the Japanese claim that Manchukuo had been established to reflect local Chinese wishes.
- The commission wanted to protect Japanese economic interests but called for the withdrawal of Japanese forces, and refused to recognise Manchukuo as a separate state.

What were the consequences of the Manchurian affair?
- Japan had already recognised Manchukuo's status as an independent country and in February 1933 Japan therefore withdrew from the League.
- Without its own armed forces the League could not compel Japan to comply with the commission's demands.
- Distracted by the Great Depression the European powers and the United States lacked the will and the resources to oppose Japanese militarism.
- Japan ignored the Lytton report and began to rearm for a more general war against China.
- The League's dependence upon the world's major powers to take action and support League decisions was

clearly exposed by the Manchurian crisis. Neither
Britain nor France was prepared to take action over an
incident that did not directly affect their immediate
interests.
- The League's weakness was also noted by Mussolini and
  Hitler.

The Abyssinian crisis 1935–6

The Great Depression also hit the Italian economy.
Mussolini's decision to maintain the value of the lira as a
symbol of Fascist strength only made it more difficult to
export Italian produce. In this context Mussolini sought to
raise the prestige of his government by invading Abyssinia.
Abyssinia was one of only two African areas (the other
being Liberia) that was not under European rule; it had
also defeated Italy in 1896 at the battle of Adowa. Since
Italy was the only European power to have been defeated
by Africans, this was an opportunity for Fascist Italy to
prove its superiority over earlier Italian democratic
regimes.

The invasion.

- On 3 October 1935 an Italian army of 100,000 men
  invaded Abyssinia. Haile Selassie, the Emperor of
  Abyssinia, appealed to the League of Nations, which
  agreed to impose economic sanctions. However, the
  sanctions did not include steel, coal and oil, which were

Destruction caused by
an Italian bombing raid
on Abyssinia in
December 1935.

vital to the Italian war effort. Moreover, some countries such as Austria and Germany refused to impose sanctions at all.

- On 14 November the National Coalition won the British general election having campaigned on the slogan, 'all sanctions short of war'. Labour had said it would shut the Suez Canal which would have blocked oil and other supplies to Mussolini. Four days later Britain imposed the sanctions agreed in October by the League. However, for fear of upsetting Mussolini too much, Britain did not support oil sanctions when they were discussed at the League in December.

The fear of pushing Mussolini into alliance with Hitler led to the development of the **Hoare–Laval Pact** (1935). In the context of the Italian invasion the publication of these proposals in the French press led to a public outcry.

What were the consequences of Mussolini's takeover of Abyssinia?

- The League's credibility as a peacekeeping organisation was shattered. The news of the proposed Hoare–Laval Pact overshadowed the debate on oil sanctions, and the collapse of the pact did not help. So long as he had oil, Mussolini's forces would win.
- On 9 May 1936 Mussolini was able to proclaim King Victor Emmanuel of Italy as Emperor of Ethiopia (the new name for Abyssinia). The League of Nations had failed to save Abyssinia.
- Britain and France had not been prepared to risk war over Abyssinia, but public opinion had prevented them negotiating a deal with Mussolini, even though they had seen him as a possible ally against the growing threat from Nazi Germany. In 1934 Mussolini had saved Austria from a possible German takeover, and in April 1935 Italy had joined Britain and France in the 'Stresa Front' agreement to condemn Hitler for breaking the Versailles Treaty by building an air force.
- However, Mussolini then saw Britain sign a naval agreement with Germany in June 1935 that broke the Versailles Treaty by quadrupling the permitted tonnage of the German navy.

COURSEWORK SOURCE-BASED QUESTION IN THE STYLE OF EDEXCEL

Source A

...whereas hereto Germany has feigned alarm at the encircling policy against Germany falsely attributed to His majesty's government ... she is now really frightened at the growing strength of the Russian Army, and may make another military effort additional to the recent large expenditure ... or bring on a conflict with Russia at an early date before the increases in the Russian army have their full effect and before the completion of the Russian strategic railways . . .

  Foreign Office Memorandum summarising Sir Edward Grey's views, 16 July 1914.

Source B

Article 1 The High Contracting Parties [Germany, Austria-Hungary and Italy], having in mind only the maintenance, so far as possible, of the territorial status quo in the Orient, engage to use their influence to forestall, on the Ottoman coasts and islands in the Adriatic and Aegean seas, any territorial modification which might be injurious to one or other of the Powers signatory to the present treaty.

  From the Treaty of the Triple Alliance, 1887.

Source C

2 In case the forces of the Triple Alliance, or one of the powers composing it, should mobilise, France and Russia, at the first news of the event and without the necessity of any previous concert, shall mobilise immediately and simultaneously the whole of their forces and shall move them as close as possible to their frontiers.

3 The available forces to be employed against Germany shall be, on the part of France, 1,300,000 men, on the part of Russia, 700,000 or 800,000 men. These forces shall engage to the full, with all speed, in order that Germany may have to fight at the same time on the East and the West.

  Draft Military Convention between France and Russia, 1892.

Source D

There is no denying that they are intriguing and girding against us from every hole and corner. I believe, as I have always done, that England for financial and economic reasons, would be very loath to decide on war against us. I believe that Russia needs and wants peace. I believe, finally, that France, although it has not even today got over Alsace-Lorraine and the loss of 250 years of *preponderance legitime* over the continent and has not given up hope of revanche, would hesitate to run the calculated risks of war. But at the same time I believe that it is in the interests of these powers to make us look nervous and unrestful.

  Private notes by Kaiser Wilhelm II, July 1908.

Source E

The bulk of the population is anti-dynastic, because it looks upon the dynasty as being anti-Slav and as an essential part of the present regime. The feeling towards the Emperor is one of complete indifference; he is looked upon as a German with German sentiments and as being completely out of touch and sympathy with his Slav subjects. The Dalmatian Slavs feel that they are treated as an inferior race and they know too well that their country has been entirely neglected by the central government. It can hardly be expected that any affection can be felt for the Emperor who, in the mind of the peasant, is responsible for all this.

Report of the British consul in Dubrovnik on the situation in Dalmatia in 1911.

Source F

	Britain	France	Russia	Austria-Hungary	Germany	Italy
1900	133.0	48.5	54.2	21.2	———	16.0
1901	137.0	49.0	55.2	23.4	72.9	16.8
1902	111.8	47.1	58.6	24.1	70.5	16.8
1903	79.3	45.9	63.8	24.2	69.4	15.9
1904	71.7	45.5	150.0	24.5	71.4	15.8
1905	67.6	45.4	205.6	23.4	73.6	16.4
1906	63.7	47.4	122.8	23.4	76.4	16.0
1907	61.6	53.6	75.6	23.4	90.7	16.4
1908	63.4	50.9	77.5	27.4	81.4	17.3
1909	67.0	48.9	73.7	34.5	86.7	19.7
1910	70.6	54.9	74.0	29.8	94.2	20.5
1911	72.6	57.1	74.0	27.5	88.0	23.1
1912	72.5	60.4	88.0	32.3	87.2	29.9
1913	75.7	65.9	101.8	42.4	117.8	39.6

Defence expenditure of the great powers, 1900–13. Figures are given in £ million.
(Taken from D. Stevenson, *Armaments and the Coming of War*, 2000.)

Study the sources and then answer the following question.

How far do the sources support the idea that war in 1914 was the result of the alliances formed before the First World War?

Reading

Before answering this question you should read Chapters 1–7, paying particular attention to Chapters 4–7 inclusive.

How to answer this question

These six sources are designed to encourage you to consider contradictory evidence in assessing the answer to 'how far' in the question. Source A suggests that Sir Edward Grey had accurately assessed General von Moltke's concern that the balance of forces was moving against Germany. Sources B and C direct you to the alliances referred to in the question. Source E focuses on the long-term weaknesses of the Hapsburg monarchy whilst the Kaiser's notes (Source D) provide a summary of some of the main grievances influencing European relations. The table can be used in conjunction with the issue of alliances, and can also be used to explore the issue of the arms race having its own momentum. Higher level essays will formulate a response to the question that draws from all these sources and includes comment upon their context.

COURSEWORK ESSAY QUESTION IN THE STYLE OF EDEXCEL, UNIT 3

Was Fischer correct to see war in 1914 as the result of a German 'grasping after power' or did war result from short-term misjudgements?

Reading

Before answering this question you should read Chapter 7.

How to answer this question.

- **Identify key words from the question.** Key words such as 'grasping after power', 'short-term' and 'misjudgements' need to be identified in your response. These words will need to appear in your essay plan and in your introduction and conclusion, and will also be the subject of paragraphs or sections of the essay.
- **Challenge the question.** You can demonstrate a high level of understanding by exposing the assumptions which lie beneath the question. For example, the reference to 'grasping after power' alludes to the title of Fischer's book. Therefore you need to assess how far you agree with Fischer that the Germans started the war in order to become a world power. 'Misjudgements' raises the issue of how far the great powers simply failed to anticipate the consequences of their actions. For example, you might consider whether Britain could have prevented war by declaring its position sooner; conversely, you need to consider whether Austria-Hungary and Germany wanted war.
- **Refer to relevant historiography and concepts**, for example, Fischer's thesis, or the concept of the primacy of military policy.
- **Balance your argument.** Your assessment of Fischer will provide you with the core of your argument. Yet you will also need to consider whether any of those factors which contributed to the outbreak of the First World War can be discounted, and which are of greater importance.

COURSEWORK ESSAY QUESTION IN THE STYLE OF AQA

Why did tensions in the Balkans lead to war in 1914 but not in 1908–9?

Reading
Before answering this question you should read Chapters 2, 5, 6 and 7.

How to answer this question.
This question draws upon the material in Module E 3(b) and asks you to focus on what changed between these two crucial dates. The key differences lie in the responses of Austria-Hungary and Russia. At a higher level, responses will explore the legacy of Russia's humiliation in 1908–9, and will also challenge whether Balkan tensions did actually lead to war in 1914. They will also explore the extent to which Austria-Hungary and Germany manipulated the situation arising from the assassination at Sarajevo. However, it is important to remember that competition in the Balkans was the initial *casus belli* between Austria-Hungary and Russia in 1914, and also the key role that Russian rearmament played in Germany's plans for war.

ESSAY QUESTIONS IN THE STYLE OF OCR

Study Topic: The causes and the impacts of the First World War

(a) **Explain why Austria-Hungary might be blamed for starting the First World War.** [30]
(b) **How fair was the Treaty of Versailles?** [60]

Reading
Before answering question (a) you should read Chapter 7. To answer question (b) you should first read Chapters 8 and 9.

How to answer question (a)
The question is asking you to focus on how Austria-Hungary acted in response to the assassination of Archduke Franz Ferdinand in June 1914.

A rapid strike by Austria-Hungary might have avoided war; but to what extent did the assurance of German backing contribute to further aggression? You will need to assess these issues, as well as the extent of threat posed by Russia: would they have stood aside in 1914 to show their disapproval of political assassinations? The case against Austria-Hungary is strong but you need to decide how crucial Germany's 'Blank Cheque' was – once armed with this, even Serbia's conciliatory response to the Austrian ultimatum failed to avert war in 1914. Given the wording of the question your answer must focus on Austria-Hungary's role, whilst addressing the influence of other European powers.

How to answer question (b)

This question is challenging you at a number of levels. Most of what you will have learnt about Versailles will have reflected the harshness of the treaty so you need to think about issues like Alsace-Lorraine which simply reversed the gains of previous wars. The Treaty of Versailles contained a provision for reparations, and the principle of reparations was fair insofar as it was established under international law and the Germans had imposed reparations on the French in 1871. However, the exclusion of Germany from the 1919 negotiations might be considered unfair, especially as France was included in negotiations in Vienna in 1815, as might the British naval blockade. You should also consider why the Germans labelled the treaty a 'Diktat'. At a higher level, responses will question 'fairness' not only from other viewpoints but also from different chronological perspectives. For many Frenchmen the Versailles Treaty did not go far enough, but you might also consider how its 'unfairness' contributed to the policy of appeasement in the 1930s.

Study Topic: International Relations, 1919–39

(a) **Explain the nature and impact of the Dawes and Young Plans.** [30]

(b) **To what extent did British foreign policy contribute to the outbreak of war in 1939?** [60]

Reading

Before answering question (a) you should read Chapters 9. To answer question (b) you should first read Chapter 8 and Sections 5 and 6.

How to answer question (a)

The important point to note about this question is that it asks you about the 'nature and impact' of both plans. It is therefore important to cover both plans in your answer. It is also essential that you deal with the 'impact' of each plan. For example, the impact of the Depression makes it hard to judge what impact the Young Plan had on international relations. You will also need to explain the different contexts in which the plans were introduced. The Dawes Plan was a response to financial crisis in Germany and was designed to 'pump prime' the European economy by reviving Germany's, but the Young Plan was negotiated in a very different context.

How to answer question (b)

The purpose of this question is to examine the causes of the Second World War. By focusing on British foreign policy the examiner is asking you to reshape your material around the policy of appeasement. Since most people do not blame Britain, this formula should help you avoid a simple 'it was Hitler' response. You might assess how the British decision to appease Hitler came at a time when Britain feared Japanese aggression, and also how appeasement contributed to Hitler's belief that he did not have to take British guarantees to Poland seriously. The growing militarisation of Japanese foreign policy after 1931 and Japan's increasing clashes with the United States (which developed into trade wars after 1939) are other factors that might be considered. The specification refers to the foreign policies of Britain, Germany, Italy, the USSR, Japan and the USA, so you need to consider each of them and establish which countries did more than Britain to cause war to break out in 1939. In this respect, the Great Depression provides a wide-ranging factor which can be shown to have influenced the foreign policies of most of the countries listed.

A2 SECTION: BRITISH FOREIGN POLICY AND INTERNATIONAL RELATIONS, 1890–1939

INTRODUCTION

The A2 Section is designed to deepen your understanding of key themes which are covered in modules taken at A2, and to help you analyse the significance of key events and actions in the period 1890–1939. British foreign policy in this period has to be seen against Great Britain's relative decline as a world power. The big debate on British foreign policy therefore relates to whether Britain's policies should have changed, or whether Britain would have declined more quickly had it not continued to try to balance power in Europe. Section 1 looks at the political and economic aims of British foreign policy in the 1890s, whilst Sections 2 and 3 assess the nature of Britain's relations with Germany, Russia and France in the period 1890 to 1914.

Some historians have questioned why Great Britain fought at all in 1914, and this provides the subject matter of Section 4. With a worldwide empire did Britain need to worry about Belgium? Should Great Britain have left France and Germany to exhaust each other and instead have pooled its resources to meet the growing challenge from the United States? The picture changes after 1918, with Great Britain left contemplating how to maintain an empire with significantly fewer resources. Section 5 looks at Britain's foreign policy objectives at the Versailles Treaty in 1919 and asks how consistent they were with its policy objectives before 1914. The question is also raised as to whether British foreign policy at Versailles was fundamentally flawed.

Sections 6 and 7 focus on appeasement and the man who will forever be associated with it, Neville Chamberlain. A case is made for seeing Neville Chamberlain's foreign policy in the context of his domestic policies and, in line with recent research, it is suggested that appeasement was very much Chamberlain's policy. Also, the effectiveness of appeasement as 'good politics' is assessed with reference to the European political climate: if we consider that Mussolini invaded Abyssinia because war would distract Italians from their economic problems, it is surely correct to recognise that politicians in a democracy have to *win* elections. Chamberlain in the 1930s therefore had to consider the impact his decisions would have on the parliamentary position of his party. Despite

the failures of appeasement, it can be seen to have emerged from a
genuine desire to maintain Britain and its empire. However, the question
will be raised as to whether Britain would have done better to fight in
1938 over Czechoslovakia than in 1939 over Poland.

SECTION 1

What were the political and economic aims of British foreign policy in the 1890s?

Introduction
This decade is the last in which Britain tried to operate in 'splendid isolation', in which it had no formal alliances. Effectively, the period ended in 1902 when Britain signed an alliance with Japan to help protect British possessions in the Far East from the expanding empires of Russia and the United States. By 1890, Britain had been the world's leading maritime power for nearly 150 years, since it had defeated France in the Seven Years War (1756–63). Now Britain faced new and greater challenges and its economy was beginning to falter.

Key themes.
- The relative decline of Britain's economy was an important factor in determining its foreign policy in the 1890s.
- Lord Salisbury was a reluctant imperialist because he recognised the economic burden that the empire was putting upon Britain.
- By the end of the decade the naval race had caused a deep rift in Anglo-German relations.
- The Boer War made Britain recognise the changing realities in international relations by 1901. It therefore preceded, but did not cause, the subsequent change of policy.

Historiography. An excellent place to start is with John Charmley's *Splendid Isolation* (1999). This is a challenging book but it also tries to cover some of the figures that have not attracted their own biographies. Charmley is an iconoclast in the true academic sense in that he challenges received wisdom and reassesses which great figures may be judged to have feet of clay. Detailed accounts of diplomatic events can also be found in R. K. Massie's *Dreadnought* (1991). British policy is also covered by James Joll in *Europe since 1870* (1976) and by A. J. P. Taylor in *The Struggle for Mastery in Europe, 1848–1918* (1971).

WITH WHAT SUCCESS WAS BRITAIN ABLE TO FOLLOW A POLICY OF ISOLATION?

No formal alliances. During the 1890s Britain did not make any formal military alliances. The French and the Russians signed a treaty in 1894 whilst the Austrians and the Germans continued the Triple Alliance with Italy which had first been signed in 1882. Therefore this is a period when Britain is described as following a policy of 'splendid isolation' because it was free from continental entanglements. Although both **Liberals and Conservatives** were in power during the decade this was an area of policy common to both parties, although their motives differed.

Mediterranean agreements. Although Britain had not made any formal military alliances it began the decade as a signatory to the Mediterranean agreements of 1887 with Italy. Austria and Spain adhered to the agreement, then Germany and Austria–Hungary acceded to the agreements. The essential object of these agreements was to maintain the status quo in the Mediterranean against France. It was only in the period after 1902 that Royal Navy planners began to base their strategic assumptions around the idea of France as an ally. By that time the British and the French had been able to resolve their differences over Egypt and the growing German naval programme was focusing British attention on the North Sea.

The Boer War 1899–1902. By the end of the 1890s Britain was at war with the Boers in South Africa. As Lord Salisbury and Gladstone had feared, the constant drive by those on the edges of the empire to secure further territory had led to war. This time, however, the enemy was not a poorly-armed native force like the Zulu (whose bravery was inadequate against modern weapons) or the Mahdists in the Sudan (whose defeat at Omdurman in 1898 owed more to the machine-guns used to stop their attacks than the cavalry charge which the popular press emphasised). The Boer farmers were trained marksmen with modern weapons and they organised themselves into mounted 'commandos'. Leading British generals such as Redvers Buller had their reputations shattered by Boer fire at disastrous battles like Spion Kop in January 1900. Eventually the war was won by using mobile cavalry columns and strategic use of the railways coupled with the **concentration camps** which deprived the Boers of the support of their families. Britain was thus finally able to defeat this very small enemy thousands of miles from London. The Boer War shook Britain's confidence in its ability to survive as a great power without allies. If it took two years and a major recruiting drive to defeat the Boers, what would it take to defeat a major European power?

WAS BRITISH FOREIGN POLICY IN THE 1890S DESIGNED TO BE CHEAP?

Economic problems. The governments of the 1890s had to face up to the reality that their means were limited. In 1879, the agricultural sector had gone into recession. Cheap grain imports from the United States and the adoption of agricultural tariffs by Germany in 1878 had led to a slump in prices on the domestic market. As wealthy landowners spent less and kept fewer servants, the wider economy felt the shock of the economic

Liberals and Conservatives
In general, Liberals favoured less colonial development and wanted to spend less on armaments. Many Conservatives followed Disraeli's theme of 'popular imperialism'. This involved cheap wars against poorly-armed indigenous people.

KEY FACT

Concentration camps First used by the Spaniards in Cuba during the Spanish-American War (1898). Their use by the British army is the single most controversial and emotional issue surrounding the Boer War. Thousands of women and children were forced from their homes and taken to concentration camps where overcrowding and a poor diet led to the rapid spread of diseases. 5000 women and over 20,000 children eventually died.

downturn. Tax revenues decreased as the incomes of the wealthy declined and foreign wars would therefore lay a heavy burden upon the rich if income tax were raised, or the poor if consumption taxes were raised. An inactive foreign policy was cheaper and therefore avoided unpopular tax rises.

The growing economic tension in Britain was emphasised in 1889 by the dock strike. Britain was a trading nation and now it found that a strike was able to threaten that very lifeline. Britain wanted to continue to be a great power but its economic base would only support limited armaments. Britain thereby understood that it could not afford both an army and a navy so it chose to continue to be a naval power.

The limits to 'splendid isolation'. In an increasingly threatening world situation Britain's policy of 'splendid isolation' had begun to look rather tarnished. In the **Venezuelan crisis** Britain had had to recognise that it could not hope to impose its will upon the United States in the western hemisphere, which is how the American popular press viewed the episode. The Boer War emphasised how much a small war could drain the resources of the empire leaving other territories vulnerable. As evidence of the economic cost of war, Britain's expenditure on the army rose to approximately £91 million in 1900 and 1901, but was down to £38 million by 1903. The increase was equal to around 3 per cent of Britain's gross domestic product, so with an empire to maintain it was clear that the British economy would suffer badly in a conflict. The alliance with Japan (1902), which was cheap in terms of the commitments it involved, might have proved sufficient if Germany had not persisted in its decision to challenge British naval supremacy. The continuing challenge from Germany would eventually cause Germany severe financial difficulties in 1908, but in the meantime if Britain were to meet the challenge then the costs would either be punitive taxation and economic decline or an end to 'splendid isolation'. By 1904, Britain had to accept that an Entente was the price it would have to pay for maintaining its status as a great power. The Entente with France would make it possible to fund both limited social reform and the naval race with Germany, since Britain would only have to build a fleet to face Germany, not both France and Germany.

Lord Salisbury. As Prime Minister and a former Foreign Secretary, Lord Salisbury played a key role in determining Britain's foreign policy. He was pessimistic about the consequences of the way in which the **franchise** had gradually been extended, believing that there would be pressure to respond to 'democracy' with programmes of social reform. In Germany, Bismarck had introduced unemployment and sickness insurance in an attempt to resist working-class demands for greater political power. Bismarck's social programmes were used to help persuade the workers to accept the higher food prices caused by tariffs. The German tariffs had

KEY TERM

Venezuelan crisis (1895–6) This dispute arose because the US were keen to prevent the European powers from extending their influence in South America. The US reacted strongly to German pressure upon Venezuela and then threatened to go to war with Britain. The British were forced to accept that Venezuela retained control of the mouth of the Orinoco river, which the British had wanted to include in their own colony of British Guiana.

KEY THEME

Franchise extension By 1885 British men who were heads of households had the vote. This meant that working-class opinion was now important in elections.

Lord Salisbury.

William Gladstone.

been introduced to protect the farmers and money was being spent in the 1890s to develop the German navy, which provided employment. Lord Salisbury believed that if he was forced to adopt an expensive foreign policy then he would also have to introduce social reform in order to justify the necessary tax increases. Lord Salisbury's foreign policy was therefore designed to allow Britain to meet its imperial commitments without the necessity of raising taxes or introducing social reform at home.

Strategic positions. Lord Salisbury was cynical about military claims that were made about the need to garrison (occupy with troops) certain strategic positions. Indeed, this period is often referred to as the 'pro-consular period' since the local British representatives behaved like semi-independent rulers. He was well aware that British expansion in India had stemmed from the desire of various men to add neighbouring areas to the ones they already governed. For example, in Africa in 1878 Lord Chelmsford's desire to seize Zulu territory had eventually led to war and the battles of Isandhlwana and Rorke's Drift in 1879, but he had portrayed the situation as arising from Zulu aggression. In 1892, Lord Salisbury wrote to the British representative in Cairo saying that he should be wary of military advice. He warned: 'If they were allowed full scope they would insist on us garrisoning the moon to protect us from Mars.' It was for this reason that Lord Salisbury had opposed the annexation of Burma in 1886. The justification suggested for the annexation of Burma was the need to protect the borders of India; the annexation only went ahead because **Lord Randolph Churchill** announced it whilst the rest of the cabinet were enjoying their holiday between Christmas and New Year.

KEY PERSON

Lord Randolph Churchill (1849–95) Served as Secretary for India (1885–6) and as Chancellor of the Exchequer in 1886 before resigning from the government. His son, Winston Churchill, was later to become Prime Minister in May 1940.

KEY DATES

British Prime Ministers

1874–80	B. Disraeli (later Lord Beaconsfield)
1880–5	W.E. Gladstone
1885	Lord Salisbury
1885–6	W.E. Gladstone
1886–91	Lord Salisbury
1891–4	W.E. Gladstone
1894–6	Lord Rosebery
1896–1902	Lord Salisbury
1902–5	A.J. Balfour
1906–8	H. Campbell-Bannerman
1908–18	H.H. Asquith

KEY TERMS

Midlothian and Beaconsfieldism
On his first Midlothian tour in 1879 Gladstone attacked Disraeli's foreign policy. Using Disraeli's new title of Lord Beaconsfield as a label, Gladstone condemned Beaconsfieldism as a combination of financial waste and immoral self-aggrandisement.

KEY PERSON

General Charles Gordon (1833–85)
Gordon's mission was to identify the situation in Khartoum and then leave. His decision to remain resulted in his murder and a popular outcry which left Gladstone looking weak, even though Gordon had brought the disaster upon himself.

William Gladstone. William Ewart Gladstone was Prime Minister for the fourth time from 1892 to 1894, when he retired at the age of 85. During a political career of over 60 years he had retained certain basic beliefs. One such belief was in economy. It was he who had founded the House of Commons Public Accounts Committee in 1861 to discourage the government from wasting money. He also insisted that it must be chaired by a member of the opposition, to keep a close eye on him when he was Chancellor of the Exchequer. Despite being a member of the Church of England, Gladstone shared the Nonconformist concern with thrift (being economical). Armaments were therefore wasteful as well as immoral, and Gladstone finally resigned in 1894 because he did not agree with the rest of the cabinet that the naval estimates should be increased. Gladstone saw armaments and the idea of imperial expansion as a result of both greed and pride.

Morality. In 1893 Gladstone's Foreign Secretary, Lord Rosebery, wanted to send more troops to Egypt in order to overawe the new Khedive. This was exactly the kind of 'power' diplomacy that Gladstone abhorred. Earlier in his career Gladstone had criticised Lord Palmerston's desire for war against Russia in 1854 and, in 1879 in his first '**Midlothian Campaign**', had attacked Disraeli's similar policies as '**Beaconsfieldism**'. However, Gladstone and the Liberal government had been blamed for the death of **General Gordon** in the Sudan in 1885 and Rosebery was determined not to look weak again. Rosebery and his cabinet colleagues therefore ignored Gladstone's declaration that he would rather set fire to Westminster Abbey than send more troops to Egypt. Gladstone's resignation in 1894 marked a key change in Liberal foreign policy. Gladstone was the last senior cabinet minister to deal with foreign policy whose roots lay in the pre-imperialist past. Gladstone's passing from the

What were the political and economic aims of British foreign policy in the 1890s?   133 scene left the field of foreign policy open to the younger 'Liberal imperialists'. One of them, Sir Edward Grey, would follow a very different policy as Foreign Secretary from December 1905 to 1915.

Popular imperialism. Both Gladstone and Lord Salisbury had to contend with the growth of popular imperialism. One of the few things they could agree upon was that it was largely Disraeli's doing. Enthusiasm for the concept of empire had grown during a series of small colonial wars, which had very little impact on the population at home. One of the reasons for this was the absence of conscription: since the British army was a small professional one the loss of men hardly touched the population at large. There was thus a general belief that the British army would be successful all over the world and that the British were well-suited to governing others. Few of her contemporaries would have agreed with **Beatrice Webb**, whose comment on the **1897 Diamond Jubilee** was 'imperialism in the air, all classes drunk with sightseeing and hysterical loyalty'. British foreign policy could therefore rely on enthusiasm for Britain's continuing expansion overseas.

Writing to President Theodore Roosevelt in 1906, Sir Edward Grey looked back on the 1890s thus:

> *Before the Boer War we were spoiling for a fight. We were ready to fight France over Siam [Thailand], Germany about the Kruger Telegram [sent by Wilhelm II to congratulate the Boer leader Kruger], and Russia about anything. Any government here during the last ten years of the last century [the 1890s], could have had a war by lifting a little finger. The people would have shouted for it. They had a craving for it, and a rush of blood to the head.*

Certainly, the Colonial Secretary Joseph Chamberlain believed that the Conservative victory in the 1895 general election was a triumph for patriotism. The famous 'small wars' of Victoria's reign had left the British public with the impression that wars could be fought and won easily. This was reflected in the wave of volunteers who came forward to serve in South Africa during the Boer War. Popular nationalism probably helped to avert war with France over Fashoda (see Chapter 3) by convincing the French that Britain would fight. Later the same popular nationalism, coupled with the increasing hatred of Germany, was to make it easier to declare war in 1914.

WHY DID RELATIONS BETWEEN BRITAIN AND GERMANY DETERIORATE DURING THE 1890S?

The deterioration in relations between Britain and Germany was a cumulative process. Each dispute served to remind Germany of its impotence without a fleet. When it sought to remedy the problem by passing the 1898 Navy Law, a deadly naval race began with Great Britain which ended in war in 1914.

The Samoan Islands. In 1898 a colonial dispute arose between Britain and Germany over the Samoan Islands off New Zealand. Even though Joseph Chamberlain, the British Colonial Secretary, had described the islands as 'not worth twopence to either of us', he nonetheless decided to make an issue of it when faced by an equally intransigent German foreign office under the newly appointed Secretary of State of the Foreign Office, and future Chancellor, Bernhard von Bülow. The Germans wanted Britain to demonstrate its goodwill towards Germany. However, despite his later efforts to forge closer links with Germany, Joseph Chamberlain refused to recognise the German-supported **Mataafa** as king of Samoa. The British and US carried out a naval bombardment of the Samoan capital Apia, during the course of which the German consulate was damaged on 11 March 1899. The Kaiser was reportedly outraged by this insult and relations between Britain and Germany sank to new depths.

Weltpolitik. Like Chamberlain, the German Secretary of State of the Foreign Office von Bülow attached little importance to the Samoan Islands themselves but he was constrained not only by the Kaiser but also by the policy of *Weltpolitik* ('world policy'). Bülow's policy of *Weltpolitik* was designed to weld conservative opinion in Germany together and therefore it was a policy he could not afford to abandon. The goal of *Weltpolitik* was to create a united German society behind the leadership of the traditional elite. A key element in this plan was the creation of a navy paid for out of taxes on imports. Although this plan would raise manufacturing costs, manufacturers would be encouraged to back government policies by receiving highly profitable military contracts. In 1897 Admiral von Tirpitz had submitted the first German Naval Bill to the Reichstag. Tirpitz's aim was to construct a fleet that would deter Britain from intervening against Germany and preventing it from developing a powerful position in the world. The Naval Bill did not receive a warm welcome in the Reichstag because it would be expensive. Therefore Tirpitz was quick to point out that without a navy Germany would be powerless to prevent incidents like that in Samoa.

The Kaiser's letter. The Americans subsequently apologised for the joint shelling of the consulate and so German resentment began to focus on Britain. Bülow advised the British government that the continuing dispute in Samoa could have far-reaching consequences for relations between the two countries. Lord Salisbury thought the Germans were making too much of a minor issue and simply reassured the Germans that the earlier agreements (1889) over Samoa would be observed. In May the Kaiser wrote an extraordinary letter to his grandmother Queen Victoria. In it he accused the British of treating Germany as though it

---

KEY PERSON

Mataafa Mataafa had been in exile and had returned after the death of King Malietoa in August 1898. Prior to his death, Malietoa had persuaded the other chiefs to recognise Mataafa, and he was subsequently recognised as king by the German consulate.

were 'Portugal, Chile or the Patagonians'. He wrote that the British government 'must learn to respect Germany' and to 'treat her as an equal'.

The Kaiser's words summarise the desire, which underlay *Weltpolitik*, to achieve parity with Britain. It is, however, unclear what the Kaiser meant when he told Queen Victoria that he was upset by the failure of his efforts to achieve peaceful relations with Britain. The fact that the Samoan Islands were eventually divided between Britain, Germany and the United States in November 1899 removed a potential area of dispute. But a share of Samoa would never fulfil the domestic goals of *Weltpolitik* to unite Germany behind its Kaiser in the way that he had perceived Britain to be united behind Queen Victoria when he attended the naval review at Spithead in 1887 for her **Golden Jubilee**. The period 1894–1900 in Germany is seen as a sterile one. During this period there were frequent discussions at Court concerning the wisdom of a *coup d'état* in which the Kaiser would close the Reichstag and become an absolute ruler again. Whilst the growth of socialism made this idea attractive to the Kaiser, it was generally thought such a move would end in failure.

Naval rivalry. As Britain and Germany became rivals at sea, so the tension between them grew. The US proved to be a third party in this developing animosity. In 1895, the Germans had upset the US by shelling Venezuela in pursuit of a colonial dispute. The Americans were annoyed since it seemed to offend against the Monroe Doctrine of 1823 under which the United States had promised not to interfere in Europe if the European powers would refrain from increasing their influence in the western hemisphere. The British and the US had conducted a verbal war over control of the mouth of the Orinoco (1895–6) and so the dispute over the Samoan Islands provided an opportunity for Britain to repair its relations with the US. In 1898, the US was also fighting a war with Spain over Cuba and had occupied the Philippines, which was part of the Spanish Empire. In this respect the United States was happy to co-operate with Britain since this would ensure that the Royal Navy did not intervene to prevent the US navy from defeating its Spanish counterpart.

Chamberlain's speech. On 30 November 1899, Joseph Chamberlain gave a widely reported speech at Leicester in which he spoke about the opportunity to forge a new alliance. This alliance was to be one between Britain, the United States and Germany. Following the conclusion of the Samoan dispute, Chamberlain thought that this was a good opportunity to improve Anglo-German relations. However, Bülow replied to Chamberlain's overture by telling the Reichstag on 12 December 1899 that Germany must seize the opportunity to build a fleet strong enough to prevent an attack. Again the naval programme underpinning *Weltpolitik* can be seen to be the stumbling block to improved relations with Britain.

Golden Jubilee, 1887 The Kaiser saw this demonstration of British naval power as further proof of the need for Germany to have a navy with which to promote German interests.

It is necessary to appreciate the state of German politics at this time. In 1894 the Kaiser had appointed the septuagenarian Prince Hohenlohe-Schillingfürst as Chancellor. This career civil servant had used his sudden elevation to marry his relatives off to better families than his previous rank would have permitted. By late 1899 it was clear that he would have to retire soon. Von Bülow, who was to succeed him in 1900, would have been foolish at this point to upset the Kaiser by undermining the Naval Bill in the Reichstag. For Bülow, talk of an alliance with Britain would have made bad politics, as it would have given the opponents of the bill considerable ammunition to delay the expensive building programme. Therefore it can be said that the desire of the German elite to push forward with the creation of an imperial navy killed any possibility of an Anglo-German alliance in the period when a British alliance with France was not yet considered.

CONCLUSION

The political and economic objectives of British foreign policy in the 1890s were to avoid war and to maintain the British Empire at the lowest possible cost to the British taxpayer. These objectives stemmed from the weakening of the British economy after 1878 and the (related) difficulties faced by Britain, as a trading nation, in a world in which tariff barriers were increasingly being used to protect domestic industry, e.g. in Germany. The Boer War demonstrated that even a small war could absorb 3 per cent of gross domestic product. Furthermore, British investors were increasingly channelling their funds into overseas ventures, for example in the United States. As Britain moved towards a **negative trade balance** in manufactured goods its ability to sustain its empire became more doubtful. To pay for the necessary armaments Britain would need to raise taxes. In a parliamentary democracy this ran the risk of causing social and political upheaval even on the restricted franchise of 1885. Relatively few people paid income tax but taxes on consumables reached further down the social scale.

> ### KEY TERM
>
> **Negative trade balance** This means that Britain was moving towards a position where it bought more manufactured goods than it sold. Britain would therefore be dependent on the flow of money from overseas investments and from sales of services such as banking.

Britain was able to continue to follow its traditional policy of making no formal alliances until the close of the century. The Boer War illuminated Britain's weakness at a time when Germany's naval programme was creating a permanent rift between the two countries. The impact of the Anglo-German naval race would see a swift end to 'splendid isolation' in practice if not in theory. The naval race was decisive in leading to Britain opposing Germany in 1914.

SECTION 2

What was the impact of naval and imperial rivalry between Britain and Germany, 1890–1914?

Introduction

In discussing British foreign policy on television, the historian A. J. P. Taylor suggested that in 1870 the French question had become the German question. By this he raised the concern as to how Britain would avoid Germany dominating the continent of Europe, as Spain and then France under Napoleon had tried to do? This section is designed to explain why, after 1870, the British came to see Germany rather than their traditional rival, France, as a threat. In particular this section will deal with the decision by Germany to build a battle fleet and to acquire colonies.

WHAT WAS *WELTPOLITIK*?

German leaders such as Bülow and Tirpitz talked about a 'world policy' in which Germany would secure 'a place in the sun'. All the great powers were building colonial empires (except Austria-Hungary) and so they believed that Germany too should enter the colonial arena. Germany was here following France and Britain's example, but it was unlikely that these powers would make another competitor welcome. *Weltpolitik* was therefore a policy designed to raise Germany to equal the status of Great Britain as a world power. To achieve this it was necessary, according to Captain Mahan (see below), to have a navy, so the two issues are inextricably linked.

Captain Mahan. The person whose ideas are most frequently quoted as influencing military leaders at this time is Captain Mahan. Mahan was a US naval officer and in 1890 he published his very influential book, *The Influence of Seapower upon History, 1660–1783*. The book provided a theoretical explanation of how sea power had enabled Britain to create and sustain its huge empire. Amongst those who read the book were Kaiser Wilhelm II and Admiral von Tirpitz. The logic of the book pointed to sea power as the means to build an empire. It is important to remember that the British cabinet decided to increase naval expenditure in 1894. It was on this issue that the Liberal Prime Minister Gladstone had decided to resign after a political career lasting 62 years. The British response to Mahan's book is interesting, as he had speculated whether

Britain, as a democracy, would have the political strength to maintain its advantage and predicted that it would not.

What have been historians' views of *Weltpolitik*? In his book, *Grasping after World Power* (1961), Fritz Fischer put Germany's desire to be a world power at the centre of the causes of the First World War. This view was especially controversial in Germany since it meant Germany was primarily responsible for the war and that Germany's aims under the Kaiser were similar to its aims under Hitler. Historians generally accept the existence of *Weltpolitik*. However, in *War of Illusions* (1974) Fischer supports the idea that domestic issues may also have led to war. In *Juli 1914* (1965) I. Geiss, too, gives greater weight to the domestic pressures that led to the decision to declare war (see Chapter 7). This idea is referred to as the *Primat der Innenpolitik*. This argument centres upon the crisis in German government (and those of other states) as old-established elites were threatened by social and economic change. Such a crisis was the result of growing industrialisation leading to pressures for social reform, which could only be financed by progressive taxation. The impact of naval rivalry plays a key role in this debate.

WHAT WERE THE EFFECTS OF THE NAVAL ARMS RACE?

Why was Britain so concerned with naval power?

The sinew which held the empire together was trade, whilst the muscle was the Royal Navy. Triumphant over the French and Spanish fleets at Trafalgar in 1805, the Royal Navy was, during the rest of the nineteenth century, recognised as the largest in the world. As Britain's 'Senior Service' it enjoyed a special place in the British national psyche or self-image. This is shown in the words of *Rule Britannia*:

> *Rule Britannia, Britannia rules the waves, Britons never, never, never shall be slaves.*

This exhortation presents the Royal Navy as Britain's barrier against foreign invasion. As an island on the edge of Europe this was a natural perception, and it was reinforced by Britain's history. After 1846 when Peel repealed the Corn Laws, Britain needed cheap imports to support its growing industries and the ability to export its manufactured goods to pay for the raw materials. The Royal Navy guaranteed that commerce would be able to continue to provide Britain with supplies and markets. Therefore Great Britain maintained squadrons in the West Indies, China, Hong Kong, South Africa and the Mediterranean as well as a squadron in the Falkland Islands, to ensure free passage to British merchant ships.

Understanding how the navy contributed to Britain's self-image helps us to understand how easily Germany's fleet could cause Britain concern.

After 1897, the growth of the Imperial German Navy posed a substantial challenge to the supremacy of the Royal Navy. How Britain and Germany dealt with this competition would determine the course of European history. From the British perspective, the need to concentrate battle ships in the Western Approaches and the North Sea weakened Britain's presence elsewhere.

Why did Germany become interested in naval power after 1898?

In 1897 the Spithead Review celebrated Queen Victoria's Diamond Jubilee and the splendour and size of the Royal Navy were there for all to see. The spectators included many foreign dignitaries aboard the Royal Yacht. Only the home fleet was on display, that is the fleet designed to prevent any direct threat to the British Isles. Even so, the ships on review occupied lines totalling 30 miles in length. If one wanted to find out about the details of the Royal Navy in 1897 it would have been possible to buy *Jane's Fighting Ships* which was first published in that year. The publication in peacetime of a new edition every year since demonstrates the interest in the balance of naval power. The 1897 edition listed 53 'ironclads' (ships with plate armour on the sides) in service with the Royal Navy. The next biggest power was France with 32. It was this demonstration of naval power that Admiral von Tirpitz had in mind as he planned the German high seas fleet.

The Kaiser. As the illustration confirms, Kaiser Wilhelm II took a close personal interest in naval affairs. In February 1895 the Kaiser had 'nothing but the navy in his head', according to his Foreign Secretary. In 1896 Admiral von Müller drafted a memorandum for the Kaiser's brother on future policy. In this memorandum, Müller accepted the goal of breaking up the British Empire. He wrote:

> *The war which could – and many say must – result from this situation of conflict would according to the generally accepted opinion in our country have the aim of breaking England's world domination in order to lay free the necessary colonial possessions for the central European states who need to expand.*

As Müller states, he is not actually saying that war was inevitable, only that many people thought so. However, he is saying that the goal of German policy was to break the domination of Great Britain. The only way in which this would not lead to war was if the British were voluntarily to surrender some of their colonial possessions. Since it would not be reasonable to expect any great power to surrender so easily the policy proposed by Müller is, effectively, to have a war with Britain.

Wilhelm II's notes on the naval build-up, 1897.

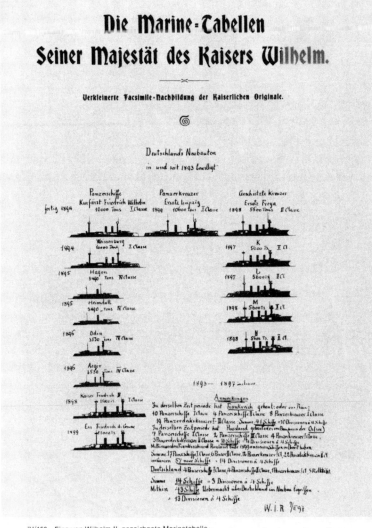

IV/158   Eine von Wilhelm II. gezeichnete Marinetabelle

How did naval rivalry prevent Britain and Germany becoming allies before 1902?

In October 1897, only four months after the Spithead Review, the Kaiser insisted that the Navy Bill be sent to the Reichstag because he would not accept any further discussion on the issue. Meanwhile, in Britain, Joseph Chamberlain, the Colonial Secretary, was concerned about Russian expansion in Asia; more specifically that Britain would be unable to prevent Russian expansion. Since Russia was a land power, Chamberlain did not feel that the Royal Navy alone could maintain Britain's position. In 1898, Chamberlain therefore wanted to make friendly overtures to Germany. Through his friend Baron von Eckardstein, who was the first secretary of the German Embassy in London, Chamberlain was able to meet the German Ambassador, Paul von Hatzfeldt. Hatzfeldt had been instructed by the German government to be pleasant but not to reach an agreement with Britain too quickly. The reason for this was that the Reichstag was debating the **Navy Bill**. Although the Navy Bill was not popular, it was important not to embarrass the Kaiser by making relations with Britain seem too friendly; opponents of the bill would use friendship with Britain to argue that the expensive navy was not necessary.

Hatzfeldt therefore told Chamberlain that Germany would prefer to see progress on colonial issues before pursuing discussions on broader matters such as naval programmes. This is therefore an example of where naval issues had a negative impact on Anglo-German relations. (It should be noted that colonial issues were the area in which Germany sought to pressurise Britain.)

Eventually Britain's problems with Russian expansion were to be solved through an alliance with Japan in 1902: much of the modern Japanese fleet, which destroyed the Russians in 1905, was built in Britain. It was easier for Britain to reach an alliance with Japan because the agreement in 1902 was designed to maintain the status quo in China and Korea, and Britain was therefore not being asked to surrender anything. Also the agreement had no specific impact on the 'narrow seas' – the English Channel and the North Sea. In his book, Mahan had identified that control of the English Channel and North Sea waters allowed Britain to control trade between Europe and the rest of the world. (Any compromise with Germany would inevitably touch upon this strategically sensitive area.)

In July 1905, Wilhelm II's attempts to forge an alliance with Russia through a personal meeting with Nicholas II became known to the British. This meeting at Björkö Sound was part of the Kaiser's attempt to balance the **Anglo-Japanese Alliance** in the Pacific.

Why did Britain succeed in meeting Germany's challenge despite Mahan's predictions?

Mahan's prediction was that Britain, a democracy, would be unable or unwilling to spend enough taxpayers' money to maintain the Royal Navy's dominance. In this he correctly gauged the temper of the electorate, which generally favoured low spending, e.g. Gladstone's win in 1880 and the later success of Lord Salisbury. However, Mahan overlooked the British understanding of the importance of safe trade routes. These routes were worldwide, and included the most important area – the seas around Britain. These seas, the English Channel and the North Sea, were also Britain's 'borders', and just as continental powers jealously looked to their frontiers, so the British looked to theirs. Hence support for a dominant Royal Navy was widespread.

KEY TERM

Navy Bill The 1897 Navy Bill, like subsequent bills, was drawn up in order to secure funding for the expansion of the German Imperial Navy. The bill laid out a plan to create a battle fleet. Ships which were designed to protect commerce, such as cruisers, were not a threat to Britain, but a battle fleet would be.

KEY THEME

Anglo-Japanese Alliance This was signed in 1902 and renewed in 1905 partly because of Wilhelm's overtures to Nicholas II.

During the first years of the twentieth century, under the command of Admiral Lord Fisher, the First Sea Lord (Britain's senior naval officer), a new battleship was launched – the *Dreadnought* (see page 39). As the *Dreadnought* slid into the water in 1906 she was held to have made all other battleships obsolete. This was a momentous decision for two reasons. The first reason was that, as Britain had the largest fleet, it now had more obsolete ships than anyone else. The second reason was that it had reduced its lead over other fleets to one ship, i.e. one Dreadnought to nil. By making the lead so numerically small Fisher did a great deal to fuel public concern about the importance of Britain's naval supremacy.

The German naval programme had considerable effect, nonetheless. In 1909 David Lloyd George, as Chancellor of the Exchequer of the Liberal government in Britain, proposed introducing social reforms. These reforms included pensions and unemployment insurance. Bismarck had introduced similar schemes in Germany in the 1880s. The Liberal government faced stiff opposition, especially in the House of Lords where the Conservatives had a large majority. During the election campaign in 1905 the Liberals had promised to spend more on social reform and less on armaments. At a cabinet meeting on 8 December 1908, there had been sharp disagreement because the First Lord of the Admiralty, Reginald McKenna, requested six new Dreadnoughts for each of the next three years. At £1 million each this was a very expensive demand.

McKenna told his cabinet colleagues that his request was a response to the increased German naval building plan. Since coming to power the Liberals had cut four Dreadnoughts from the British building programme. McKenna contrasted this with the four Dreadnoughts started by Germany by 1907 and the three planned for 1908. In addition the Germans had begun to build one battlecruiser in each year. McKenna gave his colleagues the Admiralty estimate that by 1912 the Royal Navy would have 16 Dreadnoughts to the Germans' 13. It had also been noted that the German yards were **laying down the keels** even before the Reichstag had passed the appropriate bills.

Fearing that the Germans were in fact secretly **building components** in advance of the keels being laid the Admiralty decided to increase its demands. Therefore in January 1909 it asked for eight Dreadnoughts in 1909. McKenna emphasised to the Prime Minister, H. H. Asquith, the public outcry that was likely to occur if all these points were made public. Once the debate opened in Parliament the Conservative opposition was able to stir up public concern. One MP, George Wyndham, coined the slogan 'We want eight and we won't wait'.

KEY TERMS

Laying down the keels This refers to setting out the framework of the ship on the slipway where it is to be built. The great powers recorded keels laid as definite future ships and, using known building speeds, it was possible to estimate when the ships would be launched. Tirpitz was thought (correctly) to be encouraging the shipbuilders to lay down keels before the money was passed so that once the money was passed the ships would be ready sooner.

Building components Another way of speeding up the delivery of ships was to stockpile components, e.g. gun mountings or precious metals, so that assembly would take less time once firm orders were placed.

What was the impact of naval and imperial rivalry between Britain and Germany?   143

The speech to the House of Commons by the Foreign Secretary, Sir Edward Grey, on 29 March 1909, shows how the logic of the arms race had taken hold. He said:

> If we, alone among the great powers, gave up the competition and sank into a position of inferiority, what good should we do? None whatever … we should cease to count for anything amongst the nations of Europe, and we should be fortunate if our liberty was left …

Grey did suggest to the German Ambassador Count Metternich that a mutual exchange of naval **attachés** should take place. However, Metternich told him that the Emperor had specifically forbidden this option. Had the Emperor agreed he would have been shocked to find that Tirpitz had accelerated the building of one Dreadnought and had decided not to tell the Emperor. Asquith subsequently warned Metternich that Britain would respond to any acceleration in the German naval programme.

Perhaps the greatest impact of the naval rivalry was on public opinion. As we have seen, the Navy League was already strong in Germany. In Britain, Wyndham's slogan became a popular music hall refrain. Parker, in *The Old Lie* (1987), lists *Dreadnought* amongst the popular comics aimed at children in the pre-1914 years. Although these comics were beyond the means of working-class children they were often given as prizes, for example in boys' clubs, so their readership was wider than might at first be thought. The publication of Erskine Childers' *Riddle of the Sands* in 1903 had led the way with a story of a British hero outwitting the Germans. The press owned by **Lord Northcliffe** supported the introduction of conscription. Therefore these newspapers made strident demands for tough measures to counter the Germans. It was this climate of fear that gave rise to the **Official Secrets Act** of 1911.

One last effort was made in 1912 to end the naval race. The pro-German Minister for War, **Viscount Haldane**, went to Germany to try to negotiate an agreement. At first it appeared that Haldane had been successful, but it was then recognised that Tirpitz was still planning to build large numbers of destroyers and submarines, so the talks broke down. As a result the naval race continued and by 1914 the British had 'won', with 22 Dreadnoughts to the 15 in the German high seas fleet (in addition Britain and Germany each had two more under construction). This lead on paper was deceptive as the British ships in each class had heavier guns than their opponents. However, between 1911 and 1914 the Germans had completed 11 Dreadnoughts to Britain's 12 so Britain's superior numbers largely consisted of slightly older ships. Also, the British had nine battlecruisers to the Germans' four with two and one, respectively, under construction. Naval rivalry with Germany ultimately

Attaché A technical expert on the diplomatic staff of their country at a foreign capital. A mutual exchange of attachés would improve understanding between the two countries about naval issues.

KEY PERSON

Lord Northcliffe Lord Northcliffe founded the Harmsworth press empire, of which the flagship was the *Daily Mail*. It also included the *Evening News* and the *Daily Mirror*.

KEY TERMS

The Official Secrets Act Section 2 allowed the government to decide what constituted a secret. Its significance was that it reflected the concern to protect technological advantages over opponents.

The Haldane Mission offered Germany the opportunity to agree to limit their war preparedness, but Wilhelm II regarded this as non-negotiable.

led Britain to forge an unwritten agreement with France and this made a crucial contribution to Britain's entry into the First World War. But the reason why Britain succeeded in meeting Germany's naval challenge, despite Mahan's prediction, was the undoubted perception that the Royal Navy was of fundamental national importance, more important than other matters of foreign and domestic policy, such as pensions and unemployment insurance.

Does the naval race show that Germany gave priority to domestic or foreign policy?

KEY TERM

1912 German Naval Law This bill provided for maintaining three battle squadrons at full strength all year round. (Previously during the winter only two were at full strength.)

Ian Porter and Ian Armour, in *Imperial Germany 1890–1918* (1991), argue that Tirpitz was clever at managing the Reichstag and note that he was able to get the majority of members of the centre to support the early **naval bills**. It should be remembered that the traditionally Catholic areas of the Rhineland voted for the Centre Party and they would support the navy because it would stimulate industrial demand in the Ruhr. The other way in which Tirpitz was able to support his plans was by funding his own pressure group called the Navy League (see Chapter 4). Hans Mommsen, in *Imperial Germany 1867–1918* (1995), sees the Navy League as reaching down into the non-political classes. He also sees the Navy League as becoming unrealistic in its demands. Whilst being unrealistic may have reduced the Navy League's value as an ally of government it did not help relations with Britain. If, as G. Eley suggests in *Reshaping the German Right: Radical Nationalism and Political Change after Bismarck* (1980), the Navy League got most of its funding from its membership then it must have enjoyed genuine support. It was difficult for political parties to ignore pressure groups like this and so they had to promise strong policies to secure support at elections. For example, the triumph of the right-wing 'Bülow Bloc' in the 1907 Reichstag elections depended partly on securing nationalist votes.

Sammlungspolitik. In parallel with the policy of *Weltpolitik* was that of *Sammlungspolitik,* which was designed to 'bring together' a conservative alliance. The navy played a key role in that it provided the manufacturers, especially in heavy industry, with guaranteed orders and high profits. In return the manufacturers accepted the tariffs, such as the Bülow Tariff of 1902, which protected the Junker landowners from overseas competition. The middle classes also benefited, since they could hope to see their sons commissioned into the navy where the need for technical proficiency meant class barriers were less rigid. In these respects, the navy played an important role in building a domestic consensus between 1897 and 1908. However, this consensus was fragile since the agricultural elite was very wary of the growing cost of the navy. Also, Britain's response began to undermine the coalition as the launch of *Dreadnought* in 1906 and the British-accelerated building programme frustrated Admiral von Tirpitz's calculations. The rising costs of the naval programme and Tirpitz's desire

KEY STATISTICS

Results of the 1912 elections

SPD	110	(+67)
Conservatives	43	(-17)
Reichspartei	14	(-10)
Centre	91	(-14)
Liberals	45	(-9)
Progressives	42	(-7)

(Scheidemann of the SPD was elected Vice-President of the Reichstag.)

KEY TERM

'Naval Iron Law'
Under the German
constitution of
1871, funding for
the army was
guaranteed under an
'Iron Law'. Tirpitz
wanted to link the
size of the navy and
a maximum life for
each ship in order to
create an automatic
programme for
renewing the fleet.

to create his own **'Naval Iron Law'** combined in 1909 to highlight the fact that Germany could no longer afford to develop the navy and maintain its traditional military supremacy on land. After 1908 the navy therefore ceased to be an instrument of domestic policy.

The elections of 1912. In 1912 the SPD (Socialists) became the largest party in the Reichstag. In defiance, the Kaiser refused to meet such people or to receive them at official receptions, thereby reflecting the attitude of the agrarian elite. The rise of the SPD had been fuelled by increased prices resulting from the tariffs imposed to protect the landowners. The landowners were now concerned to increase the size of the army but the SPD insisted that the necessary taxes should fall upon the landowners. The concession of an inheritance tax in 1913, to fund the increased army estimates, thus only confirmed the fears of the landowners that further increases would lead to revolutionary changes in the social structure of Germany and Prussia. In this respect, the landowners felt that it would be preferable to fight in 1914 than embark upon an accelerated arms race that Germany could not afford without a radical restructuring of the tax base. By 1914 the navy was therefore not the key issue but the money devoted to it, which had reduced the relative advantage enjoyed by the German army and created a situation in which war in 1914 was preferable to delay.

Without naval expansion, Britain might not have participated in the war. Ironically, the German navy had only helped to create the situation in which the British Expeditionary Force would be despatched and ultimately provide the thorn upon which the Schlieffen Plan would snag.

WHY DID COLONIAL RIVALRY NOT LEAD TO WAR BETWEEN BRITAIN AND GERMANY?

Economists view surplus capital as the money available to invest in new enterprises. Mommsen's view, in *Imperial Germany* (1995), is that the German economy lacked the surplus capital to invest in colonies, since the growth of the electrical and chemical industries helped to absorb available German capital. In order to finance economic growth, German banks had to attract foreign capital. This meant colonial ventures were a low priority. Lacking the need to secure colonies for investment reduced German interest in colonies, and this inadvertently helped to avoid too much conflict with Britain.

In 1898, the British and the Germans signed a secret convention regarding the Portuguese Empire. This established how the Portuguese Empire would be divided up in the event that Portugal was declared bankrupt. It was possible to accommodate German demands since they did not conflict with Britain's key territories, Egypt and South Africa.

Sir Edward Grey (1862–1933)
Liberal MP from 1885 and Foreign Secretary from 1905 to 1916. Grey sided with France against Germany and in 1907 concluded the Anglo-Russian entente, thus completing the Triple Entente against Germany. He again stood firmly in support of France during the Agadir crisis (1911), and concluded the secret Treaty of London (1915) which brought Italy into the war. He was made a peer in 1916. He was president of the League of Nations Union from 1918 and served as a special ambassador to the United States (1919–20).

Where issues did not directly impact upon Britain's strategic position it was possible for Britain and Germany to compromise. Colonial arrangements were a matter of constant negotiation. However, the constant negotiation showed that they were therefore easily discussed and therefore unlikely to lead to war, especially when the issues remained hypothetical such as the future of the Portuguese Empire.

The role of individuals

Faced with a choice between Germany and France, Asquith, Grey and Lloyd George led the cabinet in opposing Germany.

The crisis in Morocco of 1905–6 forced the British to choose between France and Germany. Unfortunately for Germany, Britain decided to back France. Charmley in *Splendid Isolation* (1999), sees British policy as being driven by **Sir Edward Grey**. In Charmley's view Lloyd George was correct in seeing Grey as one of two men responsible for war in 1914. However, it would be wrong to see Grey as acting alone over colonial issues. The key seems to be that Grey was anti-German, as Niall Ferguson believes (*The Pity of War*, 2000).

Yet it is also prudent to be aware of Charmley's own view, which seems to see the Entente as an error. Charmley may be seen, therefore, as one who prefers to put more of the blame upon Grey than on his Conservative predecessor as Foreign Secretary, Lord Lansdowne. However, the deviousness of Grey in withholding the details of the military discussions from his cabinet colleagues lends considerable weight to the case against Grey. It is important to remember how few people were actually involved in decision-making in the period between 1870

and 1914, and as a result, that the personal preferences of individuals carried greater weight. It is also very necessary to consider the bias of the personal accounts of these men. For example, one should treat Lloyd George's memoirs with caution: Lloyd George wished to be remembered as the Prime Minister who led Britain to victory rather than as one of the cabinet who decided to declare war in 1914.

CONCLUSION

It is reasonable to conclude that the naval rivalry between Britain and Germany had a major impact upon their relationship. Admiral von Tirpitz originally argued that a German battle fleet would deter the British from becoming involved in a war with Germany. As Müller's memorandum of 1896 shows, it was assumed that the ensuing conflict with Britain was likely if not inevitable. Grey's speech to the House of Commons in 1909 made that conflict clear. Unless Britain was simply to resign its position as a great power, it must face Germany's naval challenge.

Colonial issues in themselves created little difficulty in this period. Drawing lines on maps of distant countries was the stuff of traditional diplomacy. The governing elites, whilst always seeking to gain minor advantages, were able to conduct these negotiations discretely. Yet colonies clearly contributed in a minor way to the growing tension since they were tied up with the issue of sea power.

In 1914, Britain went to war not over colonies but because it wanted to maintain its status as a world power. Britain felt its status was under threat because Germany had been trying to build a navy which could rival the Royal Navy. Mahan had predicted that, as a democracy, Britain would not be able to meet such a challenge, but it had found the resources to do so. Germany could have given up the naval race in 1908–9; when it chose not to then conflict was almost inevitable.

The German navy was conceived as an instrument of *Weltpolitik* but in the end it undermined the financial stability of Germany and left its leaders facing a choice of war or social upheaval. At the Crown Council of December 1912 it was decided that a war would best be fought in 1914. Although the completion of the Kiel Canal would by then assist the navy, this was not a crucial factor in reaching this decision. Rather, the decision was based upon a military appraisal of the diminishing chances of success for the Schlieffen Plan after 1914. By December 1912 the navy was a peripheral issue in deciding upon war and by 1914 it was irrelevant. However, the failed German naval policy had by then irrevocably committed Britain to opposing Germany.

SECTION 3

What were Britain's relations with Russia and France, 1890–1914?

Introduction

This section explores the changing relationship between Britain and the two powers with which it entered the First World War, namely Russia and France. At the beginning of this period the relationship between the three powers was hostile. We need to examine why these relationships changed and to what extent the changes were less deep-rooted than they might appear.

Key themes.

- Britain's relations with Russia reflected Britain's continuing desire to avoid Russian expansion in the Mediterranean.
- Sir Edward Grey was integral to the forging of an Anglo-Russian agreement.
- As Foreign Secretary, Grey gave Britain's position in Europe priority.
- The Conservative government which resigned in December 1905 had already fundamentally altered British defence policy.

Historiography. John Charmley's *Splendid Isolation* (1999) is an excellent and challenging work devoted to British foreign policy from 1874 to 1914. For the period up to 1901, Andrew Roberts's biography, *Lord Salisbury: The Victorian Titan* (2000) gives further insight into a man with a deep distrust of Russia. For the period after 1905, Keith Robbins's biography of the British Foreign Secretary, *Sir Edward Grey* (1971), provides a more sympathetic view than Charmley. In *France and Britain 1900–40* (1996) P. M. H. Bell provides a genuinely Francophile view of the often difficult relationship between the two countries. Niall Ferguson's *The Pity of War* (2000) is an all-embracing and challenging assessment of this period.

WHY WERE BRITAIN AND RUSSIA HOSTILE TO EACH OTHER BETWEEN 1890 AND 1907?

Queen Victoria and Lord Salisbury. Queen Victoria's marked hostility to Russia influenced government policy. In 1875, Queen Victoria asked her ministers to make her an Empress. The Prime Minister, Benjamin Disraeli, and his cabinet colleagues wished to oblige the Queen but feared this would not be deemed a very English title. Therefore the government

Queen Victoria.

Lord Derby (1826–93) The 15th Earl of Derby, Edward Henry Stanley, followed his father into politics and held several posts in the latter's administration, including foreign secretary (1866–8). He was again foreign secretary (1874–8) under Disraeli, but resigned in protest against Disraeli's intervention in the Russo-Turkish war (1878). Derby later (1880) formally shifted his allegiance to the Liberal Party and was colonial secretary (1882–5) under Gladstone, before breaking with the Gladstonian Liberals over the issue of Home Rule for Ireland.

Dogger Bank An extensive sandbank, some 6800 square miles (17,610 sq km), positioned in the central North Sea between Great Britain and Denmark. Covered by shallow water 55–120ft (17–36 m) deep, it is a major breeding ground for many types of fish.

passed the Royal Titles Act and made Victoria Empress of India. Given that the route to India lay through the Suez Canal, it is not therefore surprising to find Queen Victoria writing to Disraeli in 1878 urging him to resist Russia's drive to the Mediterranean. He agreed with her, and they also both wanted to see the pro-Russian Foreign Secretary, **Lord Derby**, replaced by Lord Salisbury (as happened in 1878), who feared Russian ambitions to gain access to the Mediterranean at Constantinople. By 1885, Salisbury was Prime Minister and was to remain so for most of the time up to the Queen's death in 1901. He took the view that Russia should not be allowed to threaten British control of the Suez Canal, which was Britain's shortest sea link to the empire in Asia. Certainly, as the oil supplies of the Middle East grew in importance towards the end of the nineteenth century, there was even more reason to ward off Russian influence in the eastern Mediterranean.

Traditional British objectives. The efforts of Lord Salisbury from the Congress in Berlin (1878) onwards to oppose Russian ambitions in the eastern Mediterranean were a logical extension of earlier policy. In 1856 in the Treaty of Paris, which concluded the Crimean War, Russia was forced to accept the 'Black Sea Clauses'. Under these clauses, the Black Sea was demilitarised thus preventing all nations from using it in peacetime. This therefore impeded the passage of Russian warships through the Straits, despite the growth of German ambitions in the Balkans. Though recognising the threat German ambitions posed, the British avoided encouraging Russia for fear of being committed to supporting Russia against Austria. The irony is that Britain eventually went into a war triggered in part by Russian prestige in the Balkans.

Hostility to Russia. The hostility of Conservative figures like Lord Salisbury was equally shared by many on the Liberal benches. The Russian autocracy was the antithesis of traditional Liberal thinking. When the possibility of an understanding with Russia was first mooted in 1905, Margot Asquith quipped, 'Britons never, never shall be Slavs'. Her husband, H. H. Asquith, pointedly failed to refer to friendship with Russia even in his most intimate correspondence, according to his biographer Stephen Koss (*Asquith*, 1985). Popular hostility was easily fuelled by events such as the **Dogger Bank** incident in 1905. On its way to fight the Japanese in the Pacific, the Russian Baltic Fleet managed to fire upon British North Sea trawlers, imagining them to be Japanese torpedo boats.

In April 1906 a delegation of members of the Russian Duma (parliament) visited London. The positive effect this might have had upon Russia's pro-democratic image was destroyed when Nicholas II chose that week to dissolve the Duma and demonstrate that he was not committed to the reforms enshrined in the October Manifesto of 1905. Prime Minister Sir

Henry Campbell-Bannerman's 'La Douma est morte: vive la Douma!' ('the Duma is dead, long live the Duma!') was a witty adaptation of the traditional announcement of the death of a sovereign and pleased the downcast Russians when he met them. Although Grey had to stress to the Russian Ambassador in London that the Prime Minister had not been attacking the Tsar, Grey knew that Campbell-Bannerman had pleased the Liberal backbenchers who might otherwise have demanded stronger criticism of Russia.

The period of Grey's negotiations with Russia was, in truth, fraught. The Moscow insurrection and the 1905 Revolution in Russia led to the creation of the Duma, and was followed by a period of reaction and restraint. Grey's negotiations thus coincided with a period of repression under the reformer P. Stolypin, who had to achieve stability before attempting major reforms from 1907 onwards. Continuing **anti-Semitic pogroms**, some officially sanctioned, and the rise of the 'Black Hundreds', whose behaviour resembled the later Nazi SA (storm troopers), gave Liberal backbenchers frequent opportunities to condemn Russia. Nonetheless, Grey believed that the defence of British interests was more important than encouraging constitutional reform; this was *Realpolitik* (putting a country's own best interests first before ideology). That the negotiations could be conducted at all is further evidence of the extent to which senior government ministers were able to conduct policy away from the scrutiny of Parliament.

The Japanese Alliance (1902). The British relationship with Russia was not an easy one to forge. In 1902 Britain signed an alliance with Japan which aimed to provide Britain with a counterweight to the other great powers in Asia. In the subsequent war between Russia and Japan, Britain remained neutral, which at least allowed Britain and Russia to continue talking. Although the alliance had been made by the Conservatives Sir Edward Grey, more than his colleagues, openly welcomed the alliance from the opposition benches in the Commons and talked of Japan becoming Britain's partner in the East. Certainly, the Japanese offered a more convenient partnership than Germany since there were no European complications. Grey disliked the manner of German diplomacy as well, whilst believing German public opinion to be hostile to Britain. Japan was also a better ally against Russia as this allowed Britain to remain clear of the widening alliance system in Europe. For their part, the Japanese valued the status implied by an alliance with a colonial power and so their price, in this case neutrality, was lower than the Germans' demands would have been. It must also be remembered that German support for the Boers was too recent for an Anglo-German alliance to be viable.

WHY WAS AN ENTENTE BETWEEN BRITAIN AND RUSSIA POSSIBLE IN 1907?

Edward Grey. Keith Robbins, in *Sir Edward Grey* (1971), believes that Grey was not a Russophobe (hater of Russia) like his colleagues. After Russia's military defeat by Japan in 1905, Grey believed Russia would be more receptive to a possible agreement. Grey was also concerned to avoid Germany expanding its interests in Persia, and therefore took the opportunity of rumours concerning a possible Persian request to Germany for a loan to arrange to meet the Russian Ambassador. Grey suggested that Britain and Russia provide the loan instead. On 12 February 1906, Grey wrote to Sir Arthur Nicholson at the conference in Algeciras (which was being held on the Franco-German dispute on Morocco) that he wanted to keep open the possibility of a rapprochement (return to better relations) with Russia. He also foreshadowed the later agreements when he added that 'an Entente between Russia, France and ourselves would be absolutely secure'.

Three months later on 28 May 1906, Nicholson arrived in Russia as Britain's new ambassador. His predecessor, Sir Charles Hardinge, had returned to London as a strong advocate of an agreement with Russia. This was partly because Hardinge had worked in Teheran and did not believe that Britain could hope to regain its complete dominance over Persia. Nicholson's own spell in Teheran had left him with a poor impression of the Persians. Nicholson and Hardinge therefore reinforced Grey's own determination to forge an Anglo-Russian agreement, in case Russia otherwise simply took Persia over.

In cabinet, Grey could expect the support of both Campbell-Bannerman and his successor, H. H. Asquith. Since both men also supported the secret military talks with France it can be argued that the Triple Entente of Russia, France and Britain was not just the product of French diplomacy. Also with the acquiescence of successive prime ministers, Grey was able to follow a policy of seeking friendship with Russia which the Liberal backbenchers would have rejected had they known about it at the time.

Nevertheless, Grey faced numerous difficulties. One problem was that reaching an agreement depended upon Tsar Nicholas II taking a personal interest in the outcome.

Military considerations. Colonel William Robertson, later the Chief of the Imperial General Staff, submitted a report to Grey in March 1906 which argued that no concessions should be made to Russia in Persia because of the overall strategic balance. Robertson actually argued that if Russia gave up its interests in Persia, Britain could support Russia in Asiatic Turkey. Robertson was effectively urging Britain to offer Russia support in the Balkans in return for British control over Persia. In a telling assessment of how Robertson saw the future, he wrote that Germany would not like an agreement between Britain and Russia but that 'Germany's avowed aims and ambitions are such that they seem bound, if persisted in, to bring her into collision with us sooner or later'. Grey and Robertson shared a belief that conflict with Germany was likely to come and, although they differed on the offer to be made, they could both see that reaching an understanding with Russia was therefore necessary. Grey was happy to reach an agreement with Russia and the Russians met only with hostility from Germany and Austria. The Anglo-Russian relationship lacked warmth, but it offered comfort in an increasingly tense world.

Russian willingness. The Russians sounded out the Germans about the potential agreement with Britain over the loan, and no objections were raised. The Russian Foreign Minister A. P. Izvolsky was seeking to balance Russia's relations with the other powers: he hoped that Germany would accept Britain and Russia pledging to maintain the status quo in the Persian Gulf. Without informing Britain and France, Izvolsky then offered Germany a pact guaranteeing the status quo in the Baltic. Izvolsky's policy made sense in the context of Russia's weakness immediately after the Japanese defeat and the attempted revolution of 1905 but it ignored one fundamental fact: the Franco-Russian Alliance of 1894. Germany could never feel secure so long as it had to plan for a two-front war.

Russia and Germany. The Russians had hoped that it would be possible to secure British support for opening up the Dardanelles to Russian warships. However, even Sir Edward Grey was unwilling to alter British policy in this area and so the Russians were disappointed. Subsequently Izvolsky lost his job as foreign minister (in 1910), after a public outcry over his dealings with Austria over Bosnia-Herzegovina. British support for Russia had not been forthcoming but the subsequent German support for Austria on the Bosnia-Herzegovina question effectively destroyed any possibility of any sort of future Russo-German agreement.

Primacy of Europe. When the Anglo-Russian Entente was made in 1907 it was bitterly attacked by Lord Curzon, the former **Viceroy of India**, who was concerned about concessions over India's border with Tibet. Charmley argues that Lord Curzon failed to recognise that Grey was not viewing the matter from the Viceroy of India's position but rather with regard to Europe. Whilst Charmley, in *Splendid Isolation* (1999), may criticise Grey's Eurocentric view because it was ultimately to lead to war in 1914, it is important to remember that the Liberals came to office in 1905 just when the German naval threat was becoming clear. Grey's arrival at the Foreign Office thereby marked the beginning of a period when greater importance was attached to Britain's position in Europe.

KEY TERM

Viceroy of India
The man responsible for governing India. A political appointment usually given to a rich but not very ambitious politician since it involved being away from London.

TO WHAT EXTENT WAS AN ANGLO-FRENCH MILITARY ALLIANCE THE PRODUCT OF DECISIONS MADE BEFORE 1905?

Charmley on Grey. In Chapter 20 of *Splendid Isolation* (1999) John Charmley takes aim at the historical reputation of Sir Edward Grey. Charmley succinctly argues that it was Grey's accession to the Foreign Office that turned the Anglo-French conversations of Lord Lansdowne, his predecessor, into the informal military commitments which led Britain into war in 1914. As a result of Charmley's knowledge, and skill in expressing it, it would be easy to load Sir Edward Grey into the **tumbrel** and despatch him to the guillotine of history. Niall Ferguson, too, in *The Pity of War* (2000), sees Sir Edward Grey as pushing Britain into an unwritten commitment to the French despite opposition in the cabinet. This view is, however, too simplistic: decisions reached before 1905 had major consequences which were not always acknowledged by those who had made them.

KEY TERM

Tumbrel The name of a type of cart commonly used to take prisoners to the guillotine during the French Revolution.

Sir John Fisher. As early as 1901, the British naval commander in the Mediterranean was writing that 'we must reconsider the standard of our naval strength in view of the immense development of the German Navy'. The author of these comments was Vice Admiral Sir John Fisher who was to play a key role in developing Britain's response to this new threat. Fisher's ruthless and impersonal drive to improve the efficiency of the Mediterranean Fleet was to be followed by an equally uncompromising approach to the problem of Germany. He was also jealous of the First Sea Lord, Lord Kerr, who was roughly the same age as Fisher and therefore seemed to block Fisher's chances of further promotion.

In correspondence, Fisher indulged in bitter anti-Catholic invective against Kerr, which suggests that Fisher may have had a tendency to see things in unduly apocalyptic terms. For example, he kept referring to the forthcoming naval battle with the Germans as 'Armageddon', the biblical name for the final battle between good and evil. Lord Selborne, as First Lord of the Admiralty, was nevertheless prepared to appoint Fisher as Second Sea Lord in 1902 when his tour as Commander-in-Chief, Mediterranean, was due to end. Selborne wrote to Fisher making it clear that his appointment did not carry the promise of future promotion as First Sea Lord, and that details of any differences between him and Selborne must not reach the press. However, Fisher was by this time describing himself as 'an enthusiastic advocate for friendship and alliance with France' and the Conservative government was happy to appoint such a Second Sea Lord because of the need to counter the growth of the German navy.

Portsmouth. Fisher's time as Second Sea Lord lasted only until 31 August 1903, however, when he was appointed Commander-in-Chief,

Portsmouth, which was widely regarded as a stepping stone to the post of First Sea Lord. His time as Second Sea Lord had been very controversial, as he had pushed reforms for officer training which would give greater opportunity to engineers. These ideas, and an attempt to widen the social base of the naval officer corps, had made him very unpopular with many senior officers who were too old to serve at sea. However, his patrons included King Edward VII and the Prime Minister, Arthur Balfour, so he went to Portsmouth rather than into retirement. He was even appointed to serve on the 1903 Committee on the reorganisation of the army, the famous Esher Committee. Even when it would have been politically possible to drop Fisher, the Conservative government therefore chose to promote him.

Meeting the German threat. In May 1904, Fisher became First Sea Lord, despite his shortcomings, and was thus responsible for the operational planning and deployment of the Royal Navy. He began to alter the strategic redistribution of the Royal Navy to match the view that the threat came from Germany. During 1905, Fisher withdrew four new battleships from the Mediterranean Fleet and ordered the Mediterranean Fleet to prepare to fight a war alongside, rather than against, the French. Benefiting from the alliance already signed with Japan in 1902, he was also able to withdraw five battleships from the China station. Fisher concentrated his resources in a new Channel fleet, designed to meet the threat from Germany, and an Atlantic fleet, which could sail north from Gibraltar to reinforce the Channel fleet if required. Therefore a fundamental reorientation of British defence policy had taken place before the Conservative government left office.

Dreadnought. Although the Liberal government was in office by the time *Dreadnought* was launched on 10 February 1906, it had been built in record time. This was partly because the Conservative Prime Minister, Balfour, had guaranteed to Fisher that he would ensure that the **naval estimates** were approved by the House of Commons in 1905. After 1905 Grey deepened the alliance with France because the Royal Navy could not afford enough Dreadnoughts to maintain the two-power standard. However, the fundamental decision to build the first *Dreadnought,* and therefore to make the existing battle fleet obsolete, was taken by the Conservative government. It would be wrong to suggest that the Conservative government would have retained the two-power standard: Fisher's estimates for 1905 were £3.5 million less than those for 1904. However, the decision to build the *Dreadnought,* following on from the earlier redeployment of the navy, completed a fundamental redirection of British policy before the Liberals took office.

KEY TERM

Naval estimates
Each year the government had to seek parliamentary approval for the money to be spent on each of the armed services. The amount to be spent on the navy was known as the naval estimates.

IN WHAT WAYS DID THE NATURE OF THE ANGLO-FRENCH ENTENTE CHANGE AFTER 1905?

Sir Edward Grey. Grey, Foreign Secretary from 1905, favoured a closer understanding with France and therefore gave greater meaning to the Entente Cordiale which had been initiated in 1904. The difference seems, however, to be more of perception than of substance. For example, the 1902 Commons debate about the Anglo-Japanese alliance reveals the difficulty many had in recognising the changing reality of the balance of power. Only Grey accepted the need to seek an alliance; the other speakers felt it was useful but would not prove necessary. Grey was prepared to accept that Britain could no longer rely solely upon its own powers, others accepted the alliance with Japan without accepting the implications.

Germany. It is reasonable to argue that Grey's concerns about the rise of Germany were self-fulfilling: fear of Germany led to steps that increased Germany's fear of encirclement. However, the fundamental point remains that Tirpitz's plan to create a vast battle fleet was designed to challenge Britain. Politicians from both sides of the Commons wished to meet that threat, but some were more prepared to acknowledge the direction in which retaliation inevitably led. Grey recognised that the price of French naval support was an expeditionary force; others preferred to assume that the French would just be happy to oblige, even though international relations have never worked in that way.

The United States. In *Sir Edward Grey* (1971) by Keith Robbins, the author believes that Grey saw the United States as both the coming power and a future friend. Lord Salisbury had already found during the Venezuela dispute that the United States was determined to resist further European colonial influence in the western hemisphere. However, during the early 1900s the United States was only just beginning to absorb its first **imperial gains**. For strategic reasons the construction of the Panama Canal was its first priority in the years leading up to the First World War. Therefore Grey's diplomacy had to focus on European realities rather than New World potentialities, as his Conservative predecessors had done.

CONCLUSION

Because the First World War ended with the British Empire standing in a much weaker position than before 1914, it is tempting to argue that Grey's 'secret' diplomacy was ruinous to Britain. However, it seems that his arrival in the Foreign Office represents continuity rather than a dramatic change from the policies of his predecessors. Britain's relationship with France and Russia improved during the period after

A British cartoon of 1905 depicting the 'Entente Cordiale', with Germany lurking in the background.

1905 since the Conservative ministers who had dominated foreign policy before 1905 gradually came to realise that Britain needed a closer relationship with other European powers. Grey saw the need to offer something tangible to the French and that an entente with Russia would help Britain defend its position in Europe. The latter decision is closer to being Grey's unique contribution. It may be that the British Empire would have lasted longer if Britain had decided to share its status with Germany and forged an Anglo-German–Japanese alliance against the US, but that would have necessitated an entirely different perspective on world affairs. If Grey forged the alliances which took Britain to war, then it can be argued that the irons were already in the fire when he took office. If he is to travel in the tumbrel he should have plenty of companions on the journey!

SECTION 4

Why did Britain go to war in 1914?

Introduction

Postcards produced during the First World War included those emblazoned with the injunction 'Remember Belgium'. These cards sought to portray Britain as having gone to war to defend the right of small, neutral Belgium to be free from German domination. This section explores the wider issues behind the decision of Great Britain to declare war on the German Empire on 4 August 1914.

Key themes.

- The importance of the Irish Question in assessing British entry into the First World War.
- Lloyd George's decision to support war was crucial in enabling Asquith to lead the cabinet and the country into war.
- Grey's policy of supporting France against Germany ultimately led Britain into an undeclared alliance with France.
- British mobilisation plans assumed Germany was the enemy.
- The British cabinet system tended to allow a few key men to decide Britain's policy.
- Belgium was the cloak used to obscure the reality of British policy.

Historiography. In his memoirs, Lloyd George held that Sir Edward Grey, the Foreign Secretary, was one of the men guilty of leading Britain into the First World War. In *Asquith* (1985) by Stephen Koss, the author argued that Asquith (who was prime minister when Britain entered the war) was mainly influenced in his decision to go to war by the balance of power in Europe. Koss also argued that the Conservative pledge of support for the government had a greater impact upon Asquith than he was ever prepared to admit. Asquith's reticence in this area may be ascribed to the divisions in the Liberal cabinet; after the reality of the First World War became known Asquith would hardly wish to emphasise his own key role in carrying a divided cabinet into war. Niall Ferguson, in *The Pity of War* (2000), lays stress upon the divisions within the cabinet and the convenience of the issue of Belgium for those who supported war. The likelihood of the Conservatives winning the next general election is agreed upon by Koss and G. L. Bernstein (in *Liberalism and Liberal Politics in Edwardian England*, 1986) even though they are approaching the issue from different points of enquiry. Thus it was a divided and electorally insecure government that led Britain into war in 1914.

DID BRITAIN GO TO WAR TO AVOID A CIVIL WAR OVER ULSTER?

It has been argued, notably by V. R. Berghahn (*Germany and the approach of War in 1914*, 1973), that the domestic situation in Germany played a key role in the German government's deliberations. It is appropriate to ask similar questions of the British government. Since the passing of the Parliament Act in 1911, the Liberal government had faced a growing crisis in Ireland, and in particular over the future of the province of Ulster. Until the passing of the Parliament Act, those against Home Rule were able to rely upon the House of Lords to prevent any major constitutional change. The signing of the Covenant in 1912 (see page 42) showed the depth of hostility to Home Rule in some parts of Ulster.

The Curragh Mutiny. The Liberal government faced a major problem in implementing the Home Rule Bill, which was scheduled to receive the royal assent in August 1914. The Curragh mutiny of spring 1914 had shown that some of the British army was willing to stand back and allow Ulster's Unionists, led by **Edward Carson** and **James Craig**, to defy Parliament in the name of the Crown. When officers at the Curragh had also threatened to resign their commissions if ordered to Ulster to suppress the Unionists, the government had lost its nerve and had not known how to act. Conservative leader Andrew Bonar Law's response was to incite insurrection by saying that he could not envisage that his party would not back the Unionists. However, King George V had backed the Liberal government over the Parliament Bill, so the Unionists could not be certain how the King would react to an insurrection in his name.

In the summer of 1914 the crisis was so serious that King George V called a conference at Buckingham Palace, which met from 21 to 26 July. Representatives of all parties, British and Irish, were summoned to discuss the problem of Irish government. Asquith, Carson and **John Redmond** could not agree about excluding Ulster from Home Rule and the conference broke down with no agreement. The conference also happened to coincide with the Austrian ultimatum to Serbia on 23 July, and Austria's declaration of war on Serbia on 25 July. Ultimately, the declaration of war in Europe was to eclipse the Irish problem.

Parallels with Germany. James Joll has pointed out, in *The Origins of the First World War* (1992), that the German upper classes feared social revolution in 1914. This fear arose from the rise of the Socialists (SPD) to be the largest party and their ability to force the introduction of new taxes on the wealthy to pay for armaments. In Britain, the House of Lords had maintained power since non-money bills still had to pass both Houses of Parliament. The gradual extension of the franchise in 1832, 1867 and

Edward Carson (1854–1935) Irish politician and lawyer, elected to the British Parliament (1892). Carson opposed Home Rule for Ireland and organised military resistance in Ulster in 1912. He served as attorney general (1915) in Asquith's government and as First Lord of the Admiralty (1916–7) and member of Lloyd George's war cabinet (1917–8).

James Craig (1871–1940) Irish statesman who worked with Edward Carson to oppose Home Rule. In 1921 he became prime minister of the newly established government of Northern Ireland, a position he held until his death.

John Redmond (1856–1918) Irish Nationalist leader, elected to Parliament as a Home Rule member in 1881 and chosen as chairman of the combined Irish party in 1900. He gradually gained the leadership as well as the chairmanship of the Irish party. He turned down a cabinet post in the coalition government of 1915.

1884–5 had not impinged upon this power of the Lords, but removing their ultimate veto on bills via the 1911 Parliament Act destabilised their power and status. Just as in Germany, the war thus offered the British aristocracy the opportunity to unify the country in the face of an external enemy. The Ulster crisis might have offered the same opportunity, but the competitive party system in Britain meant that at this time the parties had progressively to rely on Irish votes in the House of Commons to gain a majority vote. The political battle lines between Conservatives and Liberals had been drawn in 1885–6 in response to Gladstone's first Home Rule Bill, and the growing tension in Ulster only confirmed how divisive this issue was. Lord Salisbury united the Conservative Party by opposing Home Rule, an issue on which the Liberals were divided.

The electoral imperative. The Irish Nationalists had largely replaced Liberals in Irish seats. Though agreeing on the issue of Home Rule, in the face of growing Conservative success in southern England, future Liberal governments would need Irish Nationalist votes in order to have an overall majority in the House of Commons. Ironically, if a Liberal government required Irish Nationalist support, there would be no such support in Parliament once Home Rule was implemented. The passing of a Home Rule Bill in 1914 would also mean that the Liberals would find resistance in Ulster dominating the run-up to the general election due by 1915. In comparison, the risks posed by a European war might have seemed electorally attractive. The cabinet were surprised at Lord Kitchener's pessimism about how long the war might last, but his advice was only available when he was invited to join the government on 5 August 1914, the day after war was declared. Indeed, the first electoral benefits came even before war was declared, when a party truce was declared on 30 July. This truce was extended on 28 August 1914 when the Conservative, Liberal and Labour Whips (party managers in the House of Commons) formally agreed that they would not oppose each other at by-elections during the war. In return the Conservatives had been assured that the government would take no further steps to implement Irish Home Rule or **Welsh Disestablishment**. Both bills had passed the Commons, so a future Conservative victory would be able to reverse the legislation before it was put into effect. In Britain bills need to be passed by both Houses of Parliament (Commons and Lords); as the Conservatives already controlled the Lords, control of the Commons would enable them to quickly reverse these policies.

Larne and Unionist rebels. When the King hosted an all-party conference on Ireland in July 1914 there was a real possibility, if no solution could be found, that Ireland would erupt into civil war. The Home Rule Bill would pass, but discussion now centred upon the Amending Bill, designed to diffuse armed resistance in Ulster by exempting some parts of the province from Home Rule. The issues therefore lay in the detail of

KEY TERM

Welsh Disestablishment
The Church of England had ceased to be the established (official) church in Ireland in 1869. Many Liberal voters in Wales belonged to independent Protestant churches and wanted the Church of England to lose its official status in Wales.

"WE WON'T HAVE HOME RULE"

"ULSTER WILL FIGHT

CAPTAIN CRAIG, M.P.

AND ULSTER WILL BE RIGHT."

A Unionist poster of 1912.

KEY PEOPLE

Lord Milner
Highly successful High Commissioner in South Africa up to 1905, who became a devoted Unionist. As a leading Conservative MP he became a member of the War Cabinet.

Sir Henry Wilson
Anglo-Irish Unionist who was also Director of Military Operations, War Office. It was his role to oversee the British Army's plans to implement Home Rule on an independent Ulster, but clearly the government could not rely on him to carry out such an order. He was assassinated in 1922 by Irish Nationalists.

Andrew Bonar Law (1858–1923)
Succeeded Arthur Balfour as leader of the Conservative Party in 1911 and fiercely opposed Home Rule. He became Prime Minister in 1922 but resigned through ill health the following year.

how much of Ulster would be exempted and for how long. The Nationalists were in favour of exempting as little as possible for as short a time as possible; the Unionists were divided, with Edward Carson concerned about the southern Unionists, whilst James Craig wanted the permanent exclusion of at least part of the province of Ulster.

In April 1914, 30,000 rifles and 3 million rounds of ammunition had been landed by the Ulster Unionists at Larne, north of Belfast Lough, to reinforce the Ulster Volunteer Force, which was pledged to resist Home Rule; amongst those on the quayside was James Craig. On 29 July 1914, Craig wrote to Carson that everything was ready and that they were 'in a very strong position' for active resistance. Three days later the Nationalists landed a consignment of rifles in Dublin. **Lord Milner** urged the Unionists to carry out their coup immediately, and informed them that he had spoken to **Sir Henry Wilson** who had given his opinion that the army would not march against a rebel Unionist government. This view was also reflected by Asquith's declaration that Ulster would not be coerced. It was in this context – on the brink of civil war – that Asquith received **Andrew Bonar Law**'s offer to delay any future decision on partition until after the current international crisis. Bonar Law thereby avoided a Unionist split and Asquith avoided a civil war. If Asquith

KEY PERSON

Venetia Stanley
Though already married, Asquith had fallen in love with Venetia, some 35 years his junior, and his frequent letters to her were politically indiscreet; some were written during cabinet meetings.

KEY TERM

'Orange Card'
Term used to describe how Lord Randolph Churchill had used anti-Catholic and anti-Irish feeling to gain votes for the Conservatives.

ordered the British army to go to France, he would not need to concern himself with what might follow an order to march to Belfast.

Winston Churchill. Asquith noted in his letters to **Venetia Stanley** that Churchill saw the possibility of war as a relief from the Irish Question. Winston Churchill was in a difficult position. His father had played the **'Orange Card'** in the 1880s, and more recently, his family's ancestral home, Blenheim Palace, had been used for a major Unionist rally in July 1912 (although he had had nothing to do with it). As First Lord of the Admiralty he would have a major role in a war but, because his family were so pro-Unionist, would probably have to resign if fighting broke out in Ulster. Churchill's decision to keep the fleet at readiness was strategically sound and helped Grey to move the cabinet towards opposing Germany; it also suited Churchill's political career.

WHO DECIDED BRITAIN SHOULD GO TO WAR?

Cabinet government. The British system of government has the cabinet at its apex: ultimately all policy decisions have to be determined by the cabinet. In the modern era the cabinet system has spawned a pyramid of committees to help it deal with the volume of decisions which have to be reached. However, in 1914 the whole cabinet was the decision forum. Traditionally, no votes are taken in cabinet but rather the Prime Minister 'counts the voices'. Since 'silence equals agreement' the Prime Minister has to consider the number and importance of those opposed to a policy. The Prime Minister is often described as 'first among equals' to show that he or she is the leader but draws power from the cabinet as a whole. However, there is a hierarchy within the cabinet. The three great officers of state (apart from the Prime Minister), are the Foreign Secretary, the Chancellor of the Exchequer and the Home Secretary. In any normal analysis of cabinet decision-making any issue on which these four key players are agreed will be carried in cabinet.

Lloyd George. Lloyd George was Chancellor of the Exchequer, which was arguably, in 1914, the third most senior post in the government. He had played a key role in carrying out the social reforms of the government through the 'People's Budget' of 1909. In the great struggle over the House of Lords he had further distinguished himself, taking a leading role against the Conservative majority. Asquith had then confided in Lloyd George during the long negotiations to resolve the details of the Home Rule Bill. Lloyd George's decision to back Asquith over war meant that Asquith now had the support of all the key figures in the cabinet. Lloyd George was also to become Asquith's link to the 'peace' group within the cabinet and the Liberal Party as a whole.

At the cabinet meeting on 1 August, Lloyd George held to a middle position: wanting peace but not supporting those who wanted Britain to declare peace at any price. Lloyd George then leant towards the peace party at the cabinet meeting on Sunday 2 August, when the cabinet decided to assure France that Britain would not allow the German fleet to use the English Channel as a base for hostile operations. This was important for France, not only because the German navy could have shelled France's coast but also because any British Expeditionary Force would have to cross the Channel. Denying the Germans domination of the Channel was thus a common interest of Britain and France; what concerned the pacifists in the cabinet was that it pushed Britain closer to war with Germany. Despite his apparent unhappiness at the outcome of the cabinet decision on 2 August, Lloyd George did not join several of his colleagues in tendering their resignations when the cabinet reconvened on 3 August. Stephen Koss (*Asquith*, 1985) ascribes this to news of Belgium's appeal to Britain for support in resisting German aggression. M. Pugh, however, takes a longer-term view of Lloyd George's views. In his short biography of Lloyd George, Pugh (1988) argues that by 1914 the pacifists doubted that he shared their views since he had not prevented Churchill from continuing to increase the navy estimates. Lloyd George conducted a long-term liaison with his secretary Frances Stevenson which culminated in their living together. She discounted Lloyd George's own emphasis upon the pressure of his colleagues and said:

> *My own opinion was that L.G.'s mind was really made up from the first, that he knew we would have to go in, and that the invasion of Belgium was, to be cynical, a heaven-sent excuse for supporting a declaration of war.*

The German invasion of Belgium becomes an even more cynical excuse when one considers that it was widely understood that the Germans were planning to invade Belgium. The Kaiser had asked the King of the Belgians to accept a German passage through his country at the time of the Moroccan crisis. A key to understanding Lloyd George's attitude in 1914 is to consider his political position. If Asquith were to lead the Liberals to defeat in a 1915 general election, then Asquith would have to resign as leader. Lloyd George's base lay in the radical wing of the Liberal Party; this was also the part of the party which contained the strongest pacifist sentiment. By waiting until the issue of the German invasion of Belgium was at the forefront of the discussions, Lloyd George would be able to argue that he had kept faith with the pacifist wing until a moral issue had overridden these desires. The pacifists in the Liberal Party drew strongly upon the Gladstonian tradition of a moral foreign policy; Belgium could be presented as a moral issue comparable with the Bulgarian atrocities which had drawn Gladstone out of his 'retirement' in 1876.

Lloyd George was the only senior member of the cabinet who might have led a revolt against the Prime Minister in the knowledge that he would receive the backing of the majority of the Liberal Party in Parliament. Lloyd George's decision to support Asquith was therefore crucial to Britain's decision to go to war. We might also bear in mind the manner in which Lloyd George later tempered his political alliances to benefit his career. He had every reason to blame Sir Edward Grey for Britain's entry into the war: Lloyd George wanted to be associated with Britain's eventual victory under his own leadership, and not with the failure of the Liberal government under Asquith, which had declared war and then failed to manage it properly.

Sir Edward Grey. In cabinet on 1 August 1914, Foreign Secretary Grey made it clear that he would resign if the cabinet insisted upon a policy of non-intervention in all circumstances. As a senior member of the government this could have posed a major blow to Asquith, and Grey maintained his position despite the weight of Liberal backbench opinion being against him. Amongst the Liberal press only the *Westminster Gazette* favoured intervention; general Liberal opinion was summed up by the *Manchester Guardian* newspaper which included a leader column on 31 July attacking the idea that England 'behind her back' had been committed to the 'ruinous madness' in a 'wicked gamble of a war'. If anyone could be accused of committing England to a war 'behind her back' then it was Sir Edward Grey, who had been Foreign Secretary since 1906 and, crucially, extended the military staff talks which Lord Lansdowne, his predecessor, had begun with the French in 1905. The details of these talks had remained secret from the bulk of the cabinet until the Algeciras crisis in 1911 (see Section 3) had led to a strategic review in 1912. Only then did most of the cabinet find out how far planning had gone towards sending an expeditionary force to France.

Secrecy. Keith Robbins (*Sir Edward Grey*, 1971) stresses that Grey began his office by confirming that the staff talks should continue and did not inform the Prime Minister about them. Grey's subsequent report to the Prime Minister (Sir Henry Campbell-Bannerman, 1906–8) about his conversation with the French Ambassador also omitted any reference to the continuing military talks. According to Robbins, Grey was clearly more in favour of a deeper understanding with France than Lord Lansdowne. The debate over the navy estimates for 1907 began a process in which Grey viewed friendship with France as the corollary of a limited defence budget. In choosing to build three Dreadnoughts in 1907, the cabinet effectively abandoned the two-power standard. To reduce the naval building programme to a level that would allow the Liberals to spend money on social reforms such as unemployment insurance, Grey concluded that France had to be an ally. The French Ambassador, Paul Cambon, had made it clear to Grey that British neutrality was an insufficient sign of friendship. Grey then asked R. B. Haldane at the War

Office what Britain would do if Germany invaded Belgium. The eerie prescience of this request underlines the point made about Lloyd George that Germany's plans were widely anticipated.

When, in January 1906, Campbell-Bannerman was told about the secret military talks he decided it was not necessary to inform the rest of the cabinet. Grey, Campbell-Bannerman and Haldane, the Secretary for War, then continued to develop this vital military policy in secret until Asquith replaced Campbell-Bannerman. It was this deliberate policy of friendship with France which helped to limit British options in later years. As James Joll astutely argues, in *The Origins of the First World War* (1992), each set of decisions circumscribed the options available later. Grey pushed Britain towards France when Britain faced a growing naval threat from Germany. After 1912, as Germany switched expenditure to the army, the balance of need swung towards the French. In the event of war with Germany, France could hardly afford to add Britain to its enemies. However, Grey did not use this alteration in the balance of power to make it clear that Britain would not be obliged to support France's ally Russia. Grey's concerns with the rise of Germany thus effectively locked Britain into an unwritten alliance with France.

The role of Haldane. As the international crisis deepened on 28 July 1914, Asquith sat up late discussing the situation with Grey and Haldane (by now Viscount Haldane). The British army remembers Haldane as a reformer. Whilst **Haldane's reforms** were designed to improve the army they also centred upon the concept of having an expeditionary force which was ready to aid France. The creation of a territorial army was thereby designed to ensure a reserve of men capable of undertaking home defence in the event of a British Expeditionary Force being despatched to the continent. The staff talks centred upon the BEF arriving on the left flank of the French army, and therefore helping to guard it against a German attack via Belgium. The French desire to be seen to respect Belgian neutrality appears to have prevented any consideration of Britain informing Germany that, in the event of Germany invading Belgium, then Britain would send troops to aid Belgium. Given the tight timetable in the Schlieffen Plan this might have added weight to British warnings to Germany. By 1914, Britain's plans were almost as inflexible as Germany's. It was hard for the cabinet to demand fresh thinking in 1914; the time for that was 1912 but the opportunity had not been taken.

The lessons of history. As the cabinet debated over the two days of 1 and 2 August 1914, its members would have been aware of Britain's recent history. Although there had been no general war between the European powers between 1815 and 1914 there had been a number of other wars. The most recent of these was the Franco-Prussian war in 1870–1. Britain had not intervened in that war and when it was rapidly won by Prussia,

The Haldane reforms In 1908 Lord Haldane reorganised the British army to create an expeditionary force ready to intervene in Europe if war was declared. This force of 100,000 men was based around the forces stationed at Aldershot. He also created a territorial army for home defence whilst the expeditionary force was abroad.

KEY EVENT

The decision to declare war In protest at the decisions tentatively reached at the Cabinet meeting on 1 August 1914 to declare war in response to the Belgian situation, Viscount Morley of Blackburn, the Lord President of the Council, and John Burns, President of the Board of Trade, tendered their resignations. They opposed war. Asquith believed their views were reflected in the *Manchester Guardian*'s view that 'England had been committed, behind her back, to the ruinous madness of a share in a wicked gamble of a war between two militant leagues on the continent'.

Britain found itself facing a new balance of power in Europe. However, though Gladstone's Liberal government had not intervened in 1870, it had had little reason to do so. In 1914 there was the added dimension of the German naval threat. Nevertheless, it is important to remember that Britain had a history of non-intervention so **the decision to intervene** was not automatic. It also had no obligation to do so until Belgium was invaded.

CONCLUSION

War in August 1914 saved the Liberal government from the prospect of presiding over the descent into civil war in Ireland; a situation in which the loyalty of the armed services was uncertain. The British government opted for war against Germany in 1914 because it had been leaning towards France since 1906. After 1908 the British army had been reorganised with a view to being able to send an expeditionary force to the continent. The naval race with Germany only served to highlight the growing fear that Germany was now the biggest threat to Britain. These plans were kept secret from the rest of the cabinet until 1912 by which time there was no one senior enough to question the direction policy had taken. Lloyd George could have split the cabinet and led a 'peace' party, but by 1914 he was already convinced that British involvement was inevitable if war came. The German invasion of Belgium enabled Britain to clothe its desire to act as a great power in the shroud of righteousness. Grey's 1906 vision of the future had proved, to a degree, to be self-fulfilling.

SECTION 5

What were Britain's foreign policy objectives at Versailles?

Key themes

- Britain wanted to remain the world's premier naval power.
- Britain sought to maintain Belgian independence.
- Britain would not offer France any reassurance when the Treaty of Versailles was not ratified by the United States and this contributed to hardening French demands for the fulfilment of the reparations provisions of the treaty.
- Britain wanted to maintain its pre-war aim of preventing Russia from reaching the Mediterranean.
- Britain wanted to improve its position in the Middle East.
- British policy was flawed in failing to support a strong France.

WERE BRITAIN'S AIMS IN 1919 CONSISTENT WITH ITS OBJECTIVES BEFORE 1914?

Naval supremacy. Britain was determined to maintain the naval supremacy in the North Sea and Western Approaches. The North Sea and the Western Approaches (the route from the Atlantic to the English Channel) were vital to Britain in maintaining its position at the centre of a worldwide trading empire. The First World War had proved this as

Representatives of the Allied powers at the Versailles Conference, 1919. From left to right: Ferdinand Foch, Georges Clemenceau, Lloyd George, Vittorio Orlando and Count Sonino.

Britain came closest to defeat in the summer of 1917 when it struggled to cope with the German submarine campaign. Therefore at Versailles the British insisted upon the surrender of the German high seas fleet. The German fleet subsequently scuttled itself at the British naval base of Scapa Flow. Thus was a real and symbolic end to the naval race that had begun in 1897 with the introduction of the first Navy Law in the Reichstag. This objective was completely consistent with British policy prior to 1914.

Freedom of the seas. When the Germans initially sought an armistice in 1918 it was on the basis of President Wilson's Fourteen Points. President Wilson had tried to give a noble image to the intervention of the United States by laying out his vision of a better post-war world. He included in his Fourteen Points the 'freedom of the seas'. Wilson was fully aware that during the First World War Britain had broken international law in the way the Royal Navy had imposed the blockade. The British had realised that modern coastal defences had made the 'close blockade' required under international law impossible to maintain whilst the alternative 'distant blockade' would be ineffective. Therefore Britain, with French assistance, had resorted to the more basic principle of 'might is right'. Britain had then extended the list of goods classified as 'contraband of war', that is goods which could be seized because they were part of the war effort. Britain was quick to realise that in a modern industrial war almost everything could be said to contribute to the war effort. Britain had therefore extended the blockade to the Netherlands in the belief that supplies were reaching Germany that way. Since the Netherlands was a neutral country this was a flagrant breach of international law, which resulted, for example, in no arrivals of cargoes of fresh fruit being recorded by the Dutch authorities in 1918.

The British could hardly reject the Fourteen Points because they included a reference to maintaining international law. However, the devastating impact of the blockade on Germany and its effectiveness in defeating Germany were evident to all. This is shown by the decision to maintain the blockade until the Germans signed the Treaty of Versailles. The British therefore chose not to attack international law publicly, but effectively undermined it. By insisting upon the neutralisation of the German high seas fleet the British were giving themselves the opportunity to repeat the situation of 1914–8 since their naval supremacy would allow them to impose another blockade under the cloak of war. Therefore it is reasonable to argue that British naval policy at Versailles was utterly consistent with its policies before 1914.

Control of the Channel coast. In 1914, Britain was concerned to avoid one major power controlling the whole of the Channel coast opposite Britain, including the key port of Ostend. This concern had been expressed in the original decision to guarantee Belgium's independence in the Treaty of London of 1839. The importance of this point is also shown in German peace discussions during the First World War, though the German 'Peace Note' of 1916 contained no specific details. The reason for the omission lay in the German General Staff's wish to retain Belgium (of which the Germans then occupied 95 per cent). The German Chancellor, Bethmann Hollweg, knew that German intentions over Belgium would lead to the peace proposals being rejected automatically, and so he was forced to keep his proposals very vague. Therefore at Versailles Britain was determined to see a strong and independent Belgium restored. In pursuing this objective Britain had the advantage that, in the last two months of the war, the British Second Army had liberated most of Belgium.

Strengthening Belgium. Belgium had proved to be a valuable if frail ally in 1914. In 1919, Belgium sought to capitalise upon its decision to defy Germany. E. H. Kossman (*The Low Countries 1780–1940*, 1978) describes how the Belgian government sought to extend Belgian territory in both Africa and Europe. The Belgians may have even believed that they could obtain Luxembourg. However, this clashed with French ambitions and Britain showed no interest. Belgium also wanted to gain territory at the expense of neutral Holland. Although Britain was angered by the Dutch decision to allow some German troops to retreat via Limburg and therefore avoid capture, it was uninterested in these schemes. The Belgians, too, were divided since it would disturb the linguistic and religious balance of the country. The Belgians had hoped to control all of the Scheldt but Britain followed its traditional policy of preferring to see the river divided along its length.

Eupen and Malmédy. Because of the major territorial changes made in 1919, the fate of Eupen and Malmédy has drawn little comment from historians. The raw materials they brought to Belgium are seen as small compensation for the massive destruction wrought by the German occupation. However, they also have a wider significance. They lie directly on the path that the German armies had used to enter Belgium in 1914. In order to avoid violating neutral Holland the original Schlieffen Plan had been modified to deliver the vital German 'right hook' through Belgium where a sufficiently dense railway network existed to take the enormous pressure of such traffic. The British decision to support the transfer of these small areas at Versailles was a further attempt to strengthen Belgium by denying Germany some of the military assembly areas it possessed in 1914. Britain was keen to maintain Belgian independence through strategic border adjustments, but not to dilute the Belgian state with Dutch people whose neutrality was seen as having leaned towards Germany. There was nothing inconsistent here with British foreign policy before 1914.

DID BRITAIN ACTIVELY SEEK TO LIMIT FRENCH POWER AT VERSAILLES?

The Rhineland. France sought to capitalise upon anti-Bolshevik feelings in the Rhineland. These had been stirred up by news of the revolution in Berlin, which had accompanied the departure of the Kaiser. The advent of a socialist government in Berlin and the attempted communist rising in 1919 seemed to the French to illustrate how little the Rhineland had in common with the rest of Prussia. The French commander, General Fayolle, encouraged his officers to conduct a discreet propaganda campaign and from January 1919 local industrialists were offered economic incentives to look towards France for the future. The French were trying to reverse the decision made in 1815 to give the Rhineland to Prussia as its reward for success at the Battle of Waterloo (1815). At that time Britain had wanted to curb any resurgence of French military ambitions by giving the Rhineland to Prussia. In 1919 the British decided not to reverse this decision.

The French Prime Minister, Georges Clemenceau, tried to exclude President Wilson from the peace conference, fearing an Anglo-Saxon bloc. Anthony Adamthwaite in *Grandeur and Misery* (1995) describes graphically how Lloyd George and Clemenceau clashed over the armistice from the evening of its signature onwards. His source is Clemenceau, which may lend some doubt as to whether the words exchanged were as direct as stated. Nevertheless, Adamthwaite argues cogently that the revival of French ambitions immediately led to Britain focusing upon the balance of power in Europe. Britain had no desire to see any power dominate Europe. The problem for France was that the different military traditions of the two countries would inevitably lead it in an opposite direction to its staunchest wartime ally.

KEY TERM

Mandates The territories administered by the great powers on behalf of the League of Nations. The mandated territories were from the empires of the defeated powers, for example, from the Turkish Empire. France received Syria and Britain Iraq.

Demobilisation. Clemenceau stressed to the other leaders that demobilisation would be putting them under pressure to make decisions and to conclude peace. However, demobilisation would mean different things to Britain and France. Both countries would scale their forces down from their wartime levels. However, for Britain that meant a return to a small professional army whose primary role was to police the empire; a role that would now be increased by the acquisition of League of Nations' **mandates**. Britain would have to maintain an army of occupation that would further stretch the resources of its small army. France, even after demobilisation, would retain an army of approximately 900,000 men (based upon conscription) and only be opposed by a German force restricted to 100,000 men bereft of tanks and aeroplanes. From a traditional British perspective this left the balance of power on the continent distinctly unequal. The British found it difficult therefore to understand why the French were so neurotic. This feeling is typified by

Chancellor of the Exchequer Austen Chamberlain's remark in January 1920 that the French 'lived in a nightmare horror of the Germans'. The reality, perceived by more Frenchmen than cared to admit it, was that France had not been able to defeat Germany alone and that next time it would not have Russian support. By refusing to recognise the inevitable nervousness of France, the British appeared to the French to be undermining them even when there was no clear intention to do so.

Reparations. A major area of debate after the Versailles conference centred on how much Germany should pay. During the conference itself both Britain and France accepted the concept of German guilt. Having won the 1918 general election with slogans such as 'Hang the Kaiser', Lloyd George had little reason to disagree with the notorious 'war guilt' clause. However, as John Maynard Keynes made clear in his famous *The Economic Consequences of the Peace* (1919), there was more than one way of viewing the impact of reparations. As a young Treasury economist, Keynes believed that the imposition of such massive reparations, set at £6600 million in 1921, would prevent German economic recovery. In Keynes's view the whole European economy would be damaged if German recovery were delayed. It has been assumed that his resignation from the Treasury was as a result of the British Treasury succumbing to French pressure to remove Keynes. However, part of the reason why the reparations bill rose was that Britain added the cost of pensions to widows and the disabled. France and Belgium were basing their claim upon the damage done by the Germans, for example, the mines that the Germans had destroyed during their planned withdrawal in March 1917.

Britain's argument that reparations should be set at a low figure was weakened by the fact that its share of the reparations would be very low. This was because, apart from incidents such as the bombardment of Hartlepool and air raids by Zeppelins and Gotha bombers, there had been little direct damage on Britain. As P. M. H. Bell points out in *France and Britain, 1900–40* (1996), the French were increasingly exasperated at the way in which Britain seized merchant shipping, but then felt the French were being harsh in demanding raw materials, such as coal, from Germany. The difference was that Britain had acted quickly whereas France was still claiming these reparations once the treaty had been signed. Britain was also driven by the need to offset the failure of Russia to repay its loans and by the need to repay the United States. These reasons, which were shared by France, cannot hide the fact that Britain did not act in concert with France on this issue. The failure of the United States to ratify Versailles, and therefore the lapsing of the Anglo-American guarantee, meant that by the time the reparations figure was settled France believed it to be the only stick left with which to beat Germany. Britain was not prepared to offer any alternative security, thus further encouraging French intransigence. The theme of balancing reality with idealism can also be followed by reading Margaret Macmillan's *Peacemakers* (2001).

TO WHAT EXTENT WAS BRITAIN'S POLICY IN THE MEDITERRANEAN AND THE BALKANS CONSISTENT WITH ITS POLICIES BEFORE 1914?

In discussing Versailles it is reasonable to consider the wider Versailles settlement which embraces the Treaties of St Germain, Neuilly, Trianon and Sevres. Prior to 1914, Britain's overriding objective was to prevent Russia gaining access to the eastern Mediterranean through the Dardanelles. In concluding the Versailles settlement, Britain faced less difficulty than it had before 1914 because Russia had descended into civil war and because Turkey's empire had been conquered, largely by Britain.

The Balkans. Romania, which had joined the Allied side in 1916 only to be rapidly overrun by Germany, was rewarded by a large increase in territory. Under the Treaty of Trianon (4 June 1920) Hungary was forced to cede Transylvania to Romania. This created a large Romania, which had also seized Bessarabia from Russia. The British were happy with the larger Romania because it created a large buffer state between Russia and the Straits. Also, the Treaty of Neuilly (24 November 1919) had awarded Greece territory at the expense of Bulgaria, which had allied itself with Germany. Neither Bulgaria nor Romania would permit Russia to move through their territory to the Straits. Thus Russian expansion from the eastern Mediterranean was brought to a halt.

Italy. Prior to 1914 Britain was reluctant to see Austria extend its control of the Mediterranean coastline. At Versailles it was equally concerned not to see Italy grow in importance as a naval power. However, the creation of Yugoslavia limited Italian expansion in the Adriatic as the dramatic dispute over **Fiume** highlighted. The subsequent Italian invasion of Corfu was also reversed after sufficient financial compensation was provided. This shows that Britain was determined to maintain its dominance in the Mediterranean. The chain link to Suez formed by Gibraltar, Malta and Cyprus was thus preserved as a vital part of imperial communications and protected from neighbouring powers.

The Turkish Empire. Before 1914, Britain had had to try to prevent Russia from advancing against the weak Turkish Empire. With both Russia and Austria removed from the picture, Britain was able not only to establish strong Balkan states but also to dismember the Turkish Empire in the Middle East. Oil was making this region even more important and the British had to resolve the conflicting promises they had made.

The Sykes–Picot Agreement (1916) which promised the Arabs support and the **Balfour Declaration** (1917) in favour of the Jews are a monument to the cynicism of diplomacy, but these agreements had helped to defeat Turkey. Britain secured the mandate to run Palestine, which gave it considerable influence in this oil-rich region, but its subsequent failure, perhaps inevitable, to resolve tensions in the region led to increasing problems for Britain. Britain thereby acquired a major role in the Middle East, an inheritance poisoned by wartime promises.

WAS BRITISH FOREIGN POLICY AT VERSAILLES FUNDAMENTALLY FLAWED?

Without resorting to hindsight it is possible to see that the logic of British foreign policy at Versailles was flawed. These flaws may be seen as causing the ultimate decline of Britain since it left Britain at the mercy of the imperial ambitions of the United States. However, given the state of British finances in 1919 it had little choice.

Finance. The British government's decision to set up the Geddes Committee in 1919 to find ways of limiting government expenditure reflects the recognition at the time that Britain had been fundamentally weakened by the war. One option, therefore, was for Britain to retreat from its global status; however, basking in the glory of victory, this was unthinkable. Britain wanted to reduce the costs of government because it had been more successful in raising finance through taxation to pay for the war than its allies or opponents. During the war more people had started paying income tax, and part of the Conservative Party's electoral success after 1919 is due to their realisation that lowering taxes would therefore be popular. However, the fact that Britain wanted a cheap foreign policy did not necessitate the foreign policy it actually followed.

France. The British could have followed a cheap foreign policy and still have supported France. For the French, who had been invaded three times between 1814 and 1914, it was a basic assumption that once Germany recovered France would again be threatened. Therefore the French wanted major territorial gains and to impose heavy reparations on Germany. In such circumstances, however, the British adopted a blinkered approach, insisting that to support France would have damaged their interests. If Britain had supported French demands then France would have been the dominant power in Europe. However, instead of a British military guarantee to France, Britain opted for the imposition of restrictions on Germany, such as the forbidding of the Anschluss (even though to deny the Anschluss was to deny the very principle of self-determination which was supposed to underlie the treaty).

The Sykes–Picot Agreement of 1916 between Britain and France was to establish a homeland in Palestine for the Arabs once Turkey was defeated. This was designed to ensure the Arabs assisted in the overthrow of the Turks. This agreement also protected British and French spheres of influence in the Middle East.

The Balfour Declaration In 1917, the British cabinet minister A. J. Balfour promised that Britain would support the creation of a Jewish state in Palestine. This is viewed as a cynical ploy to please American Jews, key supporters of President Wilson's Democratic Party, at a time when Britain was hoping to see the United States declare war on Germany.

British priorities
The war had
ensured that Britain
had eliminated
Germany as an
imperial and naval
competitor.
However, the hope
of ensuring that
Germany was
peaceful was by no
means certain.

More importantly, **Britain's foreign policy** left it facing a Europe in
which there was a bitter Germany and a neurotic France. Britain would
have been in a much stronger position if it had swapped a guarantee to
France for tangible concessions to Germany. Britain traditionally
supported the weaker power on the continent against the stronger. In this
case Britain only helped Germany by ameliorating French demands. Thus
the Germans could not see why they should be grateful, whilst
Anglophobes like Marshal Pétain concluded that France could never
really rely upon Britain. Allowing Austria, shorn of its empire, to join
Germany minus the Rhineland would have moved the political centre of
Germany away from Prussia. The strong separatist movement in Bavaria,
which looked to Austria, suggests that such a strategy could have led to a
very different post-war Germany. The British negotiators also failed to
recognise that to offer a defensive guarantee to a strong France would
have been a cheap policy.

The Royal Navy. A key factor in Britain's opposing Germany by 1914
was the naval race. If Britain had decided to back France in Europe in
1919, then Britain could have devoted its limited resources to expanding
the Royal Navy. France's military superiority on the continent would not
have posed any more threat to Britain than Germany's had before 1897
when it started the naval race. A strong France backed up by the threat of
a naval blockade by Britain would also have more than balanced a
reorganised Germany after 1919, even when Germany eventually
rearmed. In such circumstances, Britain could have afforded to develop
the Royal Navy, for example by building purpose-built aircraft carriers.
However, by failing to continue to develop the Royal Navy and then
acceding to US pressure to drop its alliance with Japan, Britain ultmately
sacrificed its ability to maintain its Empire.

Monroe Doctrine
US President
Monroe had
declared in 1823
that the United
States would not
interfere in
European affairs so
long as the
European powers
did not interfere in
North or South
America (the
western
hemisphere).

The United States. In 1914 Britain had gone to war because it perceived
Germany to be threatening its status as a world power. Yet in 1919 it did
not act to stem the threat from the United States. In 1823, President
Monroe had enunciated his famous doctrine which effectively meant that
the European powers had to accept US hegemony (dominance) in the
western hemisphere. In the 1890s, Britain had lost a colonial dispute over
the border of Venezuela. The US press as well as its government had
shown then how opposed it was to the British Empire. Now in 1919 the
United States was trying to dictate the peace terms in Europe. Wilson
kept reminding his fellow leaders that he had promised a peace based
upon the Fourteen Points, yet the elections of 1918 had seen his party
defeated and so his authority was fragile.

Despite having joined the war near its end, Wilson was allowed by Lloyd
George to have a large say in the peace in order to diminish France's
dominance. Britain had to defer to US opinion because of the role US

money, supplies and men had played in the Allied victory in 1918. In 1919, Lloyd George was in the position to forge a renewed Entente with France in order to concentrate Britain's resources on meeting the challenge from the United States; blinkered by history, he chose to revert to a Palmerstonian concern with a non-existent French threat.

CONCLUSION

At Versailles, Britain could have chosen to forge a global alliance with France and Japan. Instead it decided to follow a traditional policy of counterbalancing the strongest power in Europe, which was then France. Having sown the seeds of distrust with the French, the British went on to begin the process of alienating the Japanese over the issue of racial equality. Ultimately, it proved detrimental for Britain that these allies were sacrificed for the illusion of American friendship, which was not available to sustain the British Empire.

SECTION 6

What were the reasons for and what was the extent of appeasement?

Introduction

This section is designed to deal with why and how far the policy of appeasement was followed. It therefore deals with the foreign policy of Britain and France towards Italy and Germany in the 1930s. The role of **Neville Chamberlain** himself is dealt with in Section 7.

Key themes.

- Chamberlain was sincere in his desire to avoid war and he was still following that policy in 1939.
- Chamberlain wished to avoid war because of the human cost of war and out of a desire to maintain the status of the British Empire.
- US foreign policy influenced British foreign policy.
- Appeasement was a policy which represented the lowest common denominator between the views of opposing groups – Conservative and Labour, economisers and spenders.
- The policy of appeasement eventually failed because Hitler's demands were too great.
- The level of British rearmament before 1939 was substantial.
- Britain would probably have done better to fight in 1938 over Czechoslovakia than in 1939 over Poland.

WHAT WAS APPEASEMENT?

Appeasement is the name given to the policy of the British and French governments towards Hitler and Mussolini in the 1930s. The policy involved conceding to their demands. Many British diplomats felt that Germany would not settle down unless major amendments were made to the Treaty of Versailles. However, it was expected that Germany should also make concessions as a contribution towards peace, such as guaranteeing what was left of Czechoslovakia. Both Hitler and Mussolini were unhappy with the map of Europe after the Treaty of Versailles (1919). Mussolini felt Italy had not been rewarded properly for its efforts in the First World War. He wanted to create a larger Italian empire in Africa. Hitler wanted to make Germany strong again by rearming and taking back the territory which Germany lost at Versailles. Germans populated much of the territory Hitler wanted, such as the Sudetenland (part of Czechoslovakia). It was thought that if reasonable changes were made, then Hitler and Mussolini would not push Europe into another

Neville Chamberlain (1869–1940) Son of Joseph Chamberlain. Lord Mayor of Birmingham 1915–6, he went on to become Chancellor of the Exchequer in 1923–4 in the Conservative cabinet, as well as in the National Government (1931–7). In 1937 he succeeded Stanley Baldwin as Prime Minister. He resigned in May 1940 after winning a confidence vote in the House of Commons then nonetheless saw large numbers of Conservative MPs voting against him.

war. For example, it was thought that if Austria were allowed to join with Germany then Hitler would be satisfied. However, Hitler's desire for *Lebensraum* ('living space') in the east eventually pushed Europe into war.

Historical interpretations

The subject of appeasement has always been a controversial one because it became a deep political debate. When the policy collapsed in failure in 1939–40 the career of the British Prime Minister, Neville Chamberlain, was over. Chamberlain left office in May 1940 after a bitter debate in the House of Commons. The debate included a speech from the former Prime Minister, Lloyd George, telling Neville Chamberlain that he had asked the country to make sacrifices and that the best sacrifice that he, Neville Chamberlain, could make was to resign. Even though Chamberlain won the vote it was clear that many Conservatives did not support him. Clement Attlee, the leader of the Labour Party, subsequently made it clear that his party would only join a coalition if it were headed by Winston Churchill.

Winston Churchill had been Chamberlain's greatest critic, so his arrival in 10 Downing Street seemed to confirm the view that appeasement had been a bad policy. In July 1940 Michael Foot, a young Labour politician, anonymously published a book entitled *Guilty Men*, which not only portrayed appeasement as a failure but also as one which had led to the betrayal of the Czechs at Munich in 1938.

This mood contrasted sharply with the ecstatic welcome accorded to Chamberlain on his return from the Munich Conference in 1938. Looking back today, people focus on the image of Chamberlain waving his piece of paper and promising 'Peace for our time'. However, these words were a response to the cheering crowds outside 10 Downing Street; almost 20 years on from the armistice of 1918 people were delighted that Europe had stepped back from the brink of war. The main defence of the policy followed at the Munich conference therefore came to rest upon the argument that it had bought time for Britain to prepare, and that this had ultimately enabled Britain to win the Battle of Britain in 1940.

Charmley argues in his book *Chamberlain and the Lost Peace* (1989) that appeasement was the correct policy to follow. This positive view of appeasement is not widely shared. In this section it will be argued that Britain should have fought in 1938. Charmley believes there was no need to declare war over Poland since Britain could not do anything for the Poles. This is a moral judgement that raises the question of whether Britain should have simply reached a deal with Hitler to preserve the British Empire. In the light of the **Holocaust** few like to follow appeasement to its logical conclusion and therefore appeasement is denigrated. However, even if the British Foreign Office was indifferent to the Jews, it did not know, pre-1939, what was to follow.

Key events in the history of appeasement.	June 1935	Anglo-German Naval Agreement
	Autumn 1935	No action taken by Britain to oppose Italian invasion of Abyssinia
	March 1936	No response made to Hitler remilitarising the Rhineland
	July 1936	Britain ignored the Spanish Republican government's request for aid against Fascist rebels
	March 1938	No opposition to Hitler carrying out the Anschluss with Austria
	29/30 September 1938	Czechoslovakia forced to accept the loss of the Sudetenland

WAS APPEASEMENT A REACTION TO THE FIRST WORLD WAR?

The roots of appeasement lie in a number of factors but perhaps the most important of these was the First World War. In 1914 Britain had declared war on Germany. Popular sentiment was that the war would be over before Christmas, and young men rushed to join up knowing that sporting a uniform was an advantage at the weekly dances. The grim reality of the trenches soon began to manifest itself. After 1916 the casualty lists appeared alphabetically to hide the impact on individual battalions. Every day, women dreaded the arrival of a telegraph boy bearing news of the dead or missing. By 1918 the British Empire had suffered approximately 1 million dead. Of these approximately 750,000 were from the British Isles.

A book called *Covenants with Death* was published in 1934 by the *Daily Express* newspaper. It included one map that showed the Western Front and roughly how many men had died in the various places. The *Daily Express* estimated the number of wounded at over 2 million. The social cost of the war is typified by the case of Private William Hall of Middleton in Lancashire. Returning from the war having lost an arm he faced an uncertain future. Recognising that he was unlikely to be able to provide for his fiancée, he offered her the opportunity to break off their engagement; she accepted. His solitary future would have served as a daily reminder of hopes dashed in war. Parents would hardly wish the same fate on their children.

The horror of the 'Great War' was also symbolised in 1919 by the burial of the 'Unknown Soldier'. Each country buried one unidentified soldier to symbolise those who had not returned but had no known grave. At Verdun the French had so many unidentified dead that the bones were gathered together and buried in a pit or ossuary. Lutyens's Thiepval Memorial on the Somme was unveiled in 1932 and is dedicated to those lost on the Somme, who included 73,412 men whose names are on the memorial but whose bodies have never been identified. The numerous tours to the Western Front in the 1920s and 1930s would have reinforced the desire to avoid future conflicts.

Appeasement offered Chamberlain electoral success. Local groups organised visits to the Western Front where relatives could visit the graves of their lost relatives or read their names on the huge monuments to the 'missing'. Chamberlain believed that when these relatives voted in the general election (expected in 1940) they would not wish to send another generation to be slaughtered. He therefore believed that the long-term benefits of appeasement would bring him victory at the polls. As a party leader he could not be oblivious to such considerations, and certainly Lord Halifax urged him not to form a coalition government as they returned from the airport after Chamberlain flew back from Munich.

Chamberlain's personal commitment to peace. As Chamberlain himself said in a speech at Kettering on 3 July 1938: 'In war, whichever side may call itself the victor, there are no winners, but all are losers.'

Serving as Lord Mayor of Birmingham in 1915–6, Chamberlain would have witnessed the proud battalions leaving the city and the return of only some of them, many of whom were wounded or exhausted by action. He would also have stood in front of the memorials on subsequent Armistice Days. In 1916 his wife, as Lady Mayoress, took the lead in organising the provision of comforts and amusements for wounded soldiers in local war hospitals. Therefore his belief in appeasement was based on a genuine horror of the human costs of war.

The war encouraged pacifism. In 1933 pacifists founded the Anglo-German Group. The group consisted mainly of people from the centre and left of politics and was headed by the pacifist Dr Margarete Gurtner. Amongst them was **John Wheeler-Bennett** whose memoirs, *Knaves, Fools and Heroes* (1974), includes an eyewitness account of the **Enabling Bill** debate in March 1933. His unflattering portrayal of Hitler is evidence that his desire to avoid war was not a product of any Fascist sympathies.

HOW DID THE ECONOMIC IMPACT OF THE FIRST WORLD WAR CONTRIBUTE TOWARDS APPEASEMENT?

What was the economic cost of the First World War for Britain? One simple fact to ponder is that at the end of the war Britain owed £10 for every £1 it owed in 1914. This fact alone meant that a lot more of the government's income had to be spent on paying interest on its debts, interest on the National Debt costing £349.6 million by 1920.

KEY PERSON

John Wheeler-Bennett Also the author of *Wooden Titan: Hindenburg* (1936), *Munich: Prologue to Tragedy* (1948) and *The Nemesis of Power* (1953). It was during his research for his biography of Hindenburg that he attended the session in which the Enabling Bill was passed.

KEY TERM

Enabling Bill (1933) This bill allowed Hitler to rule by decree for four years. By the time it had expired in 1937 his dictatorship was complete.

KEY TERM

Geddes Committee Officially known as the Committee on National Expenditure (1921–2). Headed by Sir Eric Geddes, this was the first major review of UK government expenditure by a body composed largely of non-parliamentarians. Nicknamed the 'Geddes Axe' by contemporary critics, the Committee recommended expenditure reductions totalling £100 million. These affected national services such as the military, police force and education.

The British government spent only £302 million in 1913. By April 1915 it was spending £436 million just on military costs alone. Military expenditure during the war is tabled in the margin.

Approximately 28 per cent of the costs of the war were met through taxation, which was better than the French or German governments achieved. However, the National Debt rose from £650 million to £6142 million by 1919. In addition to this the British government owed money to foreign creditors. The USA was owed £1037 million and Canada £91 million. Other Allied governments were owed £113 million, bringing the total for inter-governmental debt to £1241 million.

Inter-war British governments therefore had to service some £7,383 million of debt. The burden was made worse by the fact that, to attract enough money, the government had been forced to offer higher rates of interest. (The government was unable to reduce interest rates on this debt until the 1930s.) The British government also had to cope with Lenin's refusal, as leader of the Soviet Union, to pay back the £794 million that Britain had loaned to the Tsar and the Russian Provisional Government.

The decision to appoint the **Geddes Committee** after the First World War was a result of the debt burden. The Geddes Committee suggested ways in which peacetime expenditure could be cut in order to balance the budget despite the heavy interest burden. During the inter-war period the Conservative Party was committed to low taxation, and as more people paid income tax after the First World War than before, this policy was popular with the electorate. As Chancellor of the Exchequer before 1937, Chamberlain had restricted navy spending to avoid tax increases. Minimalising the need for tax increases would undoubtedly have improved Chamberlain's chances of success in the general election expected in 1940.

Faced with the rise of both Japan and Germany in the 1930s it seemed to some that appeasing Hitler was a price worth paying to avoid another costly war. Indeed, the British could only afford an empire after 1918 by sacrificing further social reforms. As Chancellor, Chamberlain had insisted on a spending limit for the armed services so that the army and navy would compete with each other for the available funds. The fact that Britain was effectively bankrupt in late 1940 shows Chamberlain was correct in anticipating the impact the war would have on British finances.

Appeasement also reflected continuing economic weakness. A further way in which the First World War damaged British government finances was the long-term damage to Britain's balance of payments. The balance of payments is a term used to express the whole country's balance between income and expenditure. Before 1914 Britain had a surplus in its trade with the rest of the world. Countries earn money from abroad through exports, which can take the form of goods (visibles) or services (invisibles).

One of the ways in which Britain made invisible earnings before 1914 was investing in foreign companies. When the foreign companies made profits and declared dividends the money was sent to Britain. Many of these British investments were in US companies. During the First World War the British government persuaded British shareholders to sell their US shares to the British government. The British government then used these shares to raise money in the United States to finance wartime purchases. After the war the effect was to reduce the flow of foreign earnings to Britain. This reduction in invisible earnings made it even more difficult to meet the costs of Britain's Empire.

The impact of the Depression. The Depression made Britain's economic situation even more difficult. Between 1929 and 1931, the Labour government, led by the pacifist Ramsay MacDonald, cut spending in order to try to balance the budget. In 1931 the new National Government abandoned the **gold standard** but still held down spending on defence whilst following a policy of reducing interest rates. The US bitterly resented the British government's decision to cut the interest rate payable on existing loans, but was forced to accept it. Ultimately, cutting interest rates stimulated consumer demand which helped to bring southern Britain out of the Depression. However, the costs of unemployment pay meant the government could not raise defence spending without raising taxes. The Labour Party also resisted rearmament since they wanted to abolish the **Means Test** which forced poor people to sell their goods before they received benefit. In financial and social terms appeasement was the preferred policy.

WAS APPEASEMENT A REFLECTION OF BRITAIN'S CHANGING INTERNATIONAL STATUS?

Another reason for appeasement was the growing reliance of Britain upon the United States. In part this was due to the way in which Britain had needed US help to win the First World War. However, it was also due to the realisation that the **British Pacific Empire** was not sustainable without US support, and that such support could not necessarily be counted upon. Supporters of appeasement in the 1930s were thus also driven by the realisation that the United States would never fight to preserve the British Empire

Washington Naval Conference. The slide towards the United States had begun in 1921 at the Washington Naval Disarmament Conference. The

KEY TERMS

Gold standard
This was a system of fixed exchange rates. It minimised inflation as countries had to restrict paper currency to the amount they could support in gold. It was suspended during the First World War. Britain led a general return to the gold standard in 1925 when Winston Churchill was Chancellor, but was forced to depart from it in 1931 due to the Depression when Neville Chamberlain was Chancellor.

Means Test This was a very controversial measure where benefit claimants were forced to sell non-essential household items to raise money before they were allowed any benefit payments.

KEY AREA

British Pacific Empire As well as New Zealand and Australia, Britain's possessions included Singapore, Hong Kong, Malaya and Burma.

US Secretary of State, Charles Evans Hughes, shocked the other powers by proposing detailed plans for each of the major powers to scrap large numbers of battleships. The British settled for parity with the United States. Under the 5: 5: 3 ratio agreed at the conference, Britain and the United States would have five capital ships for every three possessed by Japan. Japan was told this was because it was a 'one ocean' power whereas Britain and the United States were 'two ocean' powers. The growth of the United States as a naval power was thus confirmed. The British had retained the status of a 'two ocean' power but in reality lacked the means to support it. Also, by failing to support Japan the British were beginning to alienate a possible rival in Asia. More importantly, the United States was encouraging Britain to rely on it, rather than Japan, in the Asia-Pacific region.

Britain's decision to offer the Germans a naval pact in 1935 can best be explained as an attempt to restrict Germany's naval forces to a level that would not force Britain to abandon the Far East. Prior to 1914 the alliance with Japan had enabled Britain to avoid this problem. But in August 1923, the British, under pressure from the United States and Australia, formally abandoned the alliance with Japan. This was a crucial decision: a financially weaker Britain now faced the possibility of a 'two ocean' war. Admiral Lord Chatfield expressed his unhappiness with this decision. He said: 'We have weakened most gravely our imperial position.' The decision to abandon Japan for a Nine-Power Pact over China gravely weakened Britain's strategic position in the Far East by alienating Japan. The Four-Power Pact (Britain, United States, France and Japan) thus helped to achieve harmony between the powers concerning China, but did not offer any security for the British Empire.

One of the main opponents of appeasement was Winston Churchill. Churchill saw the United States as Britain's natural ally, yet in tying Britain to the United States Churchill helped speed up the decline of the Empire. The United States, reluctantly, would help to preserve British independence, but it would not fight for the British Empire, as became clear to Churchill during the war.

The balance of power. After 1919, Britain aimed to promote good relations between France and Germany as a means of securing peace and stability in Europe. In world terms, the United States faced only Britain as a rival. The US persuaded Australia and New Zealand to back it when putting pressure on Britain to drop the Japanese alliance. With Britain's financial weakness, only the United States could offer these two Dominions security from Japanese expansion and thereby effectively exploited the situation. The United States also cancelled part of France's debt in 1926 but no part of the British debt was written off. During the Great Depression, President Hoover offered to cancel some British debt but only in return for British overseas possessions. Appeasement can therefore be seen as a result of errors made in the 1920s which reflected Britain's declining position while America's grew.

WAS APPEASEMENT AN ANTI-SOVIET POLICY?

Since appeasement was a policy pursued largely by Conservative politicians it could be seen as a reflection of Conservative sympathies with the Fascist powers. In this respect, appeasement could have been directed against the Soviet Union. It could also be argued that Britain's neutrality in the **Spanish Civil War**, intended or not, helped the Fascist rebels. For example, although the British and French navies stopped Italian submarines attacking neutral vessels close to Spain, they then permitted the Italian navy to join in the patrol activity, which effectively allowed Italian submarines freedom of movement. As the Soviet Union was the main supporter of the Spanish government, helping Italy or Germany can be seen as expressing opposition to the Soviet Union.

The British government's unwillingness to side with the Soviet Union is also evident at the Munich Conference in September 1938. Even though the Soviet Union had signed treaties with Czechoslovakia it was not invited to the conference. In this respect, the Soviet Union was left out and then saw Hitler gain further territory and move closer to the Soviet border. Stalin did not need to be paranoid to feel that the same western powers who had invaded his country in 1919 were now encouraging Hitler eastwards. The distrust between Britain, France and the Soviet Union created at Munich effectively prevented the creation of a broad anti-Hitler alliance until 1941.

DID THE TREATY OF VERSAILLES JUSTIFY APPEASEMENT?

Another reason why the appeasers felt they should make concessions to Hitler was recognition that some of the decisions at Versailles had been unfair. Since there was considerable justification for this view it was compelling. This popular feeling was summed up well by M. G. Balfour in a letter to the Editor of *The Times* when he wrote: 'After all, we brought the Germans their problems.'

The Treaty of Versailles was supposed to follow the idea of national self-determination, but this had to be balanced in practice by the need to calm French fears. The French were fearful that the League of Nations would not prove to be sufficiently strong and therefore wanted to break Germany up. Having failed to divide the Rhineland from the rest of Germany they sought to make Germany weaker in other ways.

Spanish Civil War (1936–9) Military rebellion led by General Francisco Franco against the Republic established in 1931. Supported by the German Nazis and Italian Fascists, Franco won the war and established a military dictatorship. While Spain was a kingdom under Franco, it was only after Franco's death in 1975 that a king was restored to the throne.

The creation of the Polish Corridor was an obvious injustice to Germany since it removed a million Germans from their homeland. It is a question to ponder as to what would have happened if Hitler had demanded the return of the Polish Corridor before he marched into the rump of post-Munich Czechoslovakia. The British guarantee to Poland was a direct response to Hitler's march into Prague in March 1939. If Hitler had restricted himself to territory taken from Germany at Versailles he would not have undermined the appeasers in London and Paris. By revealing his ambition to seize land Hitler removed a major plank from the appeasers' platform. Bohemia and Moravia had never been part of a united Germany. They had been part of the German Confederation, so seizing them made it seem that Hitler wanted to create the '*Grossdeutschland*' which had been discussed in 1848.

Ultimately, appeasement failed because Hitler was not prepared to continue to play the waiting game that he had played up to March 1938. Once Hitler tried to force the pace of change his ambition solidified the opposition to him. Prior to this France had used British reluctance to go to war to justify surrendering Czech control of the Sudetenland, despite the guarantee made by France to Czechoslovakia in 1938. The invasion of Czechoslovakia led Chamberlain's cabinet colleagues to insist on a guarantee to Poland. Thus, in 1938 the British failed to back a French guarantee to Czechoslovakia; in 1939 Hitler pushed Britain into a corner by challenging a guarantee given by the British themselves.

WAS APPEASEMENT AN INEVITABLE RESULT OF BRITAIN AND FRANCE BEING UNPREPARED FOR WAR?

The argument for this is that Britain was not ready for war even in 1939 and that therefore to have gone to war before would have been foolish. It is also very important to remember that France's views were of key importance as it had a much larger army than Britain.

This line of thought is evident at the Anglo-French meeting on 27 April 1938. Chamberlain and Halifax met their French opposite numbers, Daladier and Bonnet respectively. At the meeting Halifax followed the line established by Chamberlain in the House of Commons, and stated to the French ministers: 'His Majesty's Government regarded the military situation, viewed specifically from the military angle, with considerable disquiet. Not only was the military situation of Czechoslovakia exceedingly weak; His Majesty's Government could not regard the situation of France and Great Britain as very encouraging in the event of a German attack on Czechoslovakia.'

We should also consider the presence of Spitfires and Hurricanes in the Battle of Britain. Although the Spitfire was already being developed it

KEY TERM

Grossdeutschland
This concept envisaged the creation of a united Germany including Austria. The original unification in 1871, excluding Austria, was referred to as *Kleinedeutschland*. After 1919 the concept of *Grossdeutschland* included recovering the lands lost under the Treaty of Versailles.

A French right-wing cartoon of November 1938 entitled 'No thanks ... I'd rather "Live for France"!'

Punch cartoon of October 1938 showing Chamberlain as 'A Great Mediator'.

only entered front-line service in 1939. It is suggested that without these aircraft Britain would have lost; therefore appeasement can be seen as a success because it bought time for these aircraft to be produced.

However, the difficulty with this line of argument is twofold. It assumes that the Germans were ready for war in 1938 and that Britain was not. The memoirs of Adolph Galland, who rose to lead the German Fighter Command during the Second World War, make clear that even in 1940 the Luftwaffe (German air force) lacked the medium bombers necessary to attack Britain properly. He also notes the limited range of the German fighters, which reduced their ability to defend the bombers as they reached London. It is also true, but ignored by supporters of appeasement, that the German military were much more experienced by 1940. The successful invasions of Poland, Denmark and the Netherlands had all provided the Germans with combat experience before they met the British in Belgium and France. The argument fails to account for the other reasons for appeasement. Appeasement not only bought time for rearmament, it also enabled Chamberlain to restrict government spending with the objective of reviving the economy by avoiding a rise in interest rates and taxes.

Did appeasement lead to a significant opportunity for Britain to prepare?

Churchill naturally and correctly praised the courage and skill of 'the few' in Fighter Command who successfully defended Britain against the German threat from the skies in 1940. Churchill's speeches focused on the men rather than the equipment, partly because the technology was secret; however, the radar stations along the South Coast that began to appear from 1937 played a key role. The use of radar and the adoption of the **'wing' system** by RAF Fighter Command in 1940 made a major contribution to victory, as did Hermann Goering's error in 1940 in deciding to switch the attack away from the airfields to the cities, which allowed the RAF to survive.

How pragmatic was appeasement?

Another aspect of the practical justification for appeasement in 1938 is that it was pragmatic, i.e. it was the expedient response to the European situation as Britain was not ready for war. According to this view it was not possible to do any good by declaring war over Austria or Czechoslovakia, and appeasement was the immediately advantageous approach.

In the case of Czechoslovakia this practical argument is given in K. Feiling's *Life of Chamberlain* (1946). **Sir Samuel Hoare**, a member of the government at the time of Munich, also argues in his memoirs that the 'overriding consideration' with Chamberlain and the cabinet was that the very complicated problem of Czechoslovakia should not lead to war and should be solved at almost any price by peaceful means. Lord Halifax, Foreign Secretary at the time of Munich, quotes Hoare and Feiling as accurately portraying the thinking of Neville Chamberlain.

Chamberlain himself told the House of Commons on 24 March 1938 that he had 'abandoned any idea of giving guarantees to Czechoslovakia, or the French in connection with their obligations to that country'. According to Lord Halifax, Chamberlain believed from the beginning of the crisis that there was nothing British intervention could do to save Czechoslovakia from being overrun by Germany.

Even if one concedes that there is a certain logic in this argument it begs the question why was it subsequently worthwhile to declare war over Poland. The practical arguments that persuaded Chamberlain to compromise over Czechoslovakia applied even more strongly in the case of Poland. In 1938, the Soviet Union was neutral and could possibly have intervened to help Czechoslovakia. By September 1939, the Soviet Union had signed the Nazi-Soviet Pact (August 1939). The Poles had refused to consider Russian help and their immediate situation was hopeless. Having captured Czechoslovakia, Germany could invade Poland from three

'Wing' system To maximise the effect of the attack, fighters were concentrated in wings rather than mere squadron strength. This required careful organisation by the ground controllers.

Sir Samuel Hoare (1880–1959) Conservative MP for Chelsea 1910–44. Served in various cabinet posts 1931–40, including Foreign Secretary and Home Secretary. He was made Secretary for Air (1940) and served as special ambassador to Madrid (1940–4), with the task of keeping Spain neutral during the Second World War.

different directions. However, one can reverse the logic and conclude that war should have been declared in October 1938. The German generals were genuinely concerned about the strength of the **Czech defences** in 1938. In 1939 their concern was about British and French activity in the west, not the Poles themselves.

How significant was support in Britain for Hitler and his regime?

In July 1934, *The Times*, influenced by its late owner, **Lord Northcliffe**, wrote, 'In the years that are coming, there is more reason to fear for Germany than to fear Germany'. Such pro-Nazi sympathies were shared by a minority of British politicians. After Munich, critics of Chamberlain, like **Leo Amery**, feared that their sympathies would count against them and they would be deselected by their local Conservative Party associations. However, politicians like Amery were the minority. More typical was the civil servant Sir Horace Wilson, whom Chamberlain used to get around opposition within the Foreign Office: a well-intentioned civil servant, he believed in appeasement, not in Hitler.

For certain sections of the British upper class, appeasement was a natural way to show their sympathy for Hitler and his regime. Dinners and parties given by society hostesses such as Lady Cunard presented Nazis to their guests as if they were prize specimens of a new exotic species. Lady Cunard's informal parties held at her house imitated the political salons in France where politicians mixed with writers, thinkers and fashionable people as well as visiting foreign dignitaries. Her regular guests included the Prince of Wales (later Edward VIII) to whom she introduced Mrs Simpson, the American divorcee whom he was later to marry. According to the political diarist 'Chips' Channon, it was Lady Cunard who encouraged the Prince of Wales to be pro-German in a speech to the British Legion. The speech resulted in King George V reprimanding his son for being too political. Although von Ribbentrop (Hitler's foreign affairs adviser and Ambassador to London, 1936–8) liked to believe that the parties he was at were where policy was made, in practice there is little evidence that Lady Cunard's guests influenced foreign policy. Harold Nicholson (a well-known political diarist) criticised them for giving that impression, as he scathingly remarked, 'they convey an atmosphere of authority and grandeur when it is only flatulence of the spirit'.

Lady Cunard's rival, Mrs Ronnie Greville, numbered Sir John Simon among her guests and, as Foreign Secretary from 1931 to 1935, he did little to actively oppose Hitler. His contribution to the cabinet debate on helping Austria was to suggest more people went there on holiday. Since few would be able to afford this his recommendation offered little relief. Edward VIII was later forced to abdicate in order to marry Mrs Simpson and the pro-German element in top society lost its most fashionable icon.

Sir Oswald Mosley and the British Union of Fascists. The most strident of Hitler's British supporters were **Sir Oswald Mosley** and his Blackshirts. However, the violence accompanying the BUF rally at Olympia on 7 June 1934 damaged its image and on 14 July 1934 the press baron Lord Rothermere used the *Daily Mail* to announce that he was not **anti-Semitic** or a Fascist. Without press support the movement was reduced to causing trouble in the East End; trouble which the Conservative government curbed by introducing the Public Order Act (1936). The defeat of two violently anti-Semitic MPs, Edward Doran and Arthur Bateman, in London at the 1935 general election demonstrated the electoral weakness of anti-Semitism. One anti-Semite who fell out with Mosley was Francis Yeats-Brown, whose novel *The Bengal Lancer* was later made into a film, greatly enjoyed by Hitler.

How influential was public opinion?

The political elite determined foreign policy. Apart from 'peace for our time', Chamberlain's most famous pre-war utterance must have been to describe the dispute over Czechoslovakia as 'a quarrel in a faraway country between people of whom we know nothing'. Newsreels and press reports provided only limited coverage of the crisis, so public opinion on the matter was limited and not considered to be of influence. The political elite determined high policy – the overall aims of the government, of which foreign affairs were a key aspect. Chamberlain and his contemporaries in government thus operated at the pinnacle of a hierarchical society. The influence of the political elite was even stronger in France where Foreign Minister Georges Bonnet was able to influence newspapers which the French government subsidised.

However, it is also true that many people in Britain did not want another war. Few people went abroad for their holidays and very few travelled as far as Czechoslovakia. One could argue that the attitude to the Czechs in 1938 reflected the cynicism bred by the 1914–8 war. By misrepresenting the First World War as a crusade to defend Belgium the government made it more difficult for Chamberlain's government in 1938. Even if Chamberlain had wished to fight, which he did not, would the British people have accepted that this really was a genuine moral crusade? The ultimate irony was that in 1938 Chamberlain sacrificed central Europe's one successful (if Czech-dominated) democracy. Then in 1939 Chamberlain took Britain into a war to defend an authoritarian Poland, although by now, for the British public, it was simply that the Germans had to be stopped.

WHAT WAS THE EXTENT OF APPEASEMENT?

The greatest act of appeasement came at Munich in September 1938. Since then the Munich Agreement has become synonymous with betrayal. Such moments rarely occur without attitudes having had time to mature, and appeasement can be seen as a tide that reached its high water mark at Munich. However, earlier events had shown which way the tide was flowing.

Abyssinia (1935–6). The irony about this crisis is that it is famous for the failure of the Hoare–Laval Pact (see Chapter 10), which was in itself an attempt at appeasement. Under this plan Italy would have gained most of Abyssinia with small gains for France and Britain. Hoare and Laval were motivated by the desire to keep Italy from aligning with Germany, but such cynical *Realpolitik* was defeated when the plan was leaked to the press. Also, the situation had been made more difficult by Britain's decision in June to break the Treaty of Versailles by signing a naval agreement with the Germans. Britain had therefore signed the Versailles Treaty then breached it when it suited it. Its call to Italy to observe the covenant of the League of Nations thus seemed rather hollow.

It is obviously difficult to know whether implementing the Hoare–Laval Pact would have detached Mussolini from Hitler. However, relations between the two powers did become much closer in 1936 after Britain and France extended sanctions against Italy in support of the League. Critically, Hitler was able to secure the July 1936 agreement over Austria. This agreement began to undermine Austrian independence because Italy accepted the Austrian Nazis being given official posts, whereas in 1934 Mussolini had opposed increased Nazi influence over Austria. Mussolini's failure to enter the war in 1939 also suggests that appeasing Mussolini over Abyssinia would have borne more fruit than the appeasement of Hitler. Mussolini was aware of the weaknesses of Italy and his colonial demands could have been met. Hitler still went to war in 1939 but if Italy had remained neutral the Allied cross-channel invasion might have come sooner than 1944.

Haile Selassie's appeal to the League of Nations on 30 June 1936 aroused British public opinion as did press reports about the proposed deal. Sadly, the British public was indignant on behalf of a ruthless African dictator (see, e.g., Anthony Mockler, *Haile Selassie's War*, 1984), but Chamberlain was able to lull them to sleep as he sacrificed a central European democracy. The British were also happy to celebrate Empire Day whilst condemning the Italians for trying to establish an empire.

Austria (1938). The British Foreign Office was relatively calm about the rise of specifically Austrian Fascism under **Chancellor Dollfuss** in March

1933. A Foreign Office memorandum of 14 March 1933 stated the view that:

> *Dollfuss has in effect carried through a coup d'état though in such a way that with the usual adroitness of Austrian politicians he could no doubt easily make a return to normal parliamentary procedure and merely claim that the Austrian parliament had by its own folly stultified itself.*

This evidence suggests that Britain was not unhappy to see the rise of right-wing regimes. However, it preferred these governments to be run by respectable figures like Dollfuss rather than demagogues like Hitler.

Dollfuss's repressive policies included creating a new criminal offence of 'activities that might subvert the Roman Catholic Church'. By August 1933, the British Chargé d'Affaires in Vienna was reporting an anxious and uncertain mood in Austria. This was enough for the report to be noted by the Foreign Office in London as 'hardly encouraging'.

Anschluss (1938). It would seem that the Foreign Office was prepared for the fall of Austria to Hitler long before the Anschluss in March 1938. Appeasement here was rooted in a belief that the Austrians were incapable of ruling successfully. One suspects there is perhaps an air of resignation at the inadequacies of foreigners. The Trades Union Congress were told that they should persuade the Austrian labour movement to work with Dollfuss, but there was no attempt to encourage Dollfuss or his successor to broaden his political base in order to fend off Nazism.

The British decision not to oppose Hitler's remilitarisation of the Rhineland in March 1936 left Austria's Chancellor Schuschnigg little option but to make a deal with Hitler. When an Austro-German Agreement was published on 11 July 1936 the Foreign Office concluded that the Anschluss was more than half completed. The Rhineland issue was a classic case of guilt: denying Germany sovereignty within its own borders was just not fair and anyway the French were unwilling to act. The Anschluss, however, was a more complex matter.

In 1938 when Chancellor Schuschnigg tried to hold a referendum to avert a Nazi takeover, he was criticised by the British Ambassador in Berlin for having acted rashly. The Ambassador in Berlin was Sir Neville Henderson, who is seen as one of the main appeasers. However, the British Foreign Secretary, Lord Halifax, did not hold back when he told Ribbentrop that the Anschluss was an act of 'naked force'. Other opinions varied still. The *Manchester Guardian* roundly condemned the Nazi invasion but its influence on policy was limited. The French government suggested trying to agree a response with Italy, but since the Italians believed that Germany was now the strongest power in Europe the suggestion came to nothing. The evident enthusiasm of many

Austrians for the Anschluss and the fact that it was a *fait accompli* also prevented Britain and France from reacting more forcefully. Having failed to defend Austria earlier, by allowing Austria to be pressured into making the July 1936 Agreement with Germany, Britain and France must bear some of the blame.

Czechoslovakia (1938). The event always associated with appeasement is the Munich Conference that met on 29–30 September 1938 and reached an agreement to dismember Czechoslovakia. As part of the agreement German troops would enter part of the Sudetenland on 1 October 1938, in accordance with Hitler's original timetable for the invasion of Czechoslovakia. The poignancy of the situation was due to the attitude of the Czech government. The German army had carried out manoeuvres sufficiently close to the border to make it clear what German intentions were. With rising tension in Europe, Chamberlain had flown twice to meet Hitler. The first meeting at Berchtesgarten on 15 September 1938, and the second at Bad Godesburg on the Rhine on 22–3 September, failed to produce agreement.

Faced with having at least the substance of his demands met, Hitler added the demand that everything had to be implemented on 1 October 1938. At this Chamberlain left and Europe prepared for war. The Czechoslovakian government mobilised its forces and manned its strong mountain defences. On 25 September the British cabinet met and agreed to support France and Czechoslovakia. The historian Anthony Adamthwaite argues in *Grandeur and Misery* (1995) that the French carefully manoeuvred their way through the crisis in order to put most of the blame for humbling Czechoslovakia on Britain. He argues that the French Foreign Minister, Georges Bonnet, played a double game in which he appeared to be placing pressure on Prague, by threatening that the French would abandon the Czechs, but in fact was seeking additional assurances for France from Britain. It was therefore a major advance for France on 26 September when Britain agreed to support France in the event of war with Germany.

WHAT WERE THE PRIORITIES FOR FRANCE AND BRITAIN?

Why then, with a determined ally in Czechoslovakia, did France and Britain decide to accept Hitler's demands and therefore create a defenceless Czechoslovakia?

The priorities of the French. French foreign strategy since 1932 had been based on the Maginot Line. Mindful of the losses incurred in 1914 during the Battles of the Frontiers, France had opted to fight the next war in the shelter of concrete. The problem in 1938 was that if France was to help Czechoslovakia then it would have to attack Germany, rather than defend itself against German attack.

Had France chosen to attack, the Germans would have only had about six divisions in the west as the bulk of their forces would have been thrown against the formidable Czech mountain defences. These were so strong in the eyes of Hitler's generals that they had argued with Hitler as to whether it was feasible to attack Czechoslovakia unless Britain and France were neutral. The German generals had also contacted the British Foreign Office with an offer from **General Beck** to overthrow Hitler in the event of a war. The Foreign Office, which had stood back whilst Franco rebelled in Spain in 1936 against a Socialist Government, was strangely reluctant to use this opportunity to exploit a potential rebellion against a Fascist dictator.

The French Chief of Staff, General Gamelin, was prepared to acknowledge in private the weaknesses of the German defences, the **Siegfried Line**. However, in meetings with government ministers, he referred to pessimistic reports on how many German divisions would be in the west and how formidable the defences were. Such comments were used to publicly justify French inaction over Czechoslovakia. The French government also encouraged a press campaign in favour of peace at the price of Czechoslovakia. Since 1920 the French foreign ministry had operated a news bureau and retained journalists on its payroll, and the Havas news agency was effectively controlled by the French government. This control over Havas was strengthened in 1938, when the French government agreed to pay for the losses on the news service. To make the press more effective, radio news bulletins were reduced to three per day in 1938 and each programme was limited to seven minutes. The French government was therefore able to ensure that the French press supported appeasement.

Since the French were the major field army of the alliance and they did not want to attack, Chamberlain had an excuse for compromise ready to hand. Chamberlain was also given estimates for the number of civilian casualties that would result from air raids. These turned out to be greatly exaggerated. Chamberlain's big problem was that he knew the essence of the French plan was to instigate an economic blockade and await the arrival of an expanded British army in France. To declare war was therefore to rely upon Czechoslovakia to defend itself. The decision of the British Foreign Office not to encourage the German anti-Nazi plotters around General Beck, who had offered to depose Hitler if the Allies went to war over Czechoslovakia, made clear this reluctance to provide military support to Czecoslovakia.

Betrayal of the Czechs? Czech military strength in 1938 (with British and French support) meant that the defeat of the German army was

KEY PERSON

General Ludwig Beck (1880–1944)
As Chief of Staff he opposed Hitler's plans for war in 1937. He reluctantly carried out Hitler's instructions for Anschluss, resulting in his resignation in 1938. He devoted the rest of his life in attempts to overthrow the Nazi regime. Was executed after being implicated in the July 1944 bomb plot against Hitler.

KEY TERM

Siegfried Line
Germany's fortifications in the Rhineland, or 'west wall'. This extensive system of defences was penetrated by the Allies in the Second World War only after very heavy fighting.

entirely possible. Certainly, the Czechs were better armed and had better defences than the Poles. Also, much of the equipment used against France came from the Skoda works in Czechoslovakia which the Germans captured in March 1939. It is also well known that the German people were reluctant to support war in 1938. Hitler's bloodless triumph at Munich helped to give him the opportunity to push Germany further than it really wanted to go. During cabinet discussions, Sir Alfred Duff Cooper, the War Secretary, told Chamberlain that the terms being put to the Czechs amounted to 'one of the basest betrayals in history'. His subsequent resignation was therefore consistent with his views (see also Section 7). Certainly, in these respects, it would have been better to fight in 1938 than in 1939; that is the benefit, at least partly, of hindsight. If Chamberlain made the wrong decision it was for honourable reasons. If he gave more weight to the evidence which pointed to the conclusion he wished to reach, then let him who has never done that cast the first stone.

Appeasement had tried to give Hitler what a fair umpire might have awarded Germany in 1919. Hitler's invasion of Prague in March 1939 destroyed the rational argument that Hitler was simply a product of France's short-sighted meanness in 1919. That there was still room for manoeuvre after Munich is implied by Georges Bonnet, the French Foreign Minister. On 14 December 1938 he wrote to the French ambassadors in London, Berlin, Brussels, Rome, Barcelona and the French minister in Prague. The letter contained details of the recent visit of Joachim von Ribbentrop, German Foreign Minister, to Paris. Bonnet wrote that he had stressed the strength of agreement between Britain and France. He also explained that he had to stress to Herr Ribbentrop '… the part the improvement of Anglo-German relations must play in any development in the policy of European appeasement, which was considered to be the essential object of any Franco-German action'. Bonnet concluded his missive by saying that the recent Franco-German declaration was not only designed to improve relations between the two countries but 'should also be conducive to a general appeasement in the relations of the principal European powers'.

Bonnet may have misjudged the changing mood in London. He was probably unaware of the changing views of **Lord Halifax**, the British Foreign Secretary. After a meeting of the Foreign Policy Committee of the cabinet on 14 November 1938 Lord Halifax drew the conclusion that it was necessary to correct '… the false impression that we were decadent, spineless and could with little impunity be kicked around'. Halifax was increasingly disillusioned by the lack of a German follow-up to Hitler's signature on Chamberlain's piece of paper.

Albania (1939). On 7 April 1939 King Zog and Queen Geraldine of Albania fled as Italian troops entered their country. Sir Alexander Cadogan, the permanent secretary at the Foreign Office, concluded that this proved that Mussolini was a gangster, just as Hitler had been over Czechoslovakia. Chamberlain's response is said to have been that he wished Mussolini had arranged things to make it look more like an agreement. Presumably Chamberlain wanted Mussolini to arrange for a welcoming telegram from the Albanians, like that which had apparently summoned Hitler into Vienna. Based on such evidence, John Charmley argues, in *Chamberlain and the Lost Peace* (1989), that it was the French who now pushed Chamberlain into giving guarantees to threatened countries like Greece. He argues that Chamberlain wanted to avoid giving further guarantees, but was concerned about French morale and therefore decided to announce his agreement with the French decision to offer a guarantee to Greece when he responded to the debate in the House of Commons on 13 April.

Memel (1939). The German designs on Memelland in the Baltic were well known to the British government, but it was difficult for them to intervene. Not only was distance a problem, but also the fact that the British were under pressure from the Poles, who felt that a German seizure of Memelland would constitute an attack on Polish interests. Chamberlain was keen to avoid giving the Poles the decision on war, therefore Memelland remained a side issue and Hitler was able to occupy it on 23 March 1939.

KEY THEME

Mosley's foreign policy ideas These involved forging an agreement with Hitler and would have meant no British guarantee of Polish independence.

Poland (1939). In April 1939 Chamberlain extended a British guarantee to Poland and announced the introduction of conscription. It could therefore be thought that Chamberlain had abandoned appeasement. However, John Charmley, who praises **Mosley's ideas on foreign policy** as being the sensible option, argues differently. Charmley (1989) argues that Chamberlain was increasingly at odds with Halifax and the top civil servants in the Foreign Office. Charmley sees Chamberlain as trying to avoid an outright commitment to Poland despite the announcement of the guarantee. At a cabinet meeting on 20 March 1939, Chamberlain stressed to his colleagues that the guarantee to Poland did not necessarily mean maintaining the current borders of Poland, or that the status quo could be maintained indefinitely. To Halifax this seemed to suggest that another Munich could take place, and he was desperate to avoid such a repetition. For the same reason the British rejected Pope Pius XII's call for an international conference.

Charmley, in *Chamberlain and the Lost Peace* (1989), argues that Halifax's desire to make a moral stand effectively surrendered British policy into the hands of the Polish government. It is correct that there was no undertaking from the Polish government to consult the British government before taking steps which would lead to war. For this reason Charmley believes there was no need to declare war over Poland. This is a moral judgement but it has led to a re-examination of attitudes within the British government. In the end, Hitler's impatience to solve the 'need' for

Lebensraum drove him into war with Poland. The threat of British and French intervention had by then led Hitler to make an alliance with Stalin; Hitler knew he could outbid a reluctant West because Poland was not Stalin's ally. The reality brought about by appeasement was that having abandoned a reliable ally in 1938, Britain went to war in 1939 when Poland was invaded before Britain was ready.

As Lord Halifax had said, it was time to prove Britain could not be kicked around with impunity. However, the British had chosen not to support the Czechs and so Hitler saw no reason to hold back from attacking Poland. The fact that direct Allied military intervention was impossible following the signature of the Nazi-Soviet Pact made the British guarantee to Poland seem even less relevant to Hitler.

CONCLUSION

- Appeasement, like Nazism, was rooted in the First World War. The scale of the losses incurred by Britain made peace a popular policy.
- Appeasement was also designed to maintain the British Empire that had been weakened financially by the First World War. The rise of the United States underlined Britain's declining status.
- The French wanted to follow a policy of appeasement but wanted the British to appear to be the policy-makers.
- The decision to abandon Czechoslovakia at Munich condemned Europe to fighting a long war against a Germany greatly strengthened by its conquest of Austria and Czechoslovakia.
- Having decided that it was not militarily possible to defend Czechoslovakia, it was illogical for Britain to go to war over Poland.
- Hitler's territorial ambitions were too great to be satisfied by appeasement.

What was the role of Chamberlain in the policy of appeasement?

KEY
PERSON

**Stanley Baldwin
(1867–1947)**
British Conservative
statesman who
became an MP in
1908. Prime
Minister in 1923
and 1924–9. From
1931 to 1935,
Baldwin was
Conservative leader
in the National
Government under
Ramsay
MacDonald;
however, Baldwin
dominated the
coalition and was
again prime minister
1935–7. Baldwin
has been much
criticised for his
complacency over
events in Europe
during the 1930s.

KEY TERM

**National
Government**
Formed in 1931
after the Labour
government
resigned because
senior members of
the cabinet refused
to balance the
budget by cutting
unemployment
benefit. Headed
from 1931 to 1935
by the Labour leader
and former prime
minister, Ramsay
MacDonald, even
though only a few
Labour MPs joined
the coalition.

Introduction

Neville Chamberlain pursued a policy of appeasement during his time as Prime Minister from 1937 until the outbreak of the Second World War on 3 September 1939. Even before he became Prime Minister he had a major impact on government policy, as he was Chancellor of the Exchequer which is one of the most important posts in the cabinet. He also had influence because he was widely expected to succeed the then Prime Minister, **Stanley Baldwin**, when Baldwin retired. Since this was Baldwin's third term as Prime Minister he was not expected to stay in office for long.

Although Chamberlain was undoubtedly the main exponent of appeasement it is important to examine the part played by others in the development of the policy. It is also both fair and important to look at the pressure put upon Chamberlain by the French government.

Key themes.

- Appeasement was rooted in Chamberlain's economic policies which were based upon a realistic assessment of Britain's economic position.
- To Chamberlain, economic recovery was a priority over rearmament.
- It can be seen that appeasement was Chamberlain's policy and that his political opponents failed to stop him.
- It can be argued that Chamberlain must shoulder the responsibility for the French betrayal of Czechoslovakia at Munich.

WAS APPEASEMENT AN INEVITABLE RESULT OF CHAMBERLAIN'S RESTRICTIONS UPON DEFENCE SPENDING IN THE 1930S?

What was the impact of the Manchurian crisis? Soon after the **National Government** was formed in 1931 it was faced with a crisis in the Far East. The Japanese invasion of Manchuria threatened over £200 million of British investment in Hong Kong and the rest of south-east Asia. Baldwin chaired the Far Eastern Committee of the cabinet, which was responsible for recommending policy, and made a classic statement regarding sanctions, in this case against Japan. He said, 'You can't enforce them against a first class power'. Baldwin was not, however, arguing for outright appeasement, as he wanted to strengthen Britain's defences; rather, Baldwin argued that if Britain took action against Japan then Japan would simply seize the British colonies, so it was necessary to wait. Sir Robert Vansittart, head of the Foreign Office Staff, had recommended to Baldwin that Britain should seek co-operation with the United States. Baldwin dismissed this advice by arguing that the London Naval Treaty had included concessions to the US and that 'You'll get nothing out of Washington but words, big words, but only words'.

Chamberlain's response. Following Japan's creation of the puppet state of Manchuko in February 1932, Baldwin wanted to strengthen Britain's Far East defences and to cancel the 'Ten Year Rule', which said that Britain did not envisage a major war within ten years. The 'Ten Year Rule' was a convenient view in the 1920s when the government wanted to cut defence spending. Chamberlain's response was, in this respect, based upon financial arguments. Chamberlain informed the committee that:

> *The fact is that in the present circumstances we are no more in a position financially and economically to engage in a major war in the Far East than we are militarily... The Treasury submits that at the present time financial risks are greater than any other that we can estimate.*

The result of Chamberlain's intervention was that the committee agreed to a compromise. Baldwin's wishes were agreed but total military spending was not to rise. Therefore Chamberlain had achieved a situation in which whatever was spent on defending the empire would be deducted from the budget for defending Britain. Chamberlain's influence over the Manchuria crisis might thus be seen as a significant determinant of many of the deficiencies that were later used to justify appeasement.

The debate over military spending. One of the reasons given for following a policy of appeasement was that Britain could not provide military assistance to Austria or Czechoslovakia. It is therefore important to know the role that Chamberlain played in deciding what military resources Britain needed prior to 1938. In 1934 the Defence Requirements Committee (DRC) submitted its report to the cabinet via the War Office on its view of Britain's military requirements. The DRC proposed that Britain should have an army that was capable of intervening in a continental war. The DRC wanted to spend £40 million on an army, which would be capable, in co-operation with the French, of defending the Netherlands and Belgium against a German attack. Chamberlain, the Chancellor of the Exchequer, had two basic objections to this proposal. Firstly, he did not believe that it would be politically popular to plan for another continental war that would remind the public of the costly battles of the Somme and Passchendaele. Secondly, he wished to limit spending upon the army to £20 million.

One explanation given for Chamberlain's views is that he was influenced by General Sir John Burnett-Stuart. The two men were close friends and Burnett-Stuart held an important position as the General Officer Commanding, Southern Command. Burnett-Stuart argued that Britain's allies could not expect more than that Britain would supply the greatest navy in the world and a first-rate air force. Perhaps this view had influenced Chamberlain, who indicated to the cabinet that the government faced proposals which it was financially 'impossible to carry out'. The result was that the cabinet approved only £20 million for the army. The decision not to develop an army for a continental war was thus effectively encouraged by Chamberlain. Therefore the later claims that appeasement bought time for rearmament ignore the fact that it was the appeasers who had chosen not to prepare for war on the continent.

Stanley Baldwin's role. In 1934 the cabinet approved additional spending on the Royal Air Force. The DRC report had helped to encourage this as it said that the use of aircraft had grown significantly during the First World War. The report went on to add that the potential for aircraft had yet to be developed. However, Baldwin also played a major role: on 10 November 1932 he shocked the House of Commons by saying:

> I think it is as well for the man in the street to realise that there is no power on earth that can protect him from being bombed. Whatever people may tell him, the bomber will always get through.

Therefore when Chamberlain resisted pressure to develop the army and chose to give priority to the air force, he had strong support from Baldwin. These views, which Baldwin had gained at a meeting of the Committee on Imperial Defence, were borne out by air exercises in 1934. The fears these views generated dictated that the emphasis should be on developing fighters, since they would have the role of destroying enemy bombers. The cabinet therefore agreed to increase the Royal Air Force by 820 aircraft over the next five years. Meanwhile the navy decided, given Chamberlain's restrictions on spending, to spend its small additional funds on restoring the pay cuts that had led to the **Invergordon Mutiny** in 1931.

The French have often been criticised for believing that they could simply sit behind the concrete defences of the Maginot Line. The development of Britain's radar and fighter defences in the 1930s was 'Britain's Maginot Line', except that radar and aircraft were usable anywhere, whereas the Maginot Line was immovable. Like the French version it sent out the message that Britain's essential concern was its own defence and therefore other countries should not rely upon it. Chamberlain's military policy can thus be seen to have played a key role in bringing this situation about.

KEY EVENT

Invergordon Mutiny Key units of the Royal Navy were immobilised in September 1931 when sailors reacted to cuts in pay with a policy of passive resistance – no ships would sail from the Firth. Although the dispute was eventually settled it revealed to the government that there were limits to the sacrifices which people could be called upon to make.

WERE CHAMBERLAIN'S FINANCIAL CONCERNS JUSTIFIED BETWEEN 1931 AND 1937?

The national finances. We have already seen that Chamberlain advanced financial reasons for restricting rearmament and inevitably this limited Britain's ability to compete with Japanese or German rearmament. The weakness of Britain's economic position has already been explained in Section 6. It is now necessary to consider the financial constraints imposed upon the government's military policy by its economic policies.

Recovery and rearmament. By 1931 unemployment in Britain had risen to 3,252,000. The British government therefore decided to remove the pound sterling from the gold standard (see Section 6). This was a radical step since orthodox financial opinion regarded the gold standard as the sign of a properly run currency.

To restore the economy, the government rejected the idea of a massive scheme of public works as it was believed that this would lead to the kind of inflation which had destroyed the German mark in 1923. Rather, as Chancellor of the Exchequer, Chamberlain followed a policy of low interest rates which he hoped would lead to an economic revival through increased investment and rising consumer spending. The difficulty for Chamberlain was that rearmament could damage the chances of the economy recovering. One way to pay for rearmament was to raise taxes: this would be a sound policy in the eyes of the world's financiers but it would reduce the consumer's disposable income. By 1934 unemployment had fallen to 2,609,000 and there were clear signs that the south of England and parts of the Midlands were recovering from the Depression but before that it was likely that tax increases would have destroyed the progress made since 1931. In this respect Chamberlain was justified in holding down defence expenditure before 1934. Between 1934 and 1937, Chamberlain oversaw a rise in defence expenditure totalling £78.7 million (a rise of 72.9 per cent) which was financed from taxation.

If raising taxation was inappropriate before 1934 then was Chamberlain correct to avoid financing rearmament through borrowing? One way of answering this question is to point to the parallel process in Germany. In 1933, Hitler had come to power and had begun to rearm. Even though the internationally renowned banker Hjalmar Schacht managed Germany's rearmament programme, there were severe inflationary pressures by 1935. One of the main reasons for inflation was that Schacht financed rearmament through borrowing (**Mefo bills**). This had created excess monetary demand not matched by an increased output of consumer goods. Schacht tried to manage the situation through exchange controls which led to shortages in Germany and thereby increased prices.

> **KEY TERM**
>
> **Mefo bills** This was the name given to the financial instruments issued by Hjalmar Schacht in the name of a specially created company. Schacht used Mefo bills to hide the level of German rearmament from foreign observers.

Another argument is to look at the dilemma facing Chamberlain in managing the British economy into a position of recovery. Following Britain's departure from the gold standard on 21 September 1931, the government decided to boost domestic investment through a policy of 'cheap money', that is, low interest rates. The immediate effect of leaving the gold standard was to reduce the value of sterling and therefore to lower the level of interest rates needed to justify the exchange rate. By June 1932 the government had been able to reduce interest rates from 6 to 2 per cent. If the government had sought to finance rearmament from borrowing before 1937 this could have led to increased interest rates. Alternatively, investors might have decided to put their money into government bonds which would have represented a safer investment than businesses during the uncertainty of the Depression. Either way, financing rearmament through borrowing threatened to stifle Britain's recovery from the Depression. Appeasement, which stemmed from low defence spending, in this respect reflected Chamberlain's concern to achieve economic recovery without inflation.

In 1932 the Bank of England forced creditors, such as the United States, to accept lower interest rates on Britain's debts. So long as British government stock offered wartime (1914–8) levels of interest, it was not possible to get banks and building societies to offer lower rates to their investors. Once banks and building societies did not have to offer such high rates to investors, they could offer lower rates to borrowers. In this way, the policy of 'cheap money' helped to fuel economic recovery. By the end of 1932, £1919 million of 5 per cent war stock had been converted to 3.5 per cent. This saved the government £28.7 million per year which was approximately one-third of the costs of rearmament prior to 1937. Further rate reductions on the rest of the National Debt had achieved savings of £55.5 million per year by 1936. This means that rearmament prior to 1937 was effectively being paid for out of financial savings. Given the high social costs of the Depression this was a significant achievement. Insofar as appeasement stemmed from Britain's inability to rearm earlier, this inability was a product of Britain's financial necessities during the Depression, necessities which Chamberlain clearly understood.

The effect of domestic recovery without inflation. Chamberlain's financial concerns were justified at least until 1937; the difficulty for Chamberlain was that this reinforced his desire to avoid war. Therefore appeasement followed logically from Britain's financial weakness. Did this then lead to the major problem that war was actually more likely because Hitler did not believe that Britain would really be able to oppose his plans? Whereas Hitler insisted on increasing the pace of German rearmament after 1936 despite the growing economic problems it was causing, Chamberlain insisted that rearmament must await recovery. This left Britain needing to catch up, but by 1939 Britain was spending

22 per cent of its national income on its armed services to Germany's 23 per cent. At least Chamberlain's policies had restored the British economy after the Great Depression.

It would be relatively easy to argue that rearmament would have solved the unemployment in the North so graphically described by George Orwell in 1937 in *The Road to Wigan Pier*. But as the evidence above demonstrates, Britain's economy during the Depression was a much more complicated economy than Orwell set out to show. Therefore, although Chamberlain chose to follow a policy of appeasement, it is clear that he had only a limited number of options due to the domestic objective of recovery from the Depression without inflation.

WAS APPEASEMENT THE DOMINANT POLICY BECAUSE ITS POLITICAL OPPONENTS LACKED THE POLITICAL MUSCLE TO OPPOSE CHAMBERLAIN?

Chamberlain's dominance over his colleagues can be said to reflect the weakness of his colleagues. Certainly it is interesting to consider just how politically weak some of those advocating rearmament were.

Winston Churchill. Churchill's outright opposition towards developing limited self-government in India had placed him on the political fringe. His position was also further weakened by real doubts held about his success as Chancellor of the Exchequer. Churchill had taken Britain back onto the gold standard in 1926 and this was thought to have handicapped Britain's ability to export. Given Chamberlain's financial acumen this put Churchill at a serious disadvantage. Churchill also suffered from another major handicap in the eyes of the Conservative Party: namely, that he had been at one time a Liberal. He was therefore distrusted by many in the Tory Party and avoided by Conservative backbenchers with hopes for promotion for **crossing the floor** (of the House of Commons) and being a member of 'The Other Club', a dissident dining club. Also, the period of the National Government encouraged backbenchers to be loyal as some ministerial posts had to go to non-Conservatives, which created even more competition than usual.

Duff Cooper, Secretary of State for War, First Lord of the Admiralty. Although **Sir Alfred Duff Cooper** was to resign in protest over Munich, he too lacked significant political weight. Even those who had agreed with him in the cabinet discussions during the Munich crisis, did not resign with him. One reason for Duff Cooper's weakness was that Chamberlain disapproved of his private life. Duff Cooper was married to Diana, daughter of the Duke of Rutland, and reputedly the most beautiful woman of her generation. However, throughout their married life and

Crossing the floor
The term given to the action of MPs who switch parties and therefore have to cross the floor of the House of Commons to sit on the benches opposite belonging to the other party.

Sir Alfred Duff Cooper (1890–1954)
Entered Parliament as a Conservative MP in 1924. Secretary of State for War (1935–7). Resigned in protest against the Munich Pact in 1938 and returned to the cabinet as Minister of Information (1940–1) under Winston Churchill.

with her knowledge he indulged in a string of liaisons and affairs. Since Duff Cooper also drank heavily and gambled unwisely, many saw him as a dilettante more interested in fun than hard work. Whether this picture is entirely fair or not, Duff Cooper lost his battle over the army estimates with Chamberlain in February 1936. Chamberlain then made the surprise move, when he became Premier in June 1937, of giving Duff Cooper responsibility for the navy. However, for a Treasury-minded Prime Minister like Chamberlain this was a sound move: it meant the spending departments were in the hands of weak ministers. Duff Cooper made matters worse by ill-judged spending on redecorating his official residence (which made him look frivolous) and attacks on the Labour Party over the Spanish Civil War despite a cabinet agreement not to raise the issue (which made him look politically naïve). When Duff Cooper eventually resigned over Munich there was irony in that one of the most pro-French members of the cabinet resigned over an issue in which the government had acted very closely with the French government.

Anthony Eden, Foreign Secretary. One reason why Chamberlain was able to manoeuvre **Sir Anthony Eden** into resigning as Foreign Secretary in February 1938 over the appeasement of Italy, was that he was isolated and politically naïve. Eden thought Mussolini had to be resisted, unlike Chamberlain who wanted an Anglo-Italian bloc to oppose Hitler. Yet he was also in an embarrassing position, as it was widely believed in political circles that his remarks, during an official visit to Rome in 1935, had encouraged Mussolini to believe Britain would accept the Italian invasion of Abyssinia. This aspect of Eden's career was brought up by Sir Horace Wilson when he warned that if Eden leaked details of the US negotiations regarding Japan, the government machine would be used to destroy Eden's reputation. However, the real cause of Eden's resignation was Neville Chamberlain's decision to reject secret US proposals to oppose Japan over its attacks on China. Neville Chamberlain had rejected the proposals without consulting his Foreign Secretary for fear that the references to international law would upset Hitler and Mussolini. As Robert Rhodes James writes (in *Anthony Eden*, 1986), 'Eden ... had in his hand a political hand grenade which, if thrown, would have had shattering results'. What Chamberlain and others ascribed to weakness on Eden's part was perhaps something much better, but they had judged their man right: he would not 'stoop to conquer'.

Appeasement can therefore be seen as the product of Chamberlain's dominance over his political opponents. He pursued his policy ruthlessly, whereas his political opponents lacked unity and did not make full use of their own talents. In this respect, though appeasement was Chamberlain's policy, through his ruthlessness it became the British government's policy. Appeasement only collapsed when Chamberlain came up against an even more ruthless opponent: Hitler.

KEY PERSON

Sir Anthony Eden (1897–1977)
Eden served on the Western Front and won the Military Cross at the Battle of the Somme in 1916. He entered Parliament as a Conservative MP in 1923 and became Foreign Secretary in 1935, resigning in 1938. Eden was reappointed as Foreign Secretary under Churchill in 1940 and became deputy leader of the opposition in 1945. He replaced Winston Churchill as Prime Minister in 1955, but after his role in the Suez Crisis of 1956 resigned due to failing health in 1957. Eden was created 1st Earl of Avon in 1961.

TO WHAT EXTENT WAS APPEASEMENT SIMPLY THE POLICY THE FRENCH GOVERNMENT FORCED THE BRITISH GOVERNMENT TO ACCEPT?

The Rhineland (1936). When Hitler decided to remilitarise the Rhineland in March 1936 the reaction of France was critical. This was peacetime and Britain had no troops stationed in France. Hitler's nervous generals had been allowed to issue orders to the advancing troops that if they encountered opposition they should retire. The French Premier, Albert Sarraut, held office because his predecessor had lost a vote of confidence and someone had to hold office until the legislative elections took place in April. Faced with public hostility even to the defensive measure of manning the Maginot Line, Sarraut was unlikely to order French mobilisation. Despite this inactivity the French Foreign Minister, Pierre Flandin, went to London and asked for British support for military action and a naval blockade. At this time the British Foreign Secretary, Anthony Eden, was more interested in examining Hitler's proposals for limitations on air power and new non-aggression pacts. Therefore the British declined to back up what were in fact non-existent French measures, and, in this case, appeasement was the policy of first choice for both governments.

Austria (1938). On 11 March Hitler's puppet Nazi, the Austrian Chancellor Artur von Seyss-Inquart, invited Hitler to save Austria from chaos. On 12 March the German army entered Austria to a generally

Chamberlain holds aloft the Munich Agreement at the airport on his return from Munich to Britain, September 1938.

tumultuous welcome from the local people. On 12 March France had no government. Only on 13 March was Léon Blum able to form a government to replace that of Camille Chautemps, which had fallen two days earlier. The new French Foreign Minister, Joseph Paul-Boncour, then alarmed the British Foreign Office by summoning the Committee for National Defence, and France's ambassadors to Romania, Czechoslovakia, the Soviet Union and Poland, to a meeting in Paris. Paul-Boncour also asked to meet the British Foreign Secretary Lord Halifax, but on the advice of the Ambassador in Paris, Lord Halifax refused.

In Britain, Duff Cooper proposed to cabinet that Britain should respond by increasing the naval estimates and therefore raise the spectre of the naval blockade that had been so effective in the First World War. Chamberlain's authority over the cabinet was demonstrated when his counter-proposal to increase the air estimates left Duff Cooper with only two votes in cabinet.

In a strange sequel, on the instructions of the Foreign Office, the British Ambassador in Paris helped to block Paul-Boncour's retention as Foreign Minister when Édouard Daladier formed a new French government in April 1938. Whilst it is debatable as to what policy the French government was following in March 1938, it is clear that the British government lacked confidence in Paul-Boncour and chose to follow a policy of appeasement.

The Sudetenland (1938). The crisis which ended at the Munich Conference in September 1938 has already been discussed at length in Section 6. When Chamberlain met Hitler on 14 September 1938 at Berchtesgarden he accepted Hitler's demand for the transfer of the Sudeten Germans, rather than encouraging Hitler to accept the concessions being made to them by the Czech government. Daladier and Bonnet met Chamberlain in London four days later and accepted that Britain would only offer to guarantee the rump of Czechoslovakia. By taking the lead in negotiating with Hitler, Chamberlain was acting as though Britain was the country with obligations to Czechoslovakia – in fact it was the French. After the French and Czech governments had accepted Hitler's proposals, Chamberlain flew to a second meeting with Hitler only to find that Hitler had now raised his demands. Chamberlain then returned to London and recommended that the cabinet accept the new demands.

At this point the cabinet split because Lord Halifax would not agree to go beyond the original plan. Chamberlain had also lost the backing of the French government since Daladier now insisted that France would be forced to fulfil its obligations to Czechoslovakia. The only concession that

Chamberlain was able to obtain from his colleagues was that a final message be sent to Hitler via Sir Horace Wilson. Thus when the House of Commons assembled on 28 September 1938 the only active appeaser in the cabinet apart from Chamberlain was the Chancellor of the Exchequer, Sir John Simon. Ultimately, it was therefore Hitler's decision to accept a conference that saved Chamberlain from seeing his policy collapse. The conference was also a shrewd move in that it brought Chamberlain to meet Hitler and, as it was a meeting of heads of government, Chamberlain's anti-appeasement colleagues had to remain at home.

At their two previous meetings Chamberlain had accepted Hitler's demands and now he set about doing so again. Since Hitler, Mussolini and Chamberlain were determined to give Hitler what he wanted there was little, in such circumstances, that Daladier could achieve.

CONCLUSION

Appeasement at Munich was not the cabinet's policy but Chamberlain's alone. The public relief that war had been avoided obscured this fact until after the German invasion of Norway. Appeasement was Chamberlain's policy and, by 1938, he imposed it upon his cabinet. He was not alone but he was, perhaps, the guiltiest of 'the guilty men'.

A2 ASSESSMENT: BRITISH FOREIGN POLICY AND INTERNATIONAL RELATIONS, 1890–1939

Introduction

Understanding historical interpretations of topics as well as the main perspectives of participants is a key skill for historians to develop. This understanding is assessed at A2 both through traditional essays and through the evaluation of sources. At A2 you need to be aware of the wider context of the modules you are studying, for example, the impact of the Great Depression on policies followed by Chamberlain or the domestic pressures acting upon the leaders of the great powers in 1914. At the higher levels it will be necessary to accept that historians may differ in their views. You will need to assess whether these differences arise because the historians start from different perspectives, such as Marxists and conservatives, or whether their differences reflect the time at which they are writing (or both).

Evaluating historical sources

At A2 you will face a variety of historical sources, both primary and secondary. The primary sources may be published official records or secret documents that were never intended for publication. They may be private, personal records or the detailed memoirs of a key participant. In all cases it is vital that you analyse the source and its author(s). Many students simply try to tell the examiner what the source is saying. It may be necessary to do this, but at A2 level simply regurgitating the source will lead to a barren harvest of marks.

Who is the author? It will be helpful to ask the following questions in assessing who is the author of the source:

- is it a key individual in the events being described?
- what do you know about them that would help you to evaluate them as a source?

Examiners will be unimpressed by comments such as 'he is English so he must be reliable'. Not only could this descend into racism, it also shows a poor grasp of personal motivation. For example, General von Moltke told Wilhelm II that it was not possible to change Germany's plans at the last minute, a false statement which perhaps reveals more about Moltke's inadequacies as a staff officer that his moral approach to the truth.

Is the author's account authoritative? You will need to assess how much the author of the source is likely to know. Too many students seek to offer stereotypical answers such as 'he would know because as a journalist he was trained to find out the facts'. However, a trained reporter who had spent his working life gleaning stories from the late-Victorian divorce courts might be of limited value in assessing the impact of the *Dreadnought*. Students should also be aware of personal bias. For example, Lord Hankey accompanied Prime Minister Lloyd George to Versailles. As the former Secretary to the War Cabinet, Hankey was on intimate terms with the Prime Minister and other leading politicians, and can therefore offer us authority on what happened at Versailles. However, we should remember that Hankey was a strong advocate of a centralised form of government and was therefore unlikely to admit that it was difficult for one man to hold together all the strings of the negotiations.

Primary sources

It is necessary to consider the purpose of the author(s):

- Are they writing to explain or justify themselves? Many of those involved in the July Crisis of 1914 were keen afterwards to stress their own insignificance in the face of 'great events'. Lloyd George, for example, much preferred to have others see him as the war-winning premier than as a key member of the cabinet who plunged Britain into a war for which it was unprepared.
- Are they seeking to persuade others? When Duff Cooper gave his resignation speech to the House of Commons he was not only seeking to explain his resignation, but also to persuade others of the need to oppose Hitler's ambitions.
- What is the context of the source? Neville Chamberlain wrote regularly to his sisters and he could rely entirely upon their confidence. His letters to them are therefore an interesting insight into his mind. However, even when free to express their private opinions on matters, authors are subject to self-deception. For example, Chamberlain is likely to take a positive view of his motivations; we hardly expect him to write saying that he supported the formation of a National Government so that the Labour leader, Ramsay MacDonald, would take the blame for the cuts which Chamberlain was insisting upon.
- What is the influence of hindsight on the source? After the Second World War it was difficult for anyone to consider his or her role in appeasement dispassionately. Also, because Britain eventually won the war it was easier to be an appeaser: it was possible to argue that the policy had bought the time for rearmament. This point should help you to see how important it is to avoid sweeping generalisations.

The best candidates analyse the specific source given and avoid 'all-purpose' answers. You should also remember that referencing such as 'in lines 12 to 16' is too vague and is likely to go unrewarded.

Secondary sources

These sources will pose different challenges and they will nearly always be the writings of a historian. Key points to remember are:

- Does the historian represent a particular school of ideas (perhaps juxtaposed against an opposing source or view)?
- Is there significance attached to when the historian's views were published?

Note: if a source appears as 'adapted' this simply means that the examiner setting the paper needed to edit the source, which was never written with exam questions in mind. Candidates who dwell on the significance of some hidden plot behind the word 'adapted' should instead trust the examiner and concentrate upon evaluating the source.

SOURCE-BASED QUESTION IN THE STYLE OF OCR

Source A

Just before Christmas 1937, Duff sent Simon a detailed account of why the navy needed an extra £55.5 million in the coming year, only to receive a 'discouraging response'. He submitted a forceful Cabinet paper which described the 'New Standard Fleet' (NSF) as 'the minimum consistent with national security'. However, when the Cabinet met on 16 February [1938], a ceiling of £1650 million was set on defence spending for the next quinquenium. This was a decision which opened the way for a free-for-all among the Service departments – and also put the NSF in danger.

Adapted from John Charmley, *Duff Cooper* (Papermac, 1986).

Source B

It was essential to find out what the Nazis wanted, what they would accept as the price of peace and (if necessary) give it to them before they dragged the continent into war. This was Chamberlain's strategy for dealing with Hitler. The strategy was summed up in one word – 'appeasement'. For the most part Chamberlain's desire to avoid war matched the anxiety of the British people about being brought into a conflict like that of 1914–8. To this was added the new awareness that bombers could bring the war to their cities. On 30 September 1938, Chamberlain returned triumphantly to London, bearing his piece of paper. He received a hero's welcome. That evening he declared from Downing Street, 'I believe it is peace for our time'.

T. Howarth, *Twentieth Century History (1979)*.

Source C

The Munich dictate, enforced by the Four Powers and set up by Hitler, was never acknowledged by the Czechoslovak Parliament, which according to the constitution alone had the right to approve the territorial changes. With the protective belt of frontier-mountains Czechoslovakia lost the warrant of her independence … In these 'German' territories there remained about one million Czechs, and thousands of German anti-fascists, delivered by the British and the French to death and concentration camps. With the destruction of the Czechoslovak state Central Europe had its spine broken, the Western democracies lost more than 40 divisions of potential allies, and Germany had no obstacle in her march to the South-East.

The view of Czech historian J.V. Polisensky in
History of Czechoslovakia in Outline (1947).

Source D

Amery, who was no friend of the Munich Agreement, was perceptive enough to see that its 'real justification' lay in the liquidation of an untenable French position in eastern Europe. As Halifax told Phipps in November [1938], one of 'the chief difficulties of the past has been the unreal position which France was occupying in Central and Eastern Europe'. This position was the result of the circumstances of 1919, and those who wanted to uphold it, even at the cost of war, were simply ignoring the march of history for, in Butler's words: 'This is a period in which the peace settlement is being revised.' The Government's objective was to ensure that this was done by peaceful means.

John Charmley, *Chamberlain and the Lost Peace* (Papermac, 1991).

Study the sources and then answer the following question.

> 1 a) Explain whether Source A or Source B is the more convincing judgement
>   on why appeasement was adopted by Chamberlain as a policy.   [15]
>   b) Using sources A to D explain why the Munich Agreement of 1938
>   remains such a controversial issue for historians to approach.   [30]

Reading
Before answering this question you should read Sections 6 and 7.

How to answer this question
Part (a). To reach Band A you must answer the question by suggesting which is the 'more convincing' judgement whilst dealing directly with the 'differences'. General responses which reveal only a broad understanding are likely to languish in Band D or below. The basic difference is that Source A stresses the military roots of appeasement whereas Source B stresses the popularity of Chamberlain's policies. There is no 'right' answer to choosing A or B but you need arguments to support your choice. Source A is convincing in that Britain was weak in comparison with continental military powers, but that does not explain the Munich Agreement, Czech mobilisation, or French commitment to Czechoslovakia. Equally, Source B provides a clear link with popular opinion. Stronger responses will recognise that Chamberlain's popularity also reflected the way he had kept taxes down, and this was partly by limiting spending as described in Source A.

Part (b). To gain a mark in Band A it is necessary to use the evidence of the sources to support your argument as to why appeasement has been a matter of continuing controversy. You need to use your own knowledge to evaluate each source. Source C enables you to focus on 'controversial' in the question since it sums up the view that 'Munich' equals 'betrayal'. Since appeasement ultimately failed when war broke out its supporters tend to lean upon the argument that appeasement bought time. This is controversial because of the way it sacrificed Austria and Czechoslovakia. You should also consider how well Britain was led by Chamberlain during this period.

After 1940, Churchill made it a tenet of British politics that appeasement had been wrong. Yet Churchill was Chamberlain's arch-critic and, because he was the Prime Minister who led Britain to victory in the Second World War, it has been difficult to achieve a balanced assessment of him. Churchill had experienced failure as Chancellor of the Exchequer: in returning Britain to the gold standard he had supported the City at the expense of manufacturing industry, so that much of Britain was already in recession before the Depression came in 1929. Also, Churchill's total opposition to developing self-rule in India and his membership in 'the other club' were major reasons why few in politics would listen to his views on Hitler. Churchill was also never likely to thank Chamberlain for providing the radar and aircraft with which the RAF won the Battle of Britain.

Source A

Thank God someone has been found to take a stand against this nerveless folly; some of us who now feel largely humiliation and fear take heart again because we shall have a spokesman. Damn it, peace at this price is not worth buying and retribution will be awful and probably speedy.

> Oliver Lyttleton, writing on 3 October 1938 following Duff Cooper's resignation.

Source B

When he [Halifax] had sent Hitler's message of acceptance to Chamberlain on the floor of the House, and it had been read to the Members, he [Halifax] had looked down upon such a spectacle of emotional relief as had never been seen in the House of Commons before, upon wildly cheering men, some weeping and many who would later be anxious to forget their participation. In the country outside, men and women felt that they had awoken from some appalling nightmare, and the gratitude for the Prime Minister's courage and persistence was so profound, that in the prevailing atmosphere it seemed to many neither blasphemy, nor wild exaggeration when he was compared by a journalist to God.

> From Lord Birkenhead, *Halifax – The Life of Lord Halifax* (Hamish Hamilton, 1965).

Source C

Unlike Churchill, Chamberlain had knowledge of what passed for the French war-plan of the latest report of the British Chief of Staff. After a 'squib offensive (to bring us in)', the French plan was to wait behind the Maginot Line until the British had expanded their army and the economic blockade began to bite …

> From John Charmley, *Chamberlain and the Lost Peace* (Papermac, 1989).

Study the sources and then answer the following questions.

a Study Source A. Explain what you understand by Lyttleton's reference to 'peace at this price'. [10]

b Study Source B. Why does the Munich Agreement of 1938 remain such a controversial issue for historians to approach? [10]

c 'The British government's concern about the cost of war was the main determinant of its foreign policy towards Germany between 1937 and 1939.'
Using your own knowledge and these sources, assess the validity of this judgement. [20]

Reading

Before answering this question you should read Sections 6 and 7.

How to answer this question

Part (a). It is important to be clear about the terms of the Munich Agreement. To achieve a high level answer candidates should draw effectively upon their own knowledge to consider the reasons why Lyttleton believes the Munich Agreement was humiliating. Knowledge about the manner in which Czechoslovakia was coerced into signing the agreement will form a useful pillar of the response.

Part (b). Source B provides you with ample basis for debate. Most of the source shows you a country united in delight that war has been averted; however, the reference to those who will soon wish the Munich Agreement to be forgotten points to the controversy surrounding the agreement. The brutalities of the Nazi regime can make it difficult to argue that Britain should have sacrificed the Czechs. That Britain went to war in 1939 to defend a fascist country like Poland, adds to the view of the 1938 agreement as shameful. This was part of the argument by Michael Foot in 1940 when he published *The Guilty Men*. More recently, historians like Paul Kennedy have argued that Britain was too weak to have any choice but to appease Hitler.

Part (c). This question provides a challenging statement around which to organise your argument. As discussed above, you will only succeed in putting severe ceilings upon your marks if you fail to follow the guidance to use all the sources and your own knowledge. The sources given suggest that Chamberlain was fully in line with public opinion; therefore the 'cost of war' should be interpreted in this narrow sense. Candidates should also introduce their own knowledge relating to other factors, such as France's reluctance to fight, and widen the idea of 'cost' to consider Duff Cooper's warning to the Commons – that ultimately Britain would have to fight for its own security, which had been damaged by Munich. Other points to mention are that Conservative support for Chamberlain was strong in the House of Commons because MPs were under pressure from their constituency parties to back Chamberlain. Even though Chamberlain had exceeded the discretion given to him by the cabinet, Lord Halifax led his colleagues in congratulating Chamberlain when he recognised Chamberlain's popularity. The question does say 1937–9, so it is important to cover the whole period. You should therefore discuss whether the decision to fight over Poland reflected changing views amongst the public, or just the political elite.

QUESTIONS IN THE STYLE OF EDEXCEL

'Belgium was a 'fig leaf' to cover the nakedness of Britain's role as a key member of the Triple Entente in 1914.' How far do you agree with this view? [30]

Reading
Before answering this question you should read Sections 2, 3 and 4.

How to answer this question
The question provides a challenging statement around which to frame your argument. The traditional view of Britain in 1914 is of the Great Power forced to uphold international treaties by Germany's ruthless invasion of tiny Belgium. Candidates will need to assess whether the British government consistently regarded an invasion of Belgium as a reason for war. For example, it has been argued in Section 4 of this book that Sir Edward Grey acted as though the Entente was a binding alliance, even though it was not legally binding upon

Britain. It is also argued in this book (see Chapter 4) that events in Ireland made it easier to declare war than to stay out of the conflict. High level answers will be provided by candidates who reach a clear, well-supported conclusion; highest level answers will differentiate the finer 'shades of grey' – for example, Sir Edward Grey and Morley both believed the above statement to be true, which is why the latter resigned from the cabinet in protest.

> 'British foreign policy between 1919 and 1939 failed to secure British interests.'
> How far do you agree with this view? [30]

Reading
Before answering this question you should read Sections 5, 6 and 7.

How to answer this question
You are unlikely to rise above Level 2 without at least some overall judgement as to how successfully British foreign policy secured British interests. At Level 4, candidates will make a clear judgement about the short- and long-term successes of British foreign policy. For example, the Versailles settlement left Germany weak but refused to give France all that it had asked for; however, Britain was eventually forced to acquiesce in the rise of Germany and found itself supporting France to maintain the balance of power. Candidates might argue that between 1935 and 1939 British foreign policy was formulated to secure Britain's interests by postponing war. To reach Level 5 it is important to make precise use of evidence and to reach comparative judgements. For example, you might assess how the truth of the statement varies between 1919 and 1939.

Answers to this question might consider how British foreign policy towards Austria failed to secure British interests in the longer term. In the 1920s Austria remained independent but British appeasement in the 1930s eventually conceded Austria to Hitler. Under the auspices of the League of Nations, Great Britain played a key role in stabilising the Austrian economy which helped to stabilise Austrian democracy. Whilst Austria perched on a fragile balance between left and right politics, France's refusal to contemplate an economic Anschluss in 1931 undermined democracy in both Austria and Germany. Also, Great Britain's acquiescence in France's policies effectively abandoned Austria to Hitler once Mussolini's protection was withdrawn. It was not in Britain's interests for Germany and Austria to descend into Fascism, but by 1938 Britain's foreign policy had spectacularly failed to prevent this happening.

A. Adamthwaite, *Grandeur and Misery; France's bid for power in Europe, 1914–40* (Arnold, 1995)

L. Allen, *Japan: The Years of Triumph* (Louis Allen, 1971)

P.M.H. Bell, *France and Britain 1900–40 Entente and Estrangement* (Longman, 1996)

V.R. Berghahn, *Germany and the Approach of War in 1914* (Macmillan, 1973)

Lord Birkenhead, *Halifax – the Life of Lord Halifax* (Hamish Hamilton, 1965)

J.M. Bourne, *Britain and the Great War, 1914–8* (Edward Arnold, 1989)

R. Brazier and E. Sandford, *Birmingham and the Great War 1914–9* (Cornish Brothers, 1921)

M. Brock and E. Brock, *H.H. Asquith – letters to Venetia Stanley* (Oxford University Press, 1982)

A. Bucholz, *Moltke, Schlieffen and Prussian War Planning* (Berg, 1991)

P. Buckland, *James Craig* (Gill & Macmillan, 1980)

F.L. Carsten, *The First Austrian Republic, 1918–38* (Gower/Maurice Temple Smith, 1986)

J. Charmley, *Chamberlain and the Lost Peace* (Papermac, 1989)

J. Charmley, *Duff Cooper* (Papermac, 1986)

J. Charmely, *Splendid Isolation? Britain and the Balance of Power 1874–1914* (Hodder & Stoughton, 1999)

A. Cobban, *A History of Modern France, vol. 3: 1871–1962* (Pelican, 1965)

H. Cowper et al., *War, Peace and Social Change: Europe 1900–55; Book II: World War One and its Consequences* (Open University Press, 1990)

R.J. Crampton, *The Hollow Détente: Anglo-German Relations in the Balkans 1911–4* (George Prior, 1979)

P. Dewey, *War and Progress; Britain 1914–45* (Longman, 1997)

D. Dutton, *Austen Chamberlain; Gentleman in Politics* (Ross Anderson, 1985)

E.M. Earle (ed.), *Makers of Modern Strategy; Military Thought from Machiavelli to Hitler* (Princeton, 1971)

The French Yellow Book: Diplomatic Documents 1938–9 (Hutchinson, 1939)

M. Glenny, *The Balkans, 1804–1999: Nationalism, War and the Great Powers* (Granta, 2000)

J.P. Harris, *Men, Ideas and Tanks; British military thought and armoured forces, 1903–39* (Manchester University Press, 1995)

R. Henig, *The Origins of the First World War*, 2nd edition (Lancaster Pamphlets, 1993)

H.H. Herwig, *The First World War – Germany and Austria-Hungary, 1914–8* (Arnold, 1997)

J.W. Hiden, *The Weimar Republic* (Longman, 1974)

J.W. Hiden, *Germany and Europe, 1919–39* (Longman, 1977)

M. Hurst (ed.), *Key Treaties for the Great Powers, vol. 2: 1871–1914* (David & Charles, 1972)

J. Joll, *Europe since 1870 – An International History*, 2nd edition (Penguin, 1976)

J. Joll, *The Origins of the First World War*, 2nd edition (Longman, 1992)

H. Koch (ed.), *The Origins of the First World War* (Macmillan, 1972)

E. Kolb, *The Weimar Republic* (Unwin Hyman, 1988)

S. Koss, *Asquith* (Hamish Hamilton, 1985)

E.H. Kossmann, *The Low Countries, 1780–1940* (Oxford University Press, 1978)

V. Lenin, *Against Imperialist War* (Progress, 1978)

D.C.B. Lieven, *Russia and the Origins of the First World War* (St Martin's Press, 1983)

G. MacDonogh, *The Last Kaiser – William the Impetuous* (Weidenfeld & Nicolson, 2000)

M. Magnusson (ed.), *Chamber's Biographical Dictionary* (Chambers, 1990)

R.K. Massie, *Dreadnought – Britain, Germany and the coming of the Great War* (Jonathan Cape, 1991)

W.M. Medlicott et al. (eds), *Documents on British Foreign Policy 1919–39; European Affairs August 1934 – April 1935* (HMSO, 1972)

A. Mockler, *Haile Selassie's War* (Grafton, 1984)

I. Porter and I. Armour, *Imperial Germany 1890–1918* (Longman, 1991)

M. Pugh, *Lloyd George* (Longman, 1988)

R. Rhodes James, *Anthony Eden* (Weidenfeld & Nicolson, 1986)

K. Robbins, *Sir Edward Grey* (Cassell, 1971)

J.C.G. Rohl, *From Bismarck to Hitler* (Longman, 1970)

J.C.G. Rohl, *The Kaiser and His Court; Wilhelm II and the Government of Germany* (Cambridge University Press, 1996)

D. Stevenson, *Armaments and the Coming of War, Europe 1904–14* (Oxford University Press, 2000)

A.T.Q. Stewart, *The Ulster Crisis; Resistance to Home Rule, 1912–4* (Faber & Faber, 1979)

N. Stone, *Europe Transformed 1879–1919* (Fontana, 1984)

A.J.P. Taylor, *The Hapsburg Monarchy* (Peregrine, 1964)

A.J.P. Taylor, *The Struggle for Mastery in Europe* (Oxford University Press, 1971)

A.J.P. Taylor, *The Origins of the Second World War* (Penguin, 1964)

R. Tombs, *France 1814–1914* (Longman, 1996)

G.M. Trevelyan, *Grey of Fallodon* (Longman, 1937)

J. Weitz, *Hitler's Diplomat – Joachim von Ribbentrop* (Phoenix, 1997)

E. Wiskemann, *Europe of the Dictators, 1919–45* (Fontana, 1966)

K. Young, *Baldwin* (Weidenfeld & Nicolson, 1976)

INDEX